Australian Signpost MATHS

4 Mentals

Alan McSeveny Diane McSeveny-Foster Rachel McSeveny

Pearson Australia
(a division of Pearson Australia Group Pty Ltd)
707 Collins Street, Melbourne, Victoria 3008
PO Box 23360, Melbourne, Victoria 8012
www.pearson.com.au

First published 2018 by Pearson Australia
2025 2024 2023 2022
10 9 8 7 6 5 4 3 2 1

Content and Learning Specialist: Sophie Matta
Project Manager: Shelly Wang
Production Manager: Elizabeth Gosman
Editor: Eliza Collins
Designers: Anne Donald & Jennifer Johnston
Cover Designer: Jennifer Johnston
Rights & Permissions Editor: Samantha Russell-Tulip
Senior Publishing Services Analyst: Rob Currulli
Cover art: Michael Barter
Cover background: rf_vector/Shutterstock.com
Illustrators: Michael Barter, Wendy Gorton, John Winter

Printed in Malaysia (CTP-VVP)

ISBN 978 1 4886 2186 4

Pearson Australia Group Pty Ltd ABN 40 004 245 943

Introduction

Using the Mentals Books

Each unit of the Mentals Book is programmed to review Student Book content for the previous two weeks (based on the Suggested Program in the Teacher's Book). For example, Unit 15 of the Mentals Book can be set as homework to review weeks 13 and 14 of the Student Book while week 15 is being taught.

Presentation

- The content of the strands Number and Algebra, Measurement and Geometry, and Statistics and Probability is covered thoroughly.
- Essential skills are explained.
- Language, problem solving, graphs and tables are given a high profile.
- Mathematics is applied to real-life situations wherever possible.
- The **Arithmetic Card** (page 5) is an exciting teaching tool for practising basic number skills.
- **ID Cards** (pages 6–8) review the terms essential to success in the course.
- **Measurement examples and standards** (pages 9 and 84) are provided so that students can estimate effectively.

Mixed-topic Questions

The units present questions in a mixed-topic format.

- This is essential for thorough understanding and continuous review.
- In real life, similar questions don't often occur together.
- It allows the teacher to discover weaknesses that could otherwise pass unnoticed.
- It provides a real test of understanding.

Graded Questions

- Column 1: easier
- Columns 2 and 3: harder
- Column 4: Extension and Challenge

Motivation

- Cartoons make mathematics more appealing.
- There are two lizards hidden on each page for students to find.

Extra Activities

- Problem-solving **strategies** are introduced in a carefully planned sequence throughout the series.
- Important concepts from **Number and Algebra** and **Measurement and Geometry** are explored.
- **Measurement** concepts and activities are introduced and investigated.
- **Statistics and Probability** concepts (Data and Chance) are presented for revision and extension.

- A **tables** program for each of the four operations is included.
- It is important for students to try to learn addition and multiplication tables by heart.

Contents

Unit Activities

Unit	Content	Extra Activity	Unit	Content	Extra Activity
1:1/2 **1:3/4**	+ 2, + 3, + 4 Personal measures	+ tables Measure	**20:1/2** **20:3/4**	× 7 × 6, × 8	× tables × tables
2:1/2 **2:3/4**	+ 5, + 10, + 6 Language	+ tables ID Card C	**21:1/2** **21:3/4**	× 7, × 8 Fractions	× tables Concept
3:1/2 **3:3/4**	× 10, × 5 Time	× tables Measure	**22:1/2** **22:3/4**	× 6, × 8 Area	× tables Measure
4:1/2 **4:3/4**	+ 8, + 9, + 7 Time	+ tables Measure	**23:1/2** **23:3/4**	× 3, × 6 Problem solving	× tables Strategy Time
5:1/2 **5:3/4**	× 2, × 4 Number line division	× tables Concept	**24:1/2** **24:3/4**	Chance Roman numerals	Chance Concept
6:1/2 **6:3/4**	× 10, × 5 × 4	× tables × tables	**25:1/2** **25:3/4**	× 6, × 7 Language	× tables ID Card C
7:1/2 **7:3/4**	× 2, × 5, × 4, × 10, × 0, × 1 Language	× tables ID Card C	**26:1/2** **26:3/4**	Roman numerals Problem solving	Concept Strategy Time
8:1/2 **8:3/4**	Time Rounding (nearest 5)	Measure Concept	**27:1/2** **27:3/4**	Length Compass directions	Measure Concept
9:1/2 **9:3/4**	− 5, − 10, − 4 Chance	− tables Chance	**28:1/2** **28:3/4**	Multiplication tables Language	× tables ID Card B
10:1/2 **10:3/4**	− 6, − 7 + and − linked	− tables Concept	**29:1/2** **29:3/4**	Language Problem solving	ID Card A Strategy Time
11:1/2 **11:3/4**	− 8, − 9 Chance	− tables Chance	**30:1/2** **30:3/4**	× 7, × 8 ÷ tables	× tables Concept
12:1/2 **12:3/4**	× 2, × 4, × 8, × 5, × 10 Column graph	× tables Data	**31:1/2** **31:3/4**	× and ÷ linked ÷ 2, ÷ 4	Concept ÷ tables
13:1/2 **13:3/4**	× 4, × 8 Change from $2	× tables Concept	**32:1/2** **32:3/4**	× 6, × 9 ÷ 5, ÷ 10	× tables ÷ tables
14:1/2 **14:3/4**	× 4, × 8 Language	× tables ID Card B	**33:1/2** **33:3/4**	× and ÷ linked ÷ 3, ÷ 6	Concept ÷ tables
15:1/2 **15:3/4**	Patterns Crossnumber puzzle	Concept Concept	**34:1/2** **34:3/4**	÷ 7, ÷ 8 Language	÷ tables ID Card A
16:1/2 **16:3/4**	× 3, × 6 Problem solving	× tables Strategy Time	**35:1/2** **35:3/4**	÷ 9, × 4, × 7, × 9 Factors	÷ and × tables Concept
17:1/2 **17:3/4**	Chance × 3, × 6	Chance × tables	**36:1/2** **36:3/4**	Language × 11	ID Card A × tables
18:1/2 **18:3/4**	× 9 Division strategies	× tables Concept	**37:1/2** **37:3/4**	Language Personal measures	ID Card B Measure
19:1/2 **19:3/4**	× 9 Area	× tables Measure	**Answers**	These can be found in the middle of this book on pages A1 to A12.	

 • *AUSTRALIAN SIGNPOST MATHS 4 MENTALS* • ISBN 978 1 4886 2186 4

Arithmetic Card

	A	B	C	D	E	F	G	H	I	J
1	7	3	11	20	4	2	7	50	37	$6
2	4	7	17	16	25	10	11	80	93	$1
3	10	1	14	12	64	14	3	20	16	$7
4	3	5	19	17	16	4	15	70	55	$3
5	5	8	16	13	81	12	19	40	100	$8
6	8	6	12	18	1	16	1	60	71	$5
7	2	10	18	11	36	8	9	100	48	$9
8	6	4	15	14	9	20	17	30	82	$2
9	1	9	20	19	100	18	5	90	64	$10
10	9	2	13	15	49	6	13	10	29	$4

How to Use This Card

If students were told to "subtract B from C", they would write:

❶ 11 – 3 = 8 ❷ 17 – 7 = 10 ❸ 14 – 1 = 13 ❹ 19 – 5 = 14 ❺ 16 – 8 = 8
❻ 12 – 6 = 6 ❼ 18 – 10 = 8 ❽ 15 – 4 = 11 ❾ 20 – 9 = 11 ❿ 13 – 2 = 11

Other instructions might be:

- **Multiply column B by 4.**
- **Add columns A and C.**
- **Halve column F.**
- **What multiplied by 10 gives column H?**
- **What is the change from $10 if I spent what it is in column J?**
- **Double column G.**
- **Subtract column B from column H.**
- **What must be added to column I to make 100?**
- **Multiply column A by 5.**

The applications of this card are endless.

ID Card A

Do not write on this card.

ID Card A

1. **m** stands for m__________
2. **cm** stands for c__________
3. **L** stands for l__________
4. **g** stands for g__________
5. **kg** stands for k__________
6. **min** stands for m__________
7. **cm²** stands for s______ c__________
8. **m²** stands for s______ m__________
9. **°C** means d__________ C__________
10. **0°C** is the f__________ p______ of w______
11. **100°C** is the b__________ p______ of w______
12. **am** means b______ n______
13. **pm** means a______ n______
14. **5 groups of 7** means 5 ______ 7
15. **<** means is ______ ______
16. **>** means is ______ ______
17. **Share 20 among 5.** means 20 ______ 5
18. **How many groups of 6 in 18?** means 18 ______ 6
19. **7 + 9 = 16** is a number s__________
20. 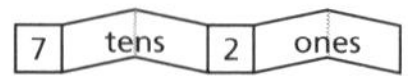

is a n__________ expander
21. **1, 2, 3, …** are the c__________ numbers
22. **2, 4, 6, …** are the e__________ numbers
23. **1, 3, 5, …** are the o__________ numbers
24. **1st, 2nd, …** are the o__________ numbers
25. **2750** has 4 d__________
26. **1, 2, 3, 4, 6 and 12** are the f________ of 12
27. **12, 24, 36, …** are the m__________ of 12
28. 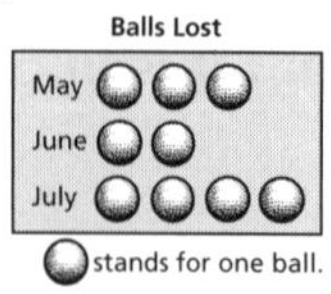

p__________ graph
29. 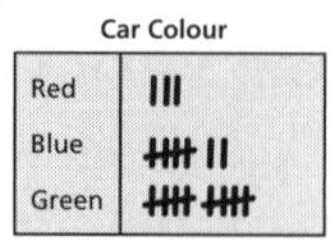

This is a t__________.
30. 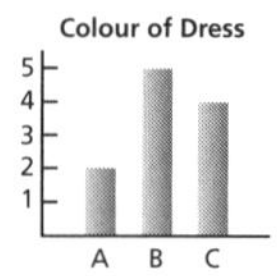

c__________ graph

See page A1 for answers.

 • *AUSTRALIAN SIGNPOST MATHS 4 MENTALS* • ISBN 978 1 4886 2186 4

ID Card B

Do not write on this card.

ID Card B

1  s_______ line	**2**  c_______ line	**3**  w_______ line	**4**  z_______ line	**5** 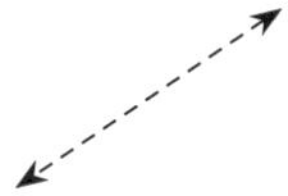 d_______ line
6 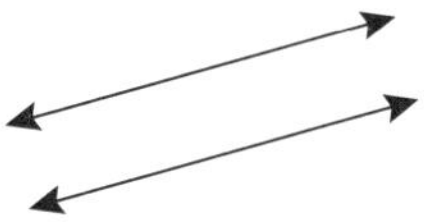 p_______ lines	**7**  p_______ lines	**8**  f_______	**9**  s_______	**10**  t_______
11 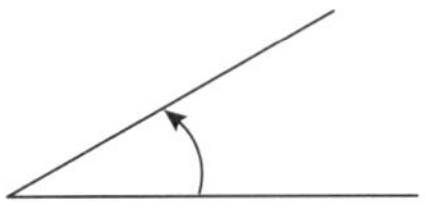 a_______ angle	**12** 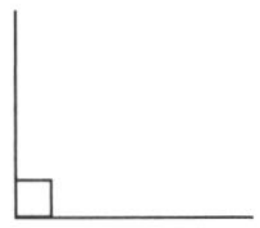 r_______ angle	**13** 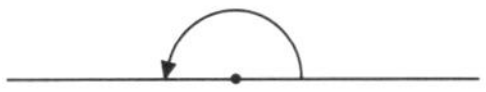 s_______ angle	**14** 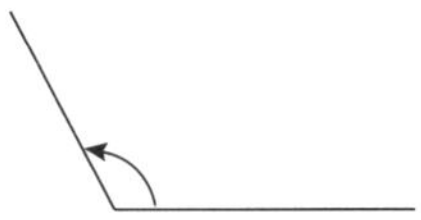 o_______ angle	**15** 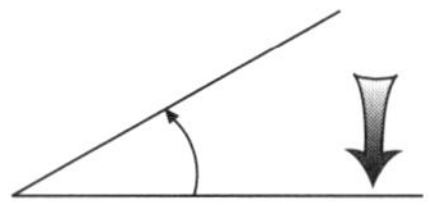 a_____ of an angle
16 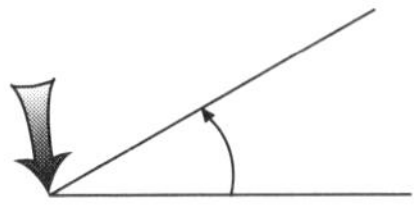 v_______ of an angle	**17**  a_____ of __________	**18**  t__________	**19** 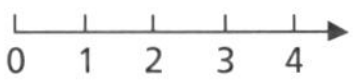 n_______ line	**20**  ____ sixths shaded
21 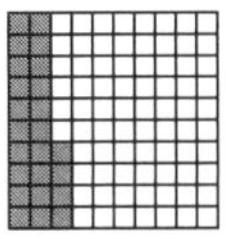 ____ hundredths shaded	**22** 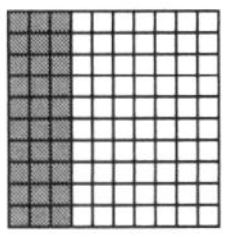 ____ tenths shaded	**23** 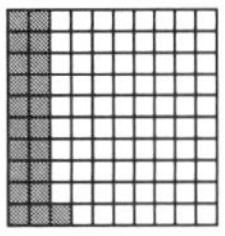 0· ____ shaded	**24** 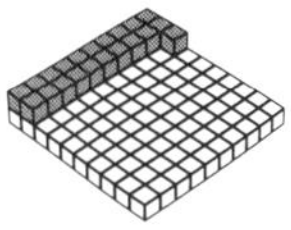 ____ hundredths covered	**25** 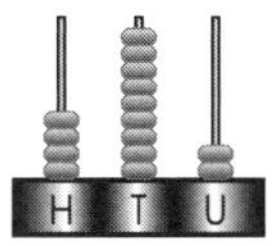 a ________
26  c ________	**27**  c ________	**28**  b _______ scales	**29**  m _______ ruler	**30**  1 square m_______

See page A1 for answers.

ID Card C

ID Card C

Do not write on this card.

1
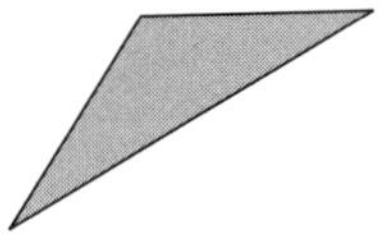
t__________

2

s__________

3

r__________

4
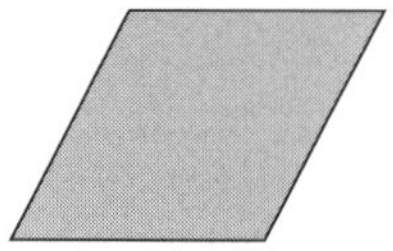
r__________

5
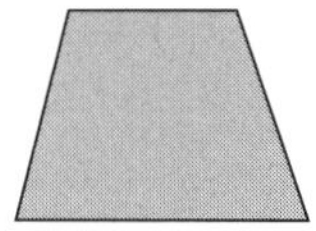
t__________

6
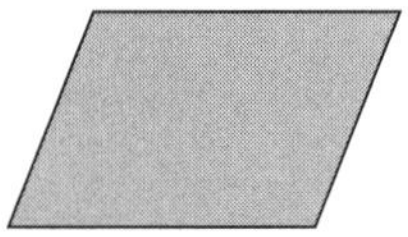
p__________

7
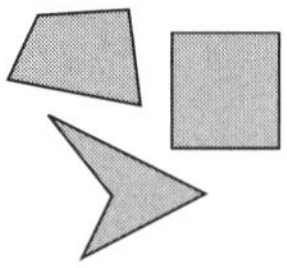
q__________

8
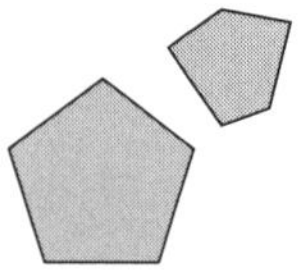
p__________

9
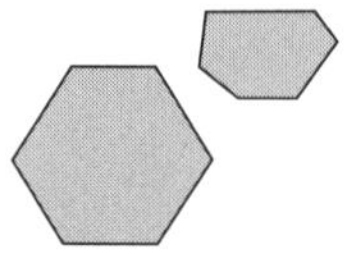
h__________

10
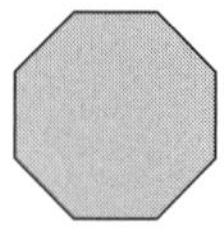
o__________

11

c__________

12
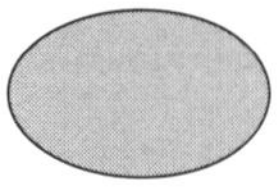
o__________

13
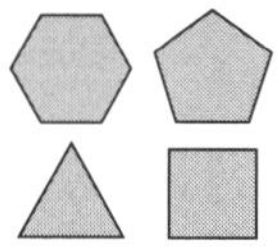
r__________ shapes

14
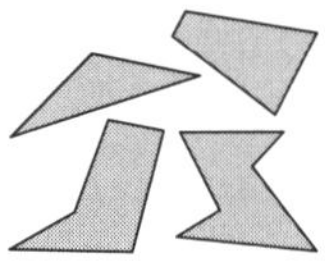
i__________ shapes

15
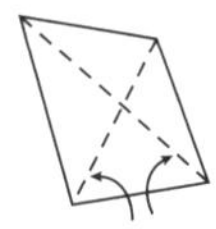
d__________

16
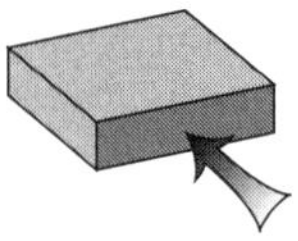
f__________

17
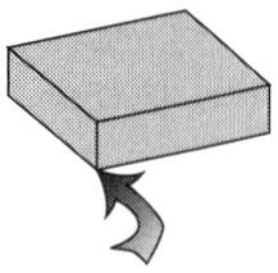
c__________

18
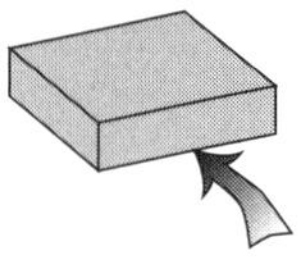
e__________

19
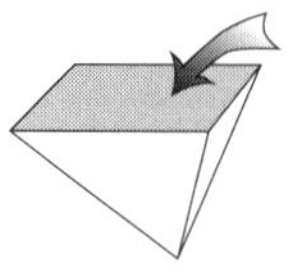
b__________

20
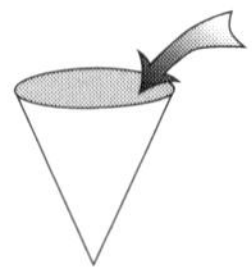
f__________ surface

21

c__________ surface

22

c__________

23
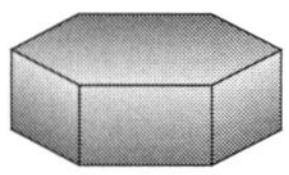
p__________

24
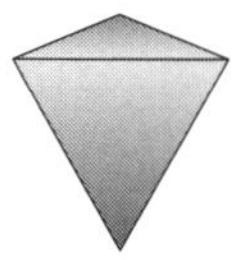
p__________

25
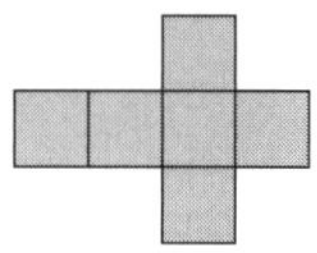
n______ of a cube

26
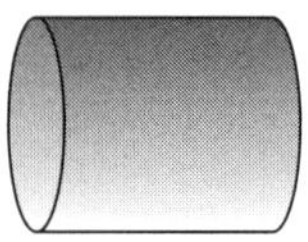
c__________

27
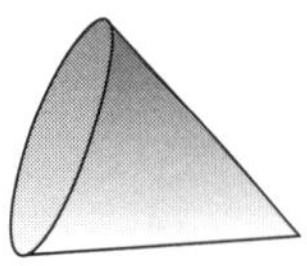
c__________

28

s__________

29

d__________ watch

30

a__________ clock

See page A1 for answers.

 • *AUSTRALIAN SIGNPOST MATHS 4 MENTALS* • ISBN 978 1 4886 2186 4

Examples of Measurements

1

2

3

4

5

6

1
- The **width of the boy's finger** is about **1 cm**.
- The **length of a place-value tens block** is **10 cm**.

2
- The **height of the girl** is a little more than **1 m**.

3
- The **container of milk** holds **2 L**.
- The **can of Fizz** holds **375 mL**.
- The **teaspoon** holds **5 mL**.

4
- The **boy** has a mass of **40 kg**.
- The **margarine** has a mass of **500 g**.

5
- The area of the **window** is about **2 m²**.
- The **top of a place-value ones block** is **1 cm²**.

6
- **30°C** is a **hot** day.
- **3°C** is a very **cold** day.

Use the pictures above to estimate the answers to these questions.

1 a How high is the glass?
b How wide is the table?

2 a How wide is the clothes line?
b How tall is the woman?

3 a How much will the bucket hold?
b How much will the cup hold?

4 a What is the mass of the dog?
b What is the mass of 2 L of milk?

5 a What is the area of the table?
b What is the the area of the top of a matchbox?

6 a What is the temperature on a very hot day?
b What is the temperature on a cool day?

1:1 out of 19

1. 2 + 2 ____
2. 3 + 6 ____
3. 9 − 5 ____
4. 10 − 4 ____
5. 19 + 0
6. 2 × 5 ____
7. 3 × 5 ____
8. Add 5 and 8. ____
9. Take 4 from 9. ____
10. 9c − 6c

11. 50, 60, 70, 80, ____, ____, ____
12. The numeral for forty. ____
13. Write 100 in words. ____
14. 7 tens + 3 ones ____
15. 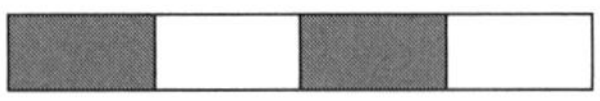

What part is shaded? ____ out of ____

16. How many minutes from 9:30 am until 9:45 am? ____
17. Which is heavier, a pencil or a tennis ball? ____
18. In one tank there are 7 fish and in the other there are 8.

How many fish are there altogether? ____

19. Draw a pentagon in this space.

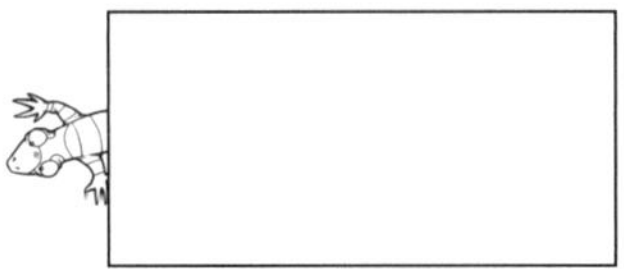

It has ____ sides.

1:2 out of 15

1. 12 + 8 ____
2. 4 + 16 ____
3. 20 − 9 ____
4. 25 − 5 ____
5. 13 + 5
6. 0 × 3 ____
7. 2 lots of 3. ____
8. 4 ÷ 2 ____
9. 10 shared by 2 ____
10. 19 − 4

11. Which height is closest to that of a fully grown elephant, 3 metres or 10 metres? ____

12. What number is modelled here? ____

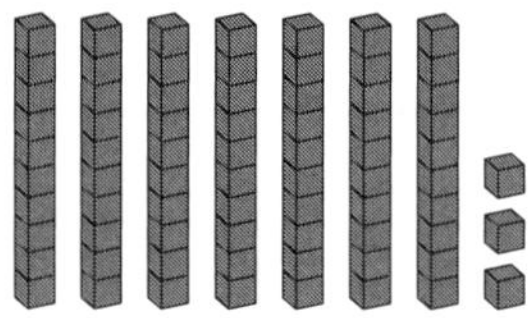

13. Draw the line of symmetry on this shape.

14. Which side is heavier? ____

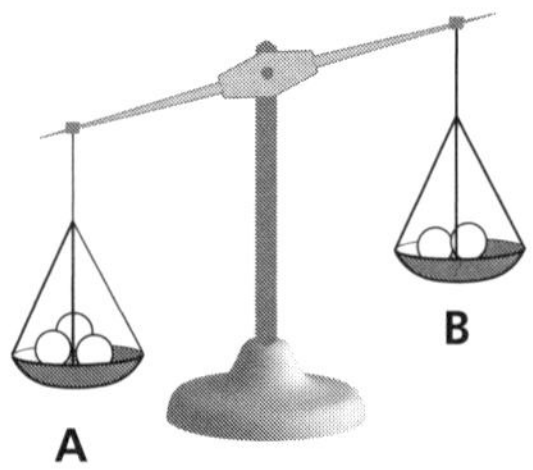

15. Which shape has the greater area? ____

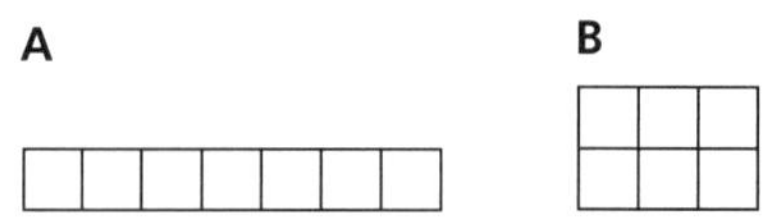

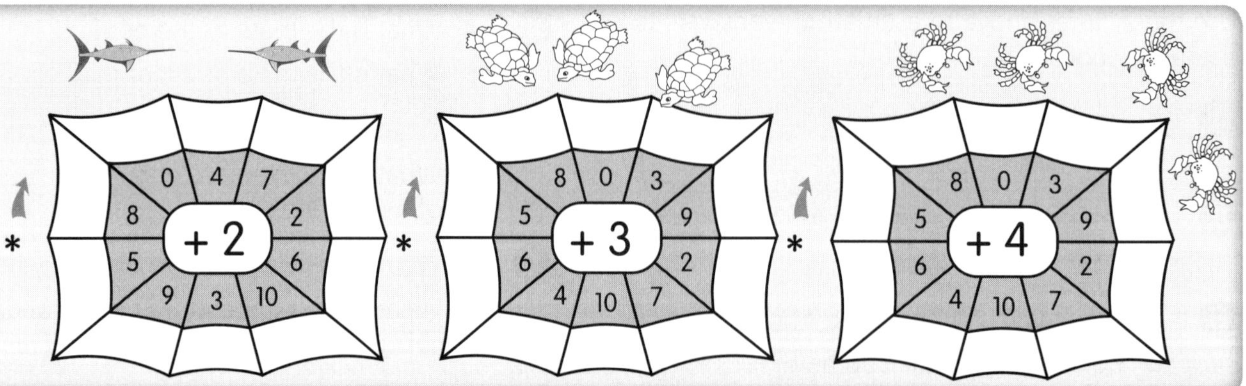

 ISBN 978 1 4886 2186 4

1:3 ☐ out of 15

1.

Tens	Ones
4	3
+2	2

2.

Tens	Ones
3	7
– 1	5

3. How many minutes past 4 o'clock?

a  ____________

b  ____________

4. 25, 30, 35, ________, ________, ________

5. Is this a pyramid, a prism or neither? ____________ 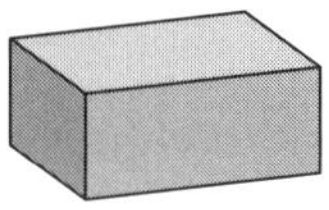

6. Write down the even numbers between 3 and 11. ____________

7. 30 + 40 + 60 + 70 ____________

8. Is 36 closer to 30 or 40? ____________

9. Are these shapes regular or irregular? 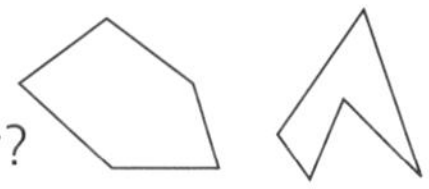 ____________

10. Is 17 odd or even? ____________

11. The "×" sign means ____________.

12. I was given 3 presents on Monday, 8 presents on Tuesday and 2 on Wednesday.

    How many presents did I get? ____________

13. 42 stamps plus 36 stamps. ____________

14. Write six hundred and twelve. ____________

15. Days in April. ____________

1:4 ☐ out of 7

Extension

1. Underline the one that is *not* a quadrilateral.

   square   rectangle   pentagon

2. Each prawn costs $1.15. How much do 5 prawns cost? ____________

3. 4 + 16 + 23 + 7 + 5 ____________

4. There are 41 houses in my street. 

   How many have odd numbers? ____________

5. Is $\frac{2}{4}$ equal to $\frac{4}{8}$? ____________

6. **a** 53 more than 121. ____________

   b 44 more than 133. ____________

7. An estimate is a good guess.

   True or false? ____________

Challenge

Draw and describe a 2D shape.

____

____

____

____

____

____

____

Fill out this table about yourself, a relative or a friend.

Name: ____________ **Date:** ____________

Age: ____________	Mass: ____________ kg	Shoe size: ____________
Height: ____________ cm	Waist: ____________ cm	Neck size: ________ cm

2:1 ☐ out of 20

❶ 2 + 3 ____

❷ 5 + 6 ____

❸ 6 − 2 ____

❹ 8 − 5 ____

❺ 2 + 5 ____

❻ 4 × 2 ____

❼ 5 × 5 ____

❽ Add 7 and 4. ____

❾ 3 less than 8. ____

❿ 8 − 1 ____

⓫ 100, 90, 80, 70, ____, ____, ____

⓬ The number after 69. ____

⓭ 

What part is shaded? ____ out of ____

⓮ 8 tens + 9 ones ____

⓯ 50c + 20c + 10c + 5c ____

⓰ Which Australian coins are coloured gold? ____

⓱ Colour two quarters of this shape.

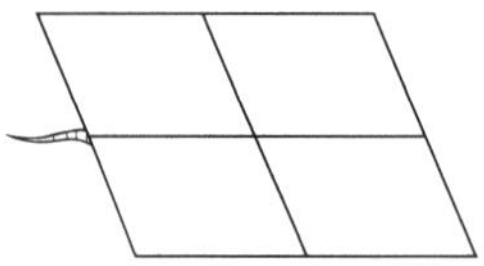

⓲ Are 10, 16, 28, and 32 even numbers? ____

⓳ The change from $20 if you buy something worth $15. ____

⓴ Sue's team scored 11 goals in a game of soccer. If they scored 4 in the first half, how many goals did they score in the second half? ____

2:2 ☐ out of 15

❶ 8 + 8 ____

❷ 21 + 7 ____

❸ 20 − 6 ____

❹ 10 − 5 ____

❺ 16 + 4 ____

❻ 5 × 1 ____

❼ 9 times 2 ____

❽ 10 ÷ 2 ____

❾ 19 subtract 12 ____

❿ 17 − 2 ____

⓫ Which of these objects have only flat surfaces? ____

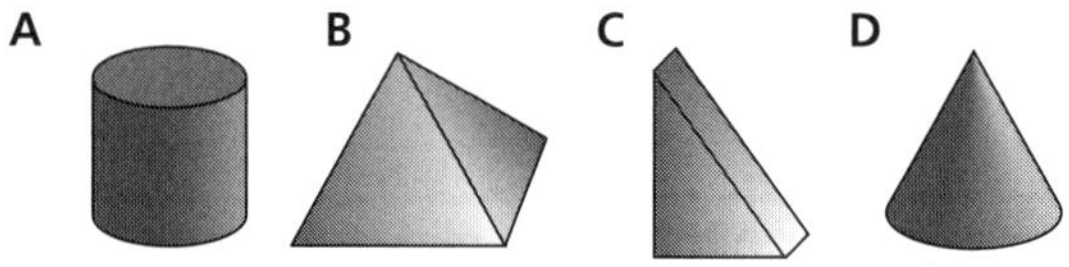

⓬ What is the time shown on this clock face?

____ past ____

⓭ A mouse was balanced by 6 coins. A book was balanced by 12 coins.

How many mice would balance the book? ____

⓮ The change from $1.00, if I buy an ice block worth 35c? ____

⓯ In a cupboard there were 18 cups, 10 bowls, 16 saucers and 13 plates.

How many more cups were there than plates? ____

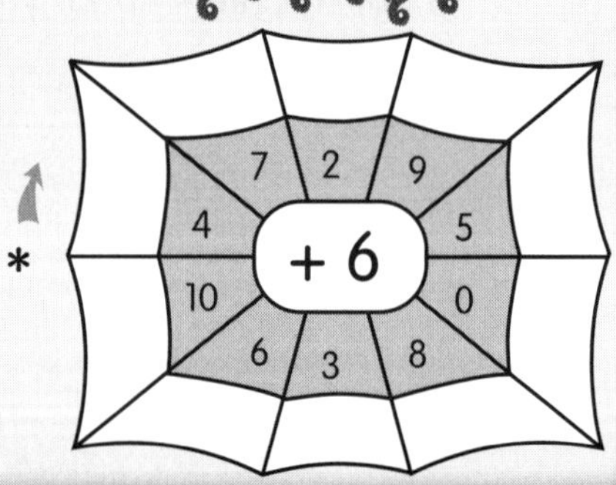

 • *AUSTRALIAN SIGNPOST MATHS 4 MENTALS* • ISBN 978 1 4886 2186 4

2:3 ☐ out of 12

❶

Tens	Ones
6	5
+3	1

❷

Tens	Ones
8	4
– 6	4

❸ Write the digital time for:

a quarter past 3 b half past 3

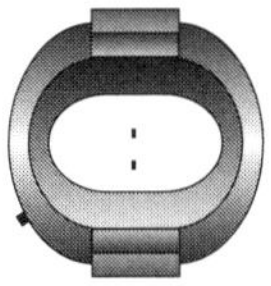
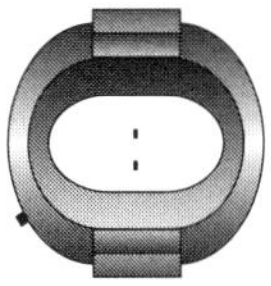

❹ From the numbers 1, 4, 8, 30 and 50, choose the best estimate for the length of a car in metres. ______

❺ What is the change from $2 if you spend:

a 35 cents? ______ b 70 cents? ______

❻ Ten less than 87. ______

❼ I live 100 m from school. How far do I walk to school and back in one school week? ______

❽ Colour $\frac{3}{4}$.

❾ a How many corners on a square? ______

b How many sides on a hexagon? ______

❿ Write 17 minutes past 3 in digital time. ______

⓫ Days in June. ______

⓬ Jim had 63 stamps. He gave 10 to his sister. How many did he have left? ______

2:4 Extension ☐ out of 6

❶ How many full weeks in 3 years? ______

❷ 85 – 15 – 15 – 15 ______

❸ Colour $\frac{3}{5}$ of these boats blue and $\frac{2}{5}$ of the boats red.

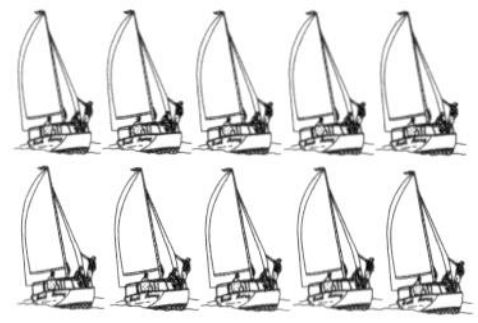

❹ The total quantity of drink held in these containers.

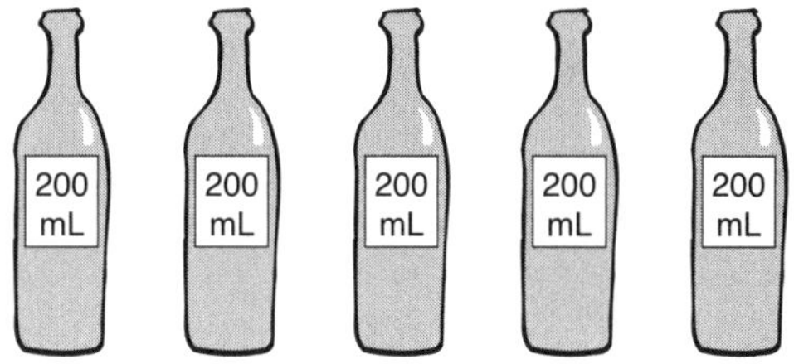

______

❺ How many 60c stamps could you buy for $2? ______

❻ 38 + 23 ______

Challenge

Draw and label some fractions of your own.

Turn to ID Card C on page 8.

Give the answers for these numbers.

(4) ______ (5) ______

(6) ______ (7) ______

(11) ______ (12) ______

(13) ______ shapes (14) ______ shapes

Make up a study card for any mistakes.

Make a study card: Put questions on one side and answers on the other.

3:1   ☐ out of 17

1. 8 + 4 ______
2. 5 + 9 ______
3. 9 − 7 ______
4. 8 − 4 ______
5. 16 + 2
6. 6 × 0 ______
7. 1 × 3 ______
8. Add 6 and 3. ______
9. Take 3 from 8. ______
10. 14 − 2
11. What number is ten more than 43? ______
12. Complete this number pattern.

    11, 13, 15, 17, ______, ______, ______
13. Write 39 in words.

    ____
14. Change from $1 if I spend 50 cents? ______
15. What number is modelled here? ______

16. Write six past nine in digital time. ______
17. Colour 3 fifths of this rectangle red.

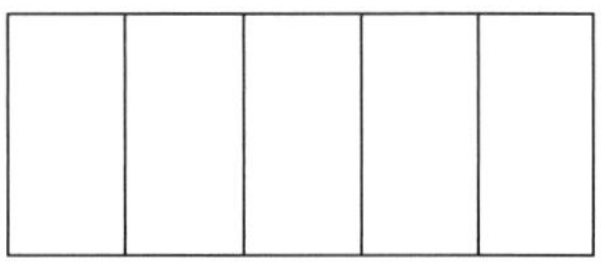

3:2   ☐ out of 15

1. 5 + 10 ______
2. 16 + 4 ______
3. 18 − 1 ______
4. 20 − 9 ______
5. 32 + 6
6. 4 × 2 ______
7. 5 groups of 2. ______
8. 6 × 2 ______
9. 14 shared by 7. ______
10. 5 × 9
11. Colour 9 out of 13.

12. 30, 35, 40, 45, ______, ______, ______
13. What is the digital time? ______

14. Complete this two-way table for these faces.

Smiley Face	Circle	Square	Rhombus
Happy			
Sad			

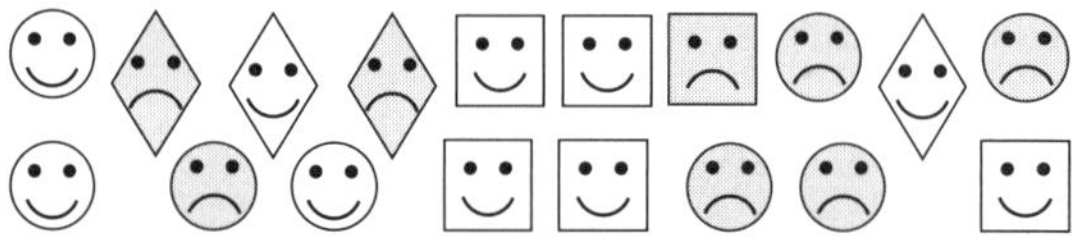

15. Draw 4 axes of symmetry.

*

*

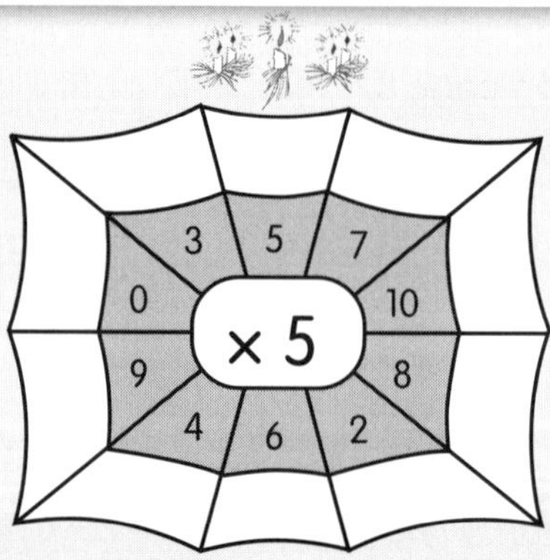

 • *AUSTRALIAN SIGNPOST MATHS 4 MENTALS* • ISBN 978 1 4886 2186 4

3:3 ☐ out of 9

1

Tens	Ones
$5	3
+ $3	5

2

Tens	Ones
$7	6
– $3	2

3 **a** 7, 14, 21, ______, ______, ______, ______

b 8, 16, 24, ______, ______, ______, ______

4 Draw the analogue time for 7:15 on this clock face.

5

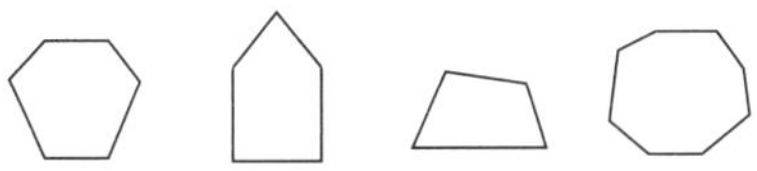

A B C D

Which shape is a pentagon? ______

6 Estimate the number of times "e" is used on this page. Check by counting.

Estimate = ______ Number = ______

7 Is this a flip, slide or turn?

______

8 The digital time half an hour after three o'clock. ______

9 **a** What fraction is white? ______

b What fraction is shaded? ______

3:4 Extension ☐ out of 5

1 **a** Millilitres in $3\frac{1}{2}$ L. ______

b Centimetres in $4\frac{1}{2}$ m. ______

2 **a** 12 + 12 + 12 + 12 ______

b 13 + 13 + 13 + 13 ______

3 9 triangles have been used to make 3 rows of this pattern. How many triangles are needed to make:

a 4 rows? ______

b 6 rows? ______

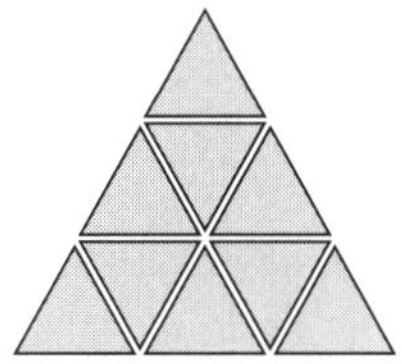

4 Hours from 9 am till noon. ______

5 For music notes (♩ = 1, 𝅗𝅥 = 2, 𝅝 = 4) putting a dot after the symbols adds an extra half of its value. Write the value of:

a ♩. ______

b 𝅗𝅥. ______

Challenge

Write your own number patterns and the rule for each.

______

______

______

______

______

How many minutes are in:

a one hour? ______ **b** half an hour? ______

c a quarter of an hour? ______

d three quarters of an hour? ______

For this clock, how many minutes:

e is it after 6 o'clock? ______

f is it before 7 o'clock? ______

4:1 ☐ out of 17

1. 3 + 5 ______
2. 6 + 4 ______
3. 7 − 3 ______
4. 5 − 3 ______
5. 16 + 3 ______
6. 4 × 10 ______
7. 9 × 1 ______
8. Add 3 and 7. ______
9. Take 5 from 9. ______
10. 15 − 4 ______
11. 5, 10, 15, ______, ______, ______
12. Does this show a flip, slide or turn? ______

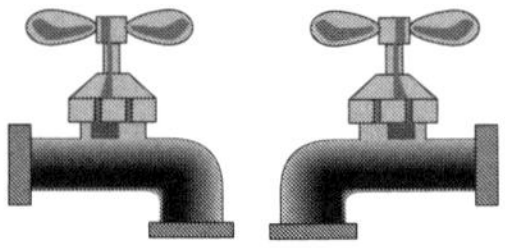

13.

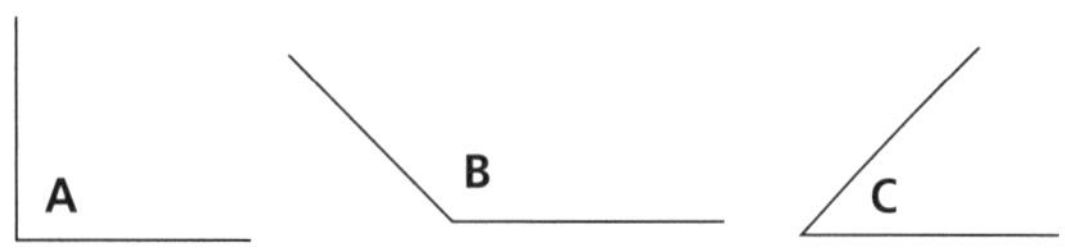

a Which angle is the largest? ______

b Which angle is the smallest? ______

14.

This shows ______ groups of ______.

15. Seconds in 1 minute. ______
16. Shade three twelfths of this shape.

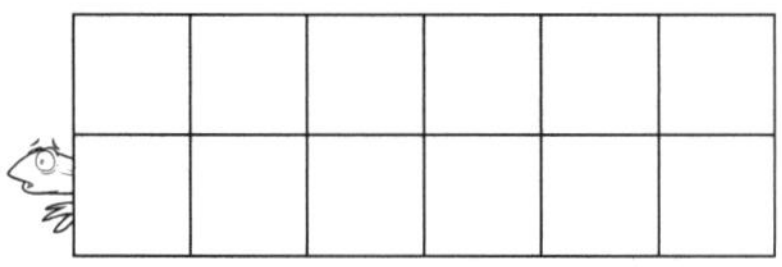

17. Jared is nine years old. How old will he be in five years? ______

4:2 ☐ out of 17

1. 12 + 12 ______
2. 20 + 10 ______
3. 14 − 7 ______
4. 20 − 5 ______
5. 53 + 5 ______
6. 4 × 5 ______
7. 6 groups of 3. ______
8. 6 shared by 3. ______
9. 12 ÷ 2 ______
10. 4 × 10 ______
11. a 6, 12, 18, ______, ______, ______

    b 15, 18, 21, ______, ______, ______
12. What analogue time is shown here? ______

13. a What part is shaded? ______

    b What part is not shaded? ______

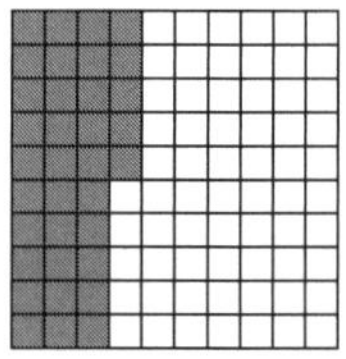

14. a What is the time 15 minutes after 4:35? ______

    b What is the time twenty minutes after 5:00? ______
15. The ordinal number before 13th. ______
16. The value of the 8 in 98. ______
17. Show 3 × 6 below.

© PEARSON AUSTRALIA 2018 • *AUSTRALIAN SIGNPOST MATHS 4 MENTALS* • ISBN 978 1 4886 2186 4

4:3 ☐ out of 8

1

Tens	Ones
$6	3
$1	0
+ $2	2

2

Tens	Ones
4	0
	7
+ 1	2

3 Here is a h ________________

s ________________.

There are ________ squares in one row.

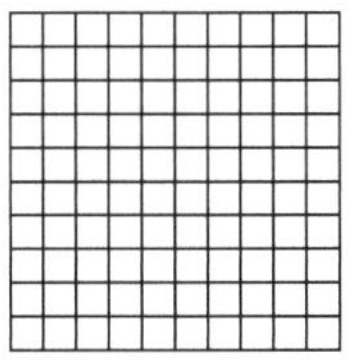

4

a 3 rows of 9. ________ **b** 5 rows of 9. ________

5 What is the day two days after Sunday? ________

6 Does the axis of symmetry divide a shape into two halves? ________

7 Complete this two-way table for these shapes.

Shapes	Rhombus	Pentagon	Rectangle
Shaded			
Not Shaded			

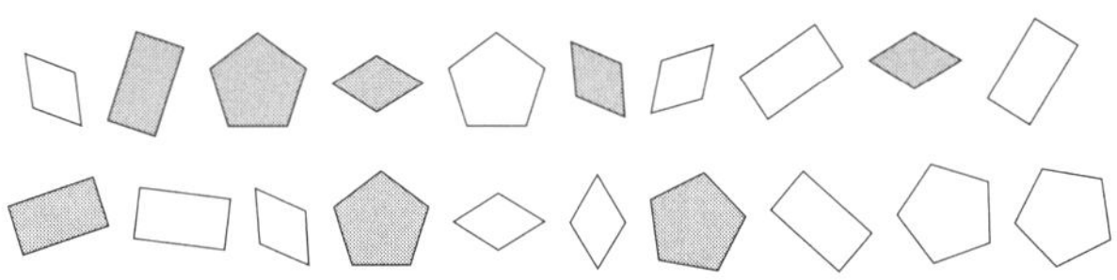

8 Show each time on the clock.

a 3:24

b 12:47

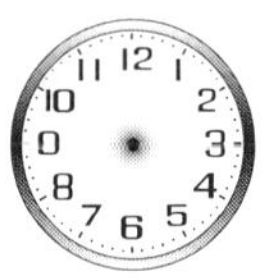

4:4 Extension ☐ out of 5

1 How many times would either of the two hands of a clock point to the numeral 3 in one day? ________

2 **a** 60 + ________ = 100

b 100 − 40 = ________

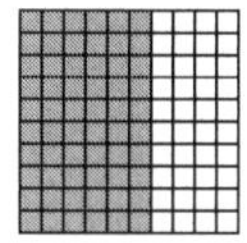

3 Complete this picture if the broken line is an axis of symmetry.

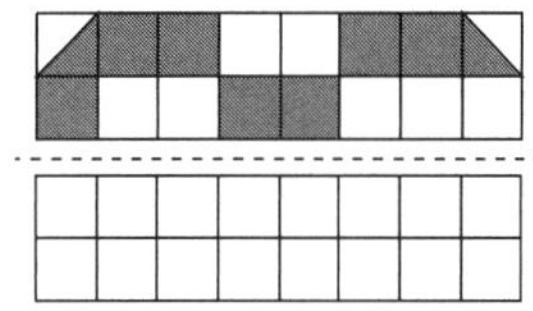

4 How many angles in 5 squares? ________

5 69 + 35 ________

Challenge

Create a simple picture that is not symmetrical. Use it to create a design using flip, slide and/or turn.

Complete, then learn these tables. (See page 84.)

a ________ seconds = 1 minute **b** ________ hours = 1 day

c ________ minutes = 1 hour **d** ________ days = 1 week

e ________ minutes = half an hour **f** 1 fortnight = ________ weeks

5:1   ☐ out of 15

1. 6 + 2 ______
2. 0 + 8 ______
3. 9 − 6 ______
4. 10 − 5 ______
5. $\begin{array}{r} 13 \\ +\ \ 3 \\ \hline \end{array}$
6. 3 × 4 ______
7. 10 × 4 ______
8. Add 5 and 4. ______
9. Take 7 from 7. ______
10. $\begin{array}{r} 17 \\ -\ \ 7 \\ \hline \end{array}$

11. Draw 4 groups of 6.

☐ ☐ ☐ ☐

12. Is this a flip, a slide or a turn?

______

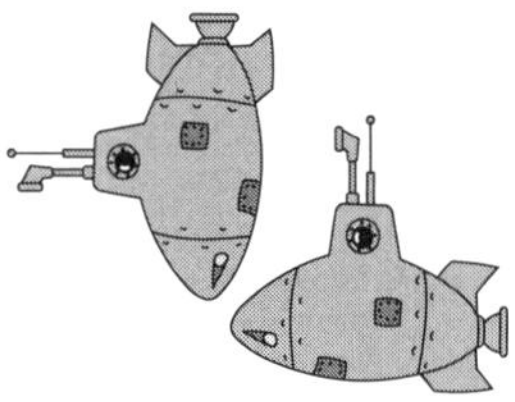

13. **a** Shade 80 out of 100.

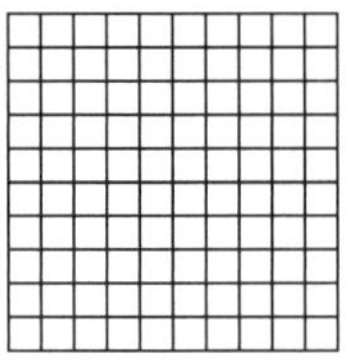

b What part is not shaded?

______ out of ______ or 0· ______.

14. This angle is called a

r ______ a ______.

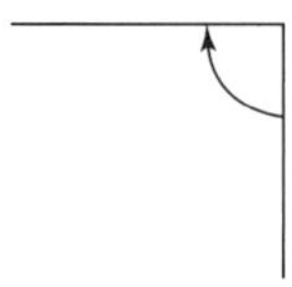

15. One minute after 4:15. ______

5:2   ☐ out of 15

1. 7 + 10 ______
2. 5 + 13 ______
3. 14 − 7 ______
4. 16 − 8 ______
5. $\begin{array}{r} 67 \\ -\ \ 3 \\ \hline \end{array}$
6. 7 × 4 ______
7. 5 lots of 4. ______
8. 24 ÷ 6 ______
9. 10 divided by 5. ______
10. $\begin{array}{r} 4 \\ \times\ \ 6 \\ \hline \end{array}$

11. The fraction shown is ____ hundredths or 0·______.

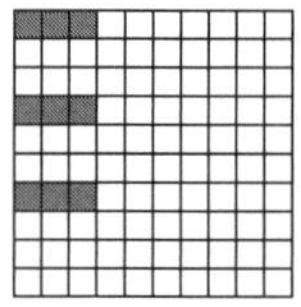

12. **a** Draw in the axis of symmetry.

b What shape would I get if I fold this diamond along an axis of symmetry?

______

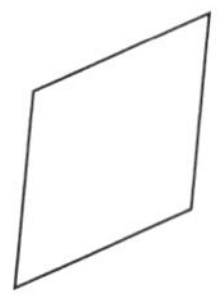

13. 6 squares have ______ corners.

14. How many axes of symmetry does this shape have?

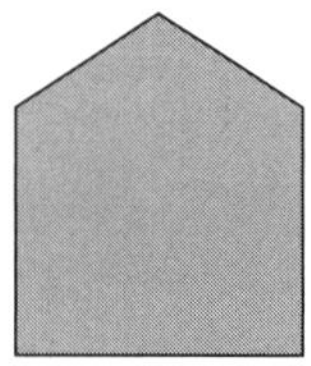

______

15. **a** 5 × 4 ______ **b** 7 × 4 ______

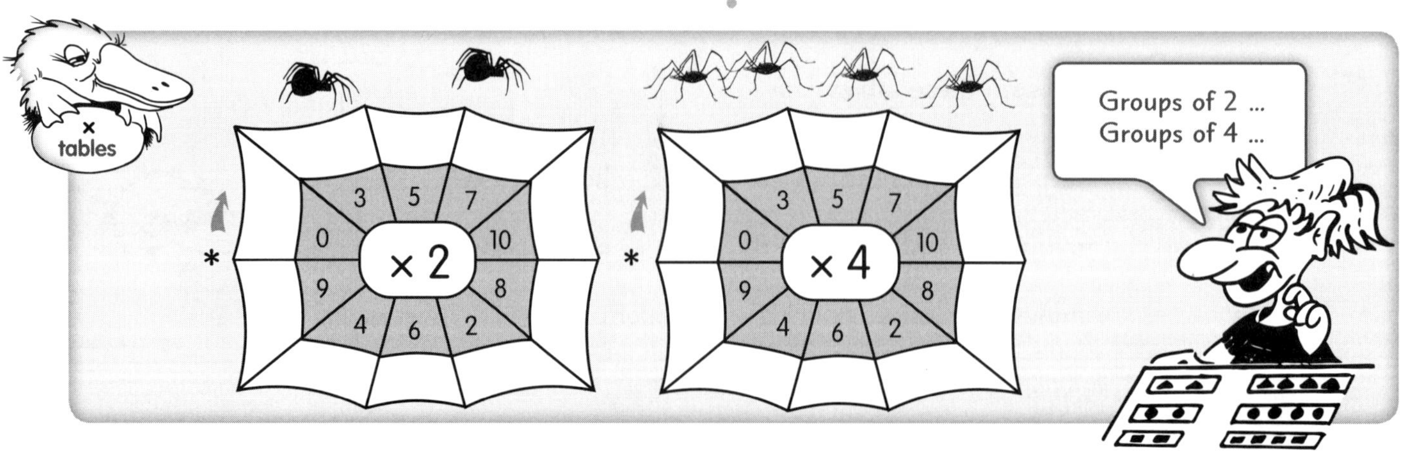

 ISBN 978 1 4886 2186 4

5:3 ☐ out of 11

1

Tens	Ones
4	2
+3	3

2

Tens	Ones
9	7
− 5	4

3 The time after 5 minutes after 20 to 8. ______

4 Draw 3 axes of symmetry on this circle.

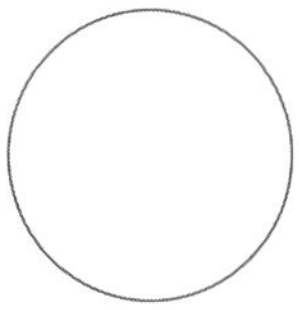

5 Name a shape that has 4 equal sides. ______

6 Months in one year. ______

7 The number two after 99. ______

8 I need $9 for one bike tyre. How much do I need for two? ______

9 How many angles do 4 squares have?

______

10

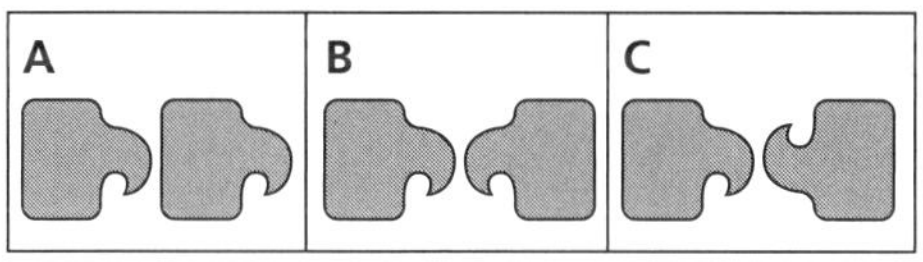

Which of these boxes shows a:

a flip? ______ **b** slide? ______

11 6 × 11 = ______

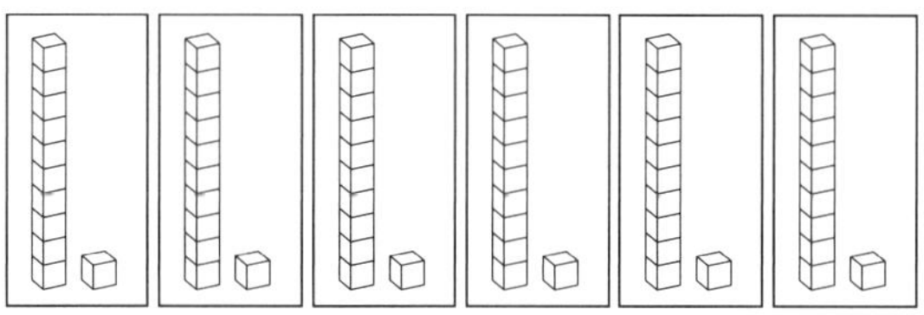

Extension 5:4 ☐ out of 5

1 13 hundredths plus 21 hundredths.

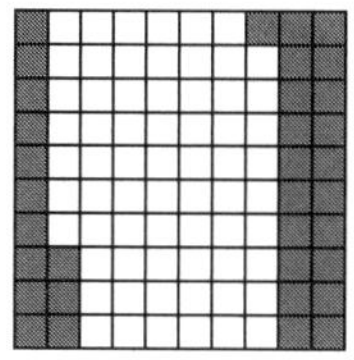

______

or 0· ______.

2 Which 2D shape has the greatest number of axes of symmetry? ______

3 Regular shapes have all angles and all sides equal. What regular shape uses this angle?

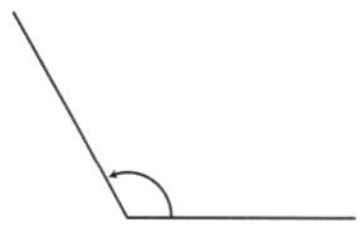

______

4 If this shape is turned, which shape below could it *not* look like?

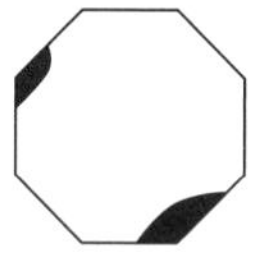

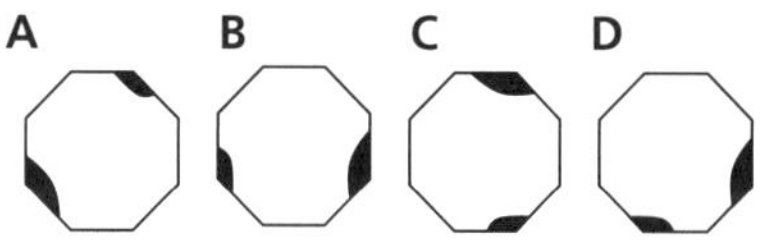

______

5 8 mugs are in each box. How many mugs would be in 12 boxes? ______

Challenge

Represent (or show) $\frac{10}{100}$ in as many ways as you can.

Division Using the Number Line

How many 4s in 12?

Jump 4 at a time.

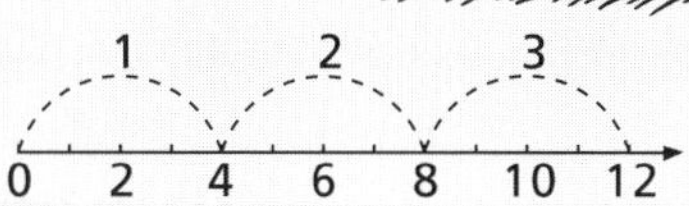

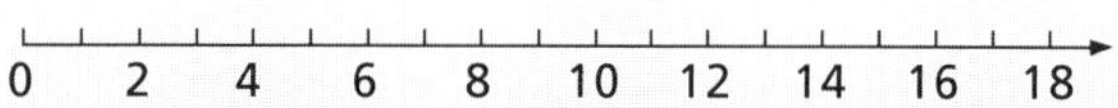

Use this number line to find how many:

a 5s in 15 ______ **b** 3s in 15 ______

c 6s in 18 ______ **d** 3s in 18 ______

e 2s in 14 ______ **f** 4s in 16 ______

6:1 ☐ out of 14

1. 4 + 9 ______
2. 7 + 3 ______
3. 10 − 2 ______
4. 9 − 3 ______
5. $\begin{array}{r} 17 \\ +\ 10 \\ \hline \end{array}$
6. 4 + 4 ______
7. 3 + 5 ______
8. 8 lots of 10. ______
9. 13 minus 6. ______
10. $\begin{array}{r} 19 \\ -\ 8 \\ \hline \end{array}$

11.

April						
Sun	Mon	Tue	Wed	Thu	Fri	Sat
	1	2	3	4	5	6
7	8	9	10	11	12	13
14	15	16	17	18	19	20
21	22	23	24	25	26	27
28	29	30				

a What day is the 19th? ______
b How many Wednesdays in the month? ______
c What is the first day of the month? ______
d What is the day three days before the 26th? ______

12. The number after 187. ______

13. Write the fraction for the part shaded.

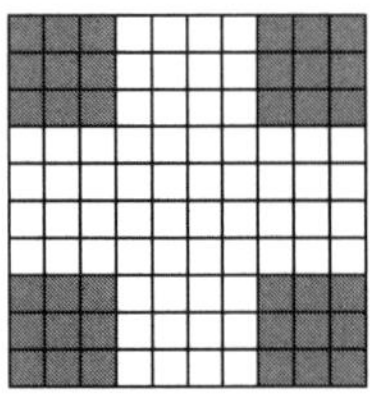

______ out of ______

or 0· ______.

14. If I toss a coin in the air, would heads be more likely than tails? ______

6:2 ☐ out of 17

1. 20 + 20 ______
2. 12 + 7 ______
3. 15 − 5 ______
4. 14 − 12 ______
5. $\begin{array}{r} 34 \\ +\ 5 \\ \hline \end{array}$
6. 5 × 4 ______
7. 10 lots of 4. ______
8. 18 divided by 2. ______
9. 4 × 4 ______
10. $\begin{array}{r} 4 \\ \times\ 7 \\ \hline \end{array}$

11. Draw a slide and a flip of this pattern.

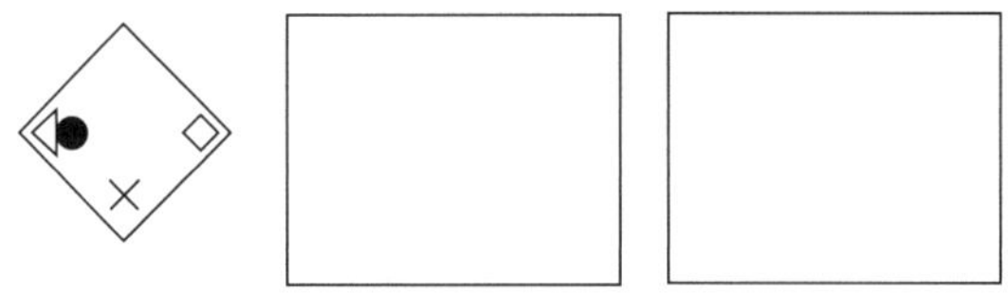

Slide Flip

12. Which angle is the largest? ______

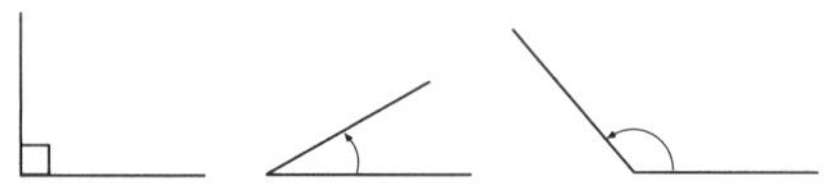

A B C

13. Which season of the year is March, April and May? ______

14. 1 006, 1 007, 1 008, ______, ______

15. The numeral for five hundred and twenty-six. ______

16. On this hundred square, the part covered is:

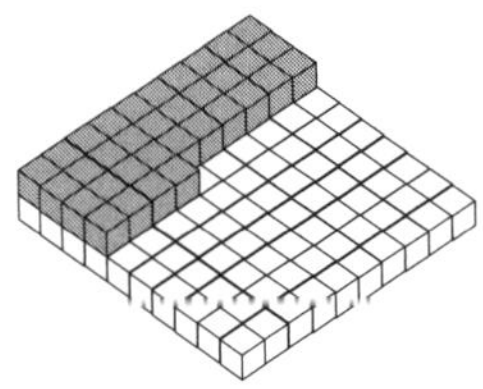

______ or 0· ______.

17. Is this a flip, a slide or a turn? ______

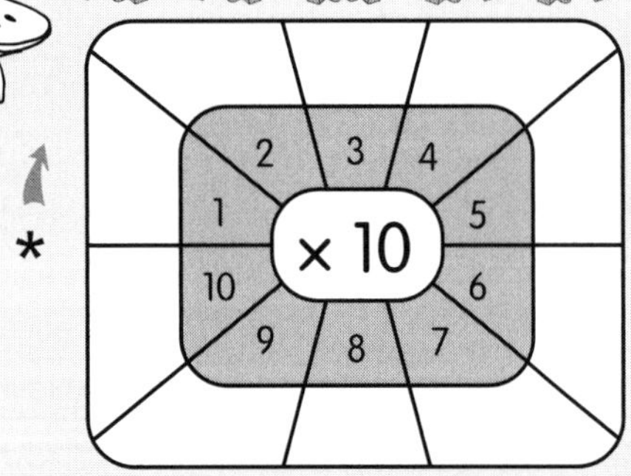

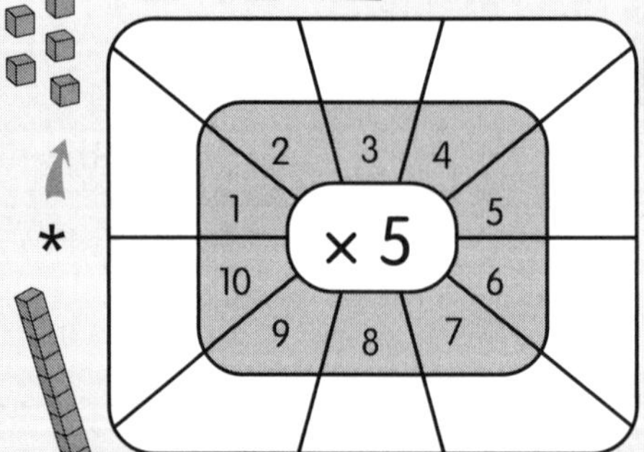

© PEARSON AUSTRALIA 2018 • *AUSTRALIAN SIGNPOST MATHS 4 MENTALS* • ISBN 978 1 4886 2186 4

6:3 ☐ out of 8

1.

Tens	Ones
\$2	4
+ \$1	5

2.

Tens	Ones
7	5
– 5	4

3. Draw the axes of symmetry of this shape.

4. What decimal is shown?

a 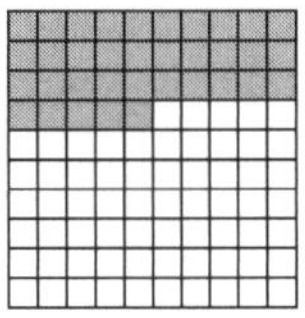

0· ______

b 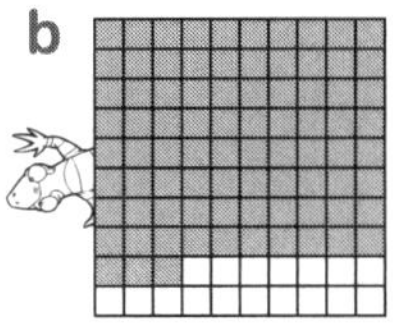

0· ______

5. List all the possible outcomes if two coins are tossed. ______

6. Complete this tile pattern by flipping tiles to the right or down.

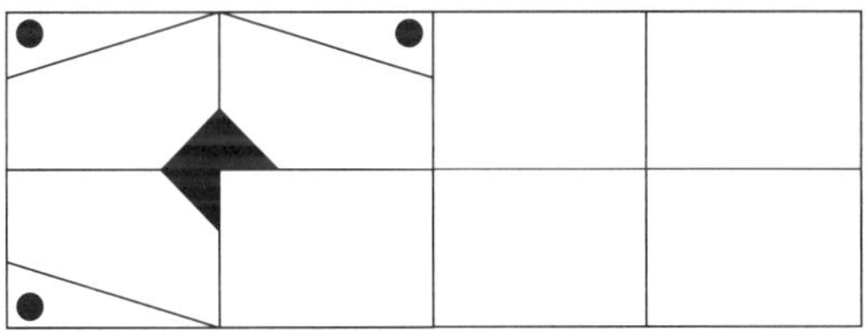

7. How many lines of symmetry does a rectangle have? ______

8. 

$4 \times 12 =$ ☐

☐ = ______

6:4 Extension ☐ out of 7

1. How many days in autumn? ______
2. How many three-digit numbers can be made using the three digits:
   a 8, 7 and 0 ______ **b** 5, 3 and 1? ______
3. 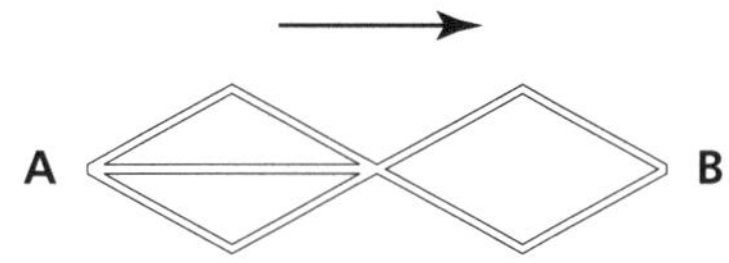

How many different ways are there of going from A to B? ______

4. 28 soldiers stood in each row. How many soldiers in three rows? ______
5. Tomorrow is Friday. What day was it 8 days ago? ______
6. How many place-value tens blocks would be needed to reach two metres? ______
7. 47 + 35 ______

Challenge

Write a list of events that are very unlikely to happen but not impossible.

______

______

______

______

______

______

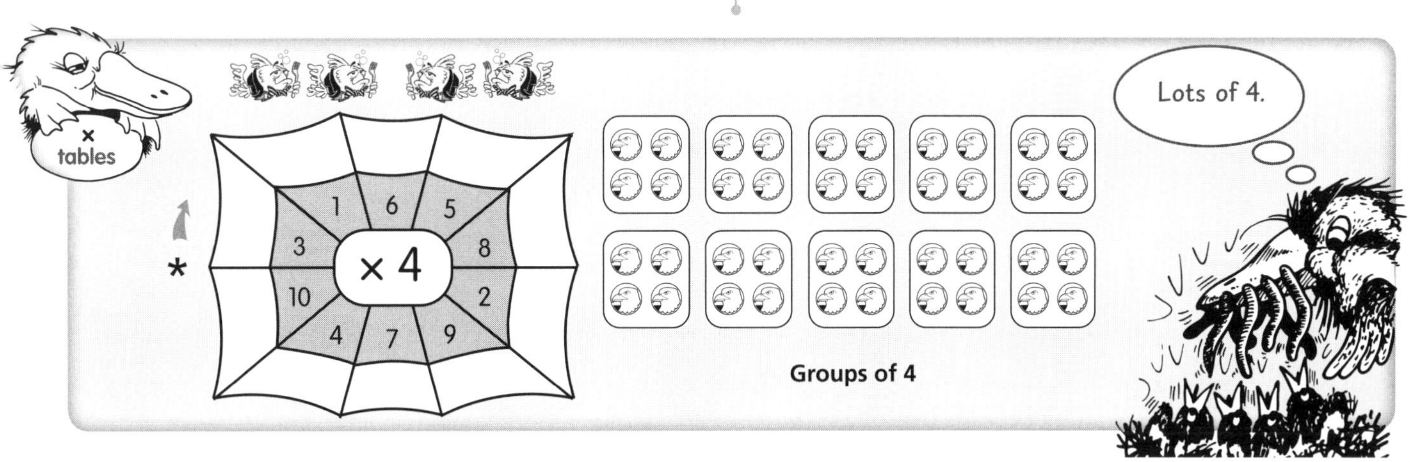

7:1 ☐ out of 17

1. 6 + 7 ______
2. 5 + 4 ______
3. 8 − 3 ______
4. 7 − 4 ______
5. 14 + 2 ______
6. 9 × 4 ______
7. 7 × 4 ______
8. Half of 10. ______
9. Subtract 3 from 6. ______
10. 18 − 6 ______
11. How many digits in the number 587? ______
12. Write the numeral shown on the abacus. ______

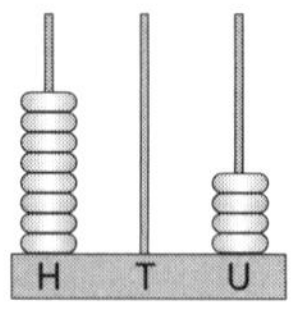

13. Write as millimetres:
    a 4 cm 3 mm = ______ mm
    b 7 cm 9 mm = ______ mm
14. List these angles in order of size, from smallest to largest. ______

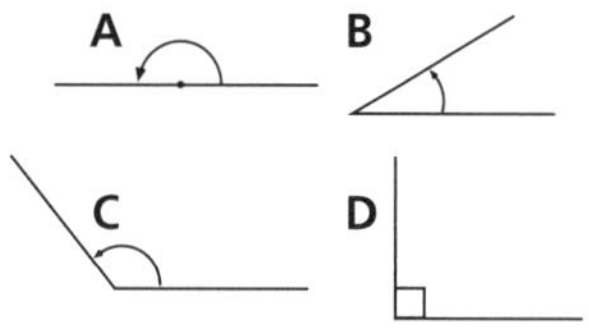

15. Days in 2 weeks. ______
16. In which month is Christmas? ______
17. What decimal is shown?

a 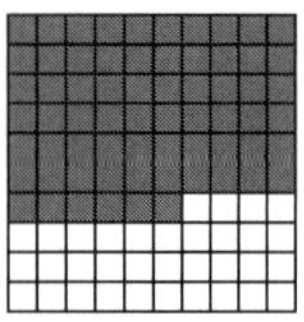

0· ______

b 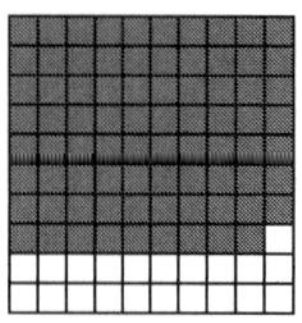

0· ______

7:2 ☐ out of 17

1. 18 + 4 ______
2. 18 − 4 ______
3. 5 × 2 ______
4. 8 × 2 ______
5. 73 − 2 ______
6. 8 × 4 ______
7. 5 × 4 ______
8. 6 + 3 − 3 ______
9. 2 + 14 − 14 ______
10. 4 × 8 ______
11. Write the fraction for the part shaded.
    ______ out of ______

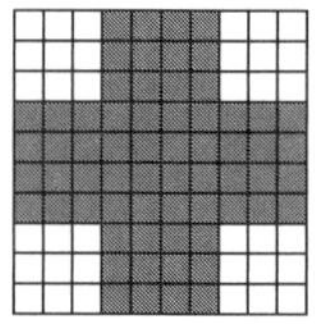

12. A shape has 4 equal sides and 4 equal angles. What is it? ______
13. Abbreviation for centimetres. ______
14. Cents in $1.25. ______
15. Four more after 3 497. ______
16. What date is the:
    a third Friday? ______
    b second Sunday? ______

DECEMBER

Sun	Mon	Tue	Wed	Thu	Fri	Sat
		1	2	3	4	5
6	7	8	9	10	11	12
13	14	15	16	17	18	19
20	21	22	23	24	25	26
27	28	29	30	31		

17. If a hat contains 2 red and 4 blue counters, how many counters would need to be drawn out, to be sure of getting a:
    a red counter? ______
    b blue counter? ______

a

	2	4	6	8	10
× 2					

b

	2	4	6	8	10
× 5					

c

	1	2	3	4	5
× 4					

d

	1	2	3	4	5
× 10					

e

	6	3	8	7	9
× 0					

f

	4	7	3	9	6
× 1					

7:3 ☐ out of 8

1.

Tens	Ones
2	8
+5	1

2.

Tens	Ones
3	5
+6	4

3. Shade 65 out of 100.
What part is not shaded? ______

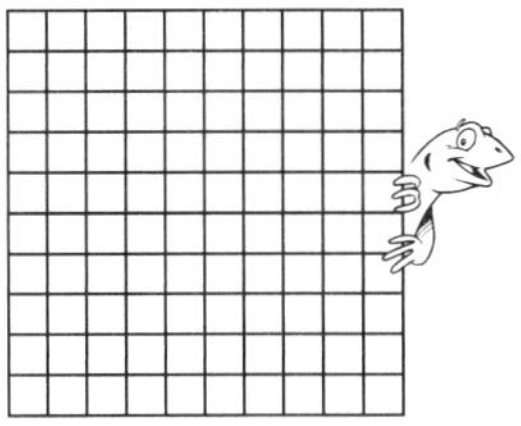

4. 

This bar is ______ mm long.

5. What is the month:
   a before August? ______
   b after March? ______

6. 643 is made up of:
______ hundreds ______ tens ______ ones

7. a The next odd number after 13. ______
   b The next even number after 13. ______

8. impossible | unlikely | even chance | very likely | certain

I throw a standard dice once. Choose a label for the chance that the dice shows:
   a a three ______
   b an odd number ______
   c larger than two ______
   d a number ______

7:4 Extension ☐ out of 5

1. How many days in 3 weeks? ______

2. $\frac{1}{4}$ plus $\frac{1}{4}$. ______

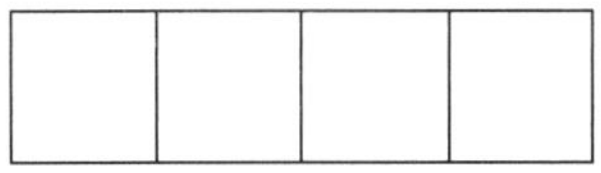

3. 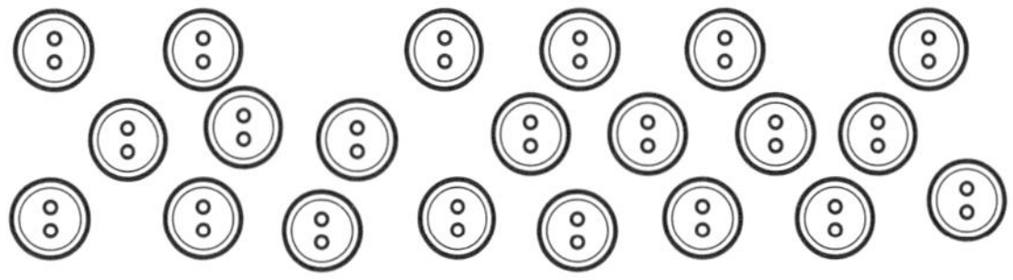

$\frac{1}{3}$ means 1 share out of 3.
What is $\frac{1}{3}$ of 21? ______

4. Twenty people stood in a straight line holding hands. How many hands were held? ______

5. What fraction of $1 is:
   a 50c? ______
   b 25c? ______

Challenge

Draw or list objects in the environment that have an angle smaller than a right angle.

Turn to ID Card C on page 8.
Give the answers for these numbers.

(23) ______ (24) ______
(25) ______ of a cube (26) ______
(27) ______ (28) ______
(29) ______ watch (30) ______ clock

8:1 — out of 16

1. 3 + 4 ______
2. 8 + 7 ______
3. 10 − 6 ______
4. 7 − 2 ______
5. 20 + 5 = ______
6. 3 × 2 ______
7. 8 × 4 ______
8. 5c plus 5c. ______
9. Add 7 and 4. ______
10. 26 − 4 = ______

11. Write the numeral for the number shown on the abacus. ______

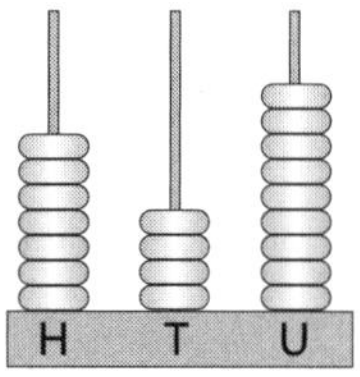

12. Is a pyramid a 3D object? ______
13. Starting at the arrow, colour as you move:
2 right, 3 down,
2 left, 2 down,
4 right, 3 down,
3 left, 1 down.

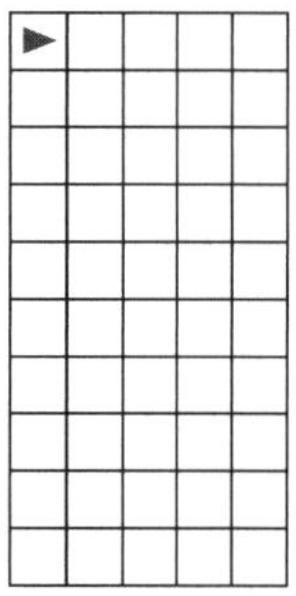

14. Which of these shapes is regular? ______

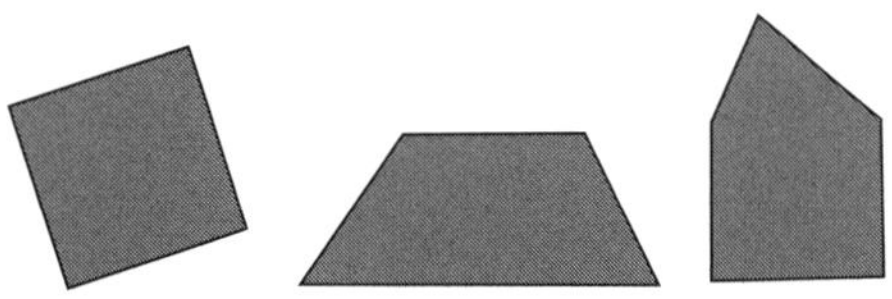

A B C

15. This line is ______ centimetres long.

16. Write six hundred and thirteen as a numeral. ______

8:2 — out of 18

1. 12 + 6 ______
2. 27 − 3 ______
3. 9 × 5 ______
4. 5 × 4 ______
5. 71 + 8 = ______
6. 9 × 4 ______
7. 4 × 4 ______
8. 14 ÷ 2 ______
9. 12 divided by 4. ______
10. 4 × 7 = ______
11. One thousand as a numeral. ______
12. Write 90 cents using a dollar sign and a decimal point. ______
13. **a** Double 4. ______
b Double 8. ______
c Double 3. ______
14. Which angle is the smallest? ______

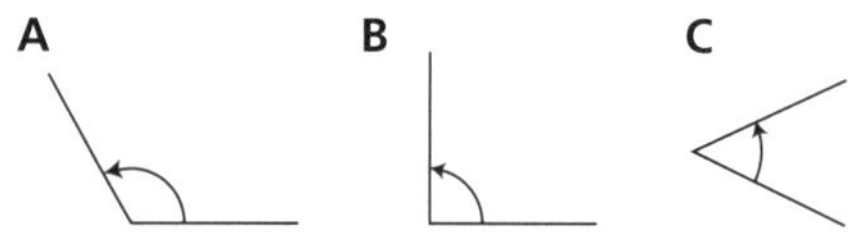

15. Days in 48 hours. ______
16. How many angles has a pentagon? ______
17. **a** How many faces has this pyramid? ______
b How many corners has this pyramid? ______

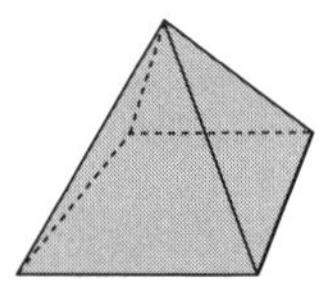

18. Write as centimetres and millimetres.
a 84 mm = ______ cm ______ mm
b 59 mm = ______ cm ______ mm

Complete, then learn these tables from page 84.

a 1 year = ______ weeks
b 1 leap year = ______ days
c 1 year = ______ months
d 1 decade = ______ years
e 1 year = ______ days
f 1 century = ______ years

 • *AUSTRALIAN SIGNPOST MATHS 4 MENTALS* • ISBN 978 1 4886 2186 4

8:3 ☐ out of 11

1

Tens	Ones
\$4	4
+ \$3	3

2

Tens	Ones
5	6
+ 3	4

3 Write the odd numbers up to 10. ____________

4 Write 143 in words. ____________

____

5 Write the biggest number you can using 3 digits. ____________

6 Name the two solids in this model. ____________

____

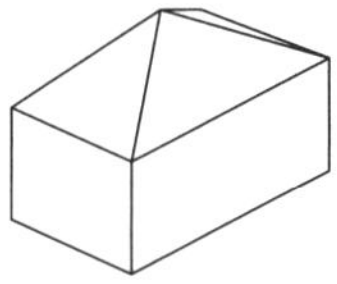

7 3000 + 800 + 50 + 7 ____________

8 Kyle had 25 toy cars and Tyler had twice as many.

How many toy cars did Tyler have?

____

9 Write 6th in words. ____________

10 The value of four 20c coins. ____________

11

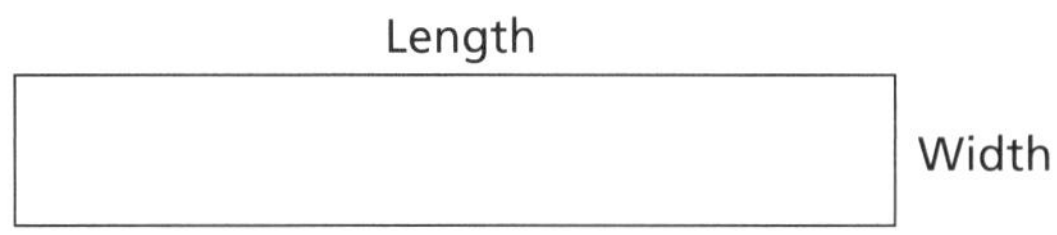

Use your ruler to measure:

a the length of this rectangle. ____________

b the width of this rectangle. ____________

8:4 ☐ out of 5

Extension

1 What am I if my faces are all rectangles? ____________

2 Amy earned \$15 more than Thanh. Lee and Thanh earned \$32 each.

How much did Amy earn? ____________

3

How many different pairs could be chosen from these people? ____________

4 This figure has squares of different sizes.

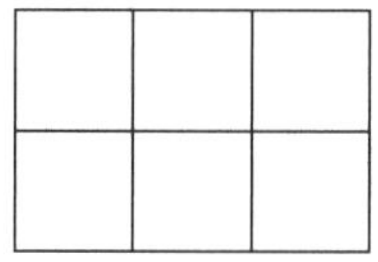

How many squares altogether? ____________

5 **a** Days in a year. ____________

b Days in a leap year. ____________

Challenge

Draw a 3D object and describe it.

____

____

____

____

____

____

____

____

____

Rounding to the Nearest 5 Cents

To round to the nearest 5 cents, give the closest answer that ends in 5 or 0.

a Is \$1.37 closer to \$1.35 or \$1.40? ____________

b Is \$1.32 closer to \$1.30 or \$1.35? ____________

Round each of these to the nearest 5 cents.

c \$2.48 ________ **d** \$8.13 ________ **e** \$6.01 ________ **f** \$1.99 ________

AUSTRALIAN SIGNPOST MATHS 4 MENTALS • ISBN 978 1 4886 2186 4

9:1 — out of 18

1. 8 + 3 ______
2. 6 + 6 ______
3. 7 − 5 ______
4. 4 − 0 ______
5. 14 + 5 ______
6. 1 × 4 ______
7. 6 × 10 ______
8. Add $3 and $2. ______
9. Double 4. ______
10. 18 − 6 ______
11. 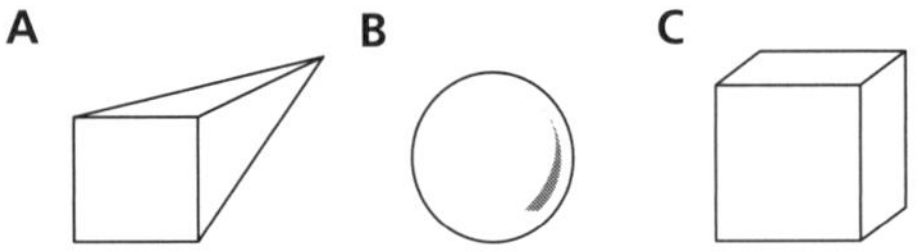

Which shape is a pyramid? ______
12. Write 3 m 25 cm as centimetres. ______
13. Write the number shown by this tally.

______
14. The numeral for 800 + 20 + 7. ______
15. Make the smallest number using 4, 7, 5 and 1. ______
16. Starting at the arrow, colour as you move:
4 up, 5 right
2 down, 3 left.
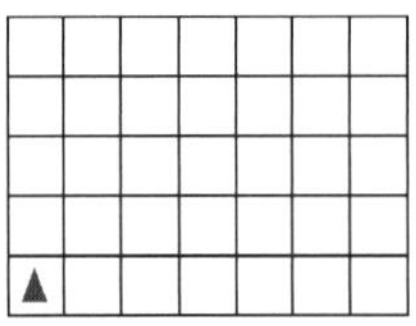
17. The total value of these coins in decimal form. ______
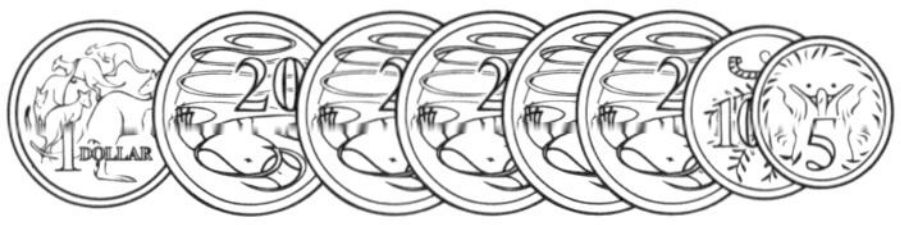
18. How many tens in 6982? ______

9:2 — out of 16

1. 9 + 9 ______
2. 15 − 5 ______
3. 0 × 4 ______
4. 20 − 8 + 8 ______
5. 62 + 7 ______
6. 8 × 1 ______
7. 11 × 4 ______
8. 6 divided by 2. ______
9. 25 divided by 5. ______
10. 10 × 4 ______

11. How many edges on a cube? ______
12. Write 7 163 in its expanded form. ______
______
______
13. Write 2 cm 7 mm as millimetres. ______
14. 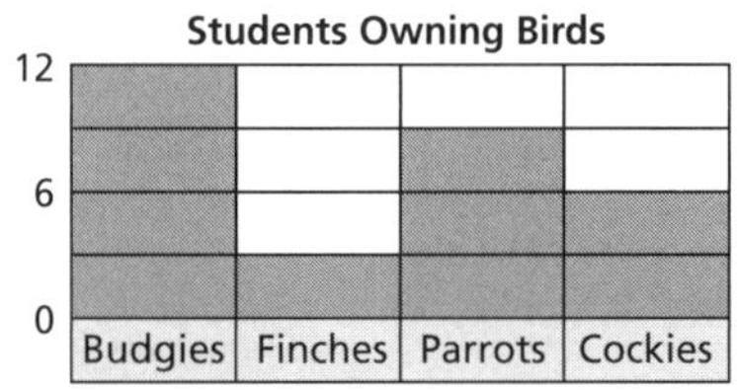

a. How many own parrots? ______
b. How many students own parrots or cockies together? ______
c. How many students altogether? ______
15. How many hundreds in 5 314? ______
16. 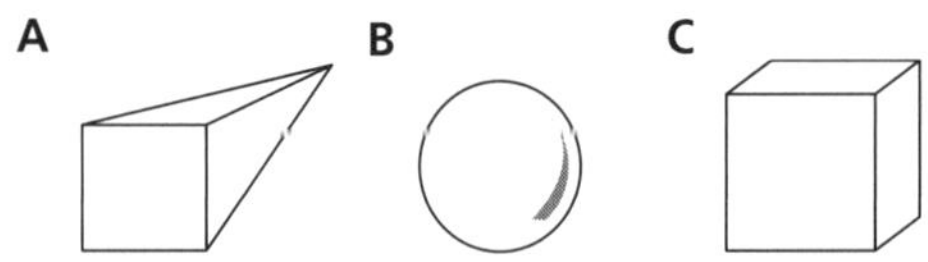

Which shape is a prism? ______

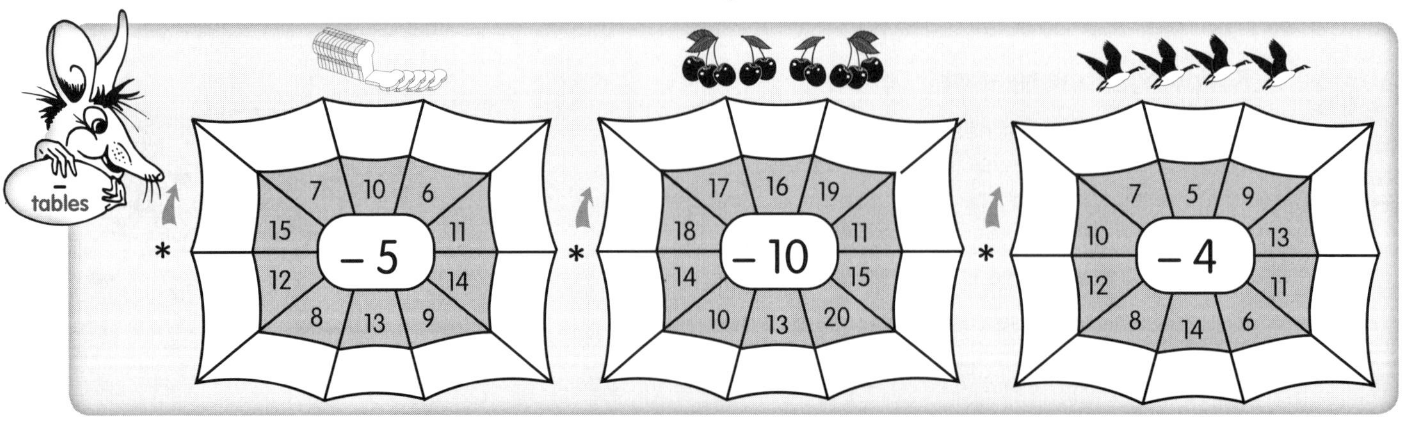

 ISBN 978 1 4886 2186 4

9:3 ☐ out of 9

1

Tens	Ones
$1	1
$5	7
+ $2	8

2

Tens	Ones
$2	3
$3	2
+ $1	7

3 9000 + 300 + 40 + 3 ________

4 Estimate then measure this bar's length.

Estimate = ____ cm Measure = ____ cm

Measure = ____ mm

5 The measure is

____ kg.

6 Write 8240 in words. ________

7 Jason drew 2 green monsters.
He gave each one 13 legs.

How many legs were there altogether? ________

8 Write as centimetres and millimetres:

a 93 mm ________

b 79 mm ________

9 Is each shape a prism, a pyramid or neither?

a 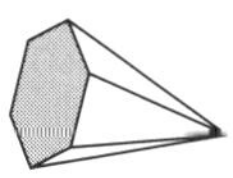

b 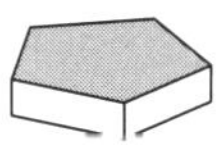

9:4 Extension ☐ out of 6

1 How many triangular faces are on:

a a square pyramid? ________

b a triangular pyramid? ________

2 How many 20c coins have the same value as:

a $7.40? ________ **b** $20? ________

3 How many sides on 12 hexagons? ________

4 **a** 76 − ☐ = 32

b 42 − ☐ = 17

5 **a** 12 + 12 + 12 + 12 ________

b 24 + 24 + 24 + 24 ________

6 89 + 47 ________

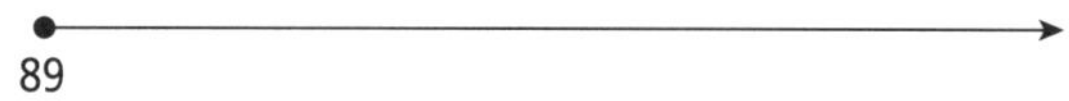

Challenge

What do you know about the number 838?

When you throw a dice, are all numbers equally likely? ________

Throw a dice 40 times and keep a tally of the results.

Number	1	2	3	4	5	6
Tally						

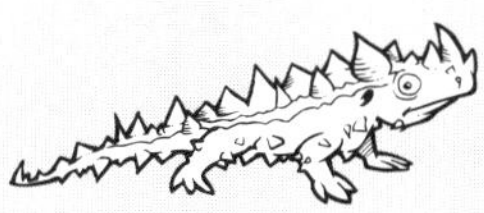

10:1 ☐ out of 19

1. 10 + 4 ______
2. 7 + 7 ______
3. 8 − 6 ______
4. 9 − 4 ______
5. 24
   \+ 4
6. 10 × 5 ______
7. 7 × 0 ______
8. Subtract 3 from 7. ______
9. Triple 2. ______
10. 25
    − 1

11. Rewrite as metres and centimetres.
    a 459 cm ______
    b 327 cm ______
12. Which number is larger, 178 or 631? ______
13. Write the next odd number after 76. ______
14. The length of this page correct to the nearest centimetre. ______ cm
15. Is 17 closer to 10 or 20? ______
16. Write 374 in words. ______

    ______
17. Which 3 coins have a total value of $5?

    ______
18. A square has ______ sides.
19. Write as millimetres.
    a 9 cm 5 mm ______
    b 4 cm 2 mm ______

10:2 ☐ out of 14

1. 30 + 70 ______
2. 20 − 10 ______
3. 3 × 10 ______
4. 4 × 10 ______
5. 12
   \+ 13
6. 6 × 10 ______
7. 10 × 10 ______
8. 6 ÷ 2 ______
9. 10 ÷ 2 ______
10. 10
    × 6

11. How many tens in 2830? ______
12. The measure is ______ kg.

13.

Goals Kicked This Year

Kym	卌 卌 卌 卌
Lisa	卌 IIII
Diane	卌 卌 III
Marta	卌 卌 II

a Who kicked 13 goals? ______
b How many did Marta kick? ______
c How many more goals did Kym kick than Lisa? ______

14. On this rectangular prism, how many:
    a faces? ______
    b edges? ______

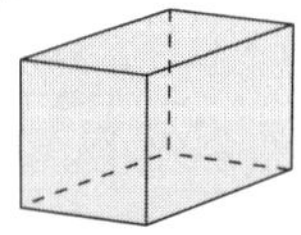

*
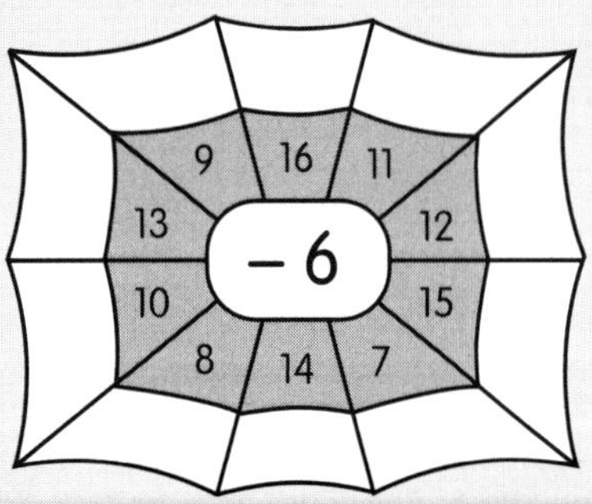

*
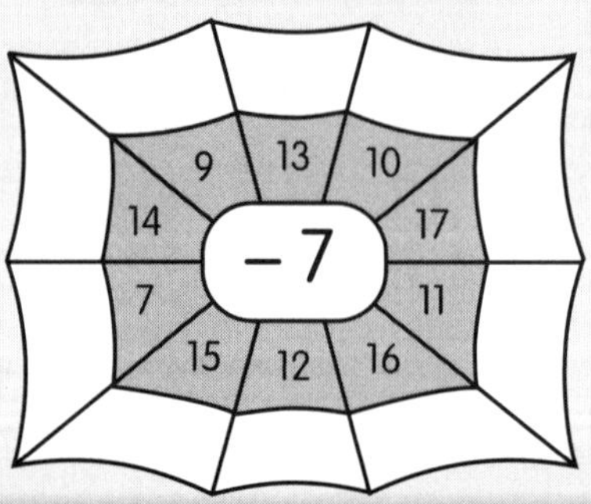

 ISBN 978 1 4886 2186 4

1.

Tens	Ones
5	4
1	9
+ 2	0

2.

Tens	Ones
6	2
1	8
+ 0	7

3. Estimate then measure the length of this bar.

Estimate = ________ cm   Measure = ______ cm

Measure = ______ mm

4. Write 5 m 21 cm as centimetres. ____________

5. Write 3621 in expanded notation.

____

____

6. If there are 10 dots in each row, how many dots are in 6 rows? ____________

7.

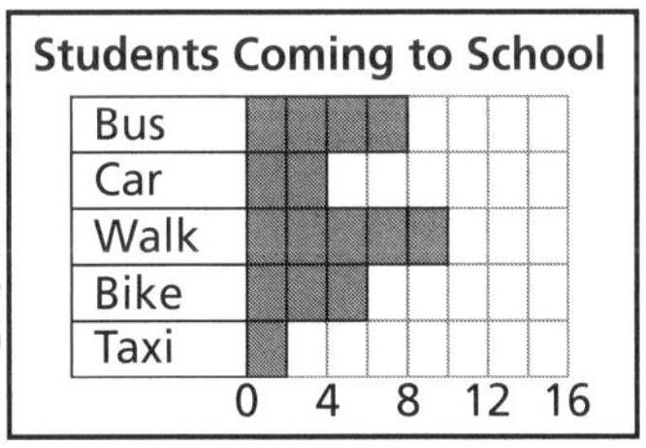

a How many students came to school by bus or bike? ____________

b How many more students walked to school than came to school by taxi? ____________

8. How many hundreds in 7832? ____________

1. How many corners has a square prism? ____________

2. 1, 10, 100, ________, ________, ________

3.

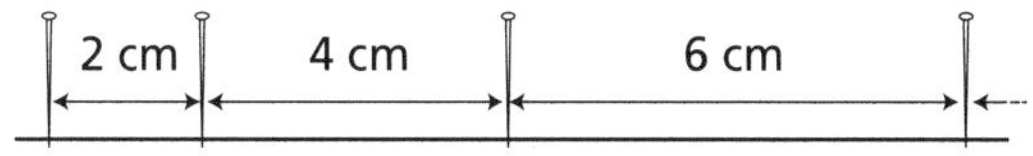

Pins were stuck into the floor using the pattern shown above.

What was the distance between:

a the 5th and 6th pins? ____________

b the 1st and 6th pins? ____________

4. How many hours in 4 days? ____________

5. 88 + 34 ____________

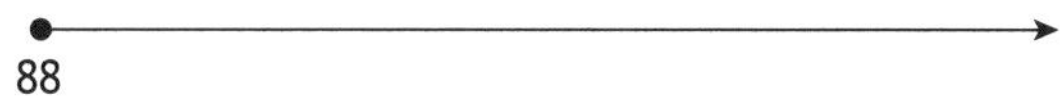

6. How many 20c coins have the same value as:

a $3.40? ______   b $12 ______

Challenge

Draw and label as many different 2D shapes as you can.

Addition Linked to Subtraction

If 6 + 7 = 13,
then 13 − 6 = 7
13 − 7 = 6

a 5 + 6 = ☐   11 − 5 = ____   11 − 6 = ____

b 5 + 7 = ☐   12 − 5 = ____   12 − 7 = ____

c 6 + 8 = ☐   14 − 6 = ____   14 − 8 = ____

d 8 + 7 = ☐   15 − 8 = ____   15 − 7 = ____

e 8 + 5 = ☐   13 − 8 = ____   13 − 5 = ____

f 7 + 6 = ☐   13 − 7 = ____   13 − 6 = ____

11:1 ☐ out of 20

1. 3 × 2 ____
2. 10 − 7 ____
3. 9 + 2 ____
4. 6 − 4 ____
5. 21 + 4 ____
6. 3 + ☐ = 10, ☐ = ____
7. 4 + 7 ____
8. 3 less than 12. ____
9. 8 more than 6. ____
10. 28 − 16 ____
11. Write the number before 825. ____
12. The value of these coins. ____

13. Minutes in an hour. ____
14. $10 and $15. ____
15. Arrange in order, from smallest to largest: 2 972, 2 927, 2 982.

____

16. Write the numeral three thousand and thirty. ____
17. This is a net for a p____.

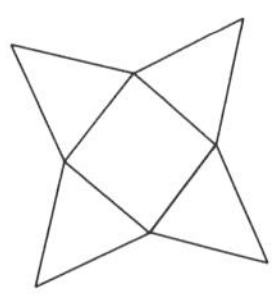

18. Round off to the nearest ten:
    a 786 ____ **b** 804 ____
19. The numeral shown below. ____

2	thousands	4	hundreds	1	tens	8	ones

20. The value of the 5 in 6 543. ____

11:2 ☐ out of 19

1. 12 + 8 ____
2. 14 − 8 ____
3. 7 × 10 ____
4. 9 × 5 ____
5. 16 + 11 ____
6. 7 × 10 ____
7. 8 × 10 ____
8. 14 ÷ 2 ____
9. 30 ÷ 10 ____
10. 2 × 9 ____

11. Thousands in 7 321. ____
12. 6 000 + 100 + 7 ____
13. Would this net make a pyramid, prism or neither? ____

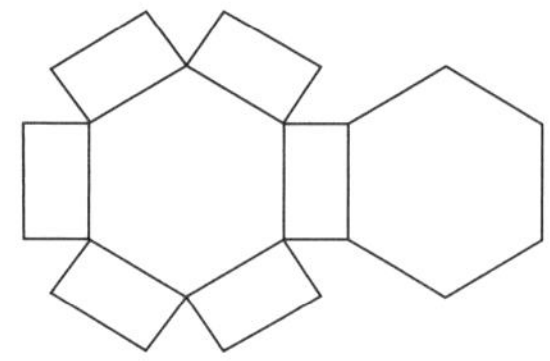

14. Could a prism be made from this set of faces? ____

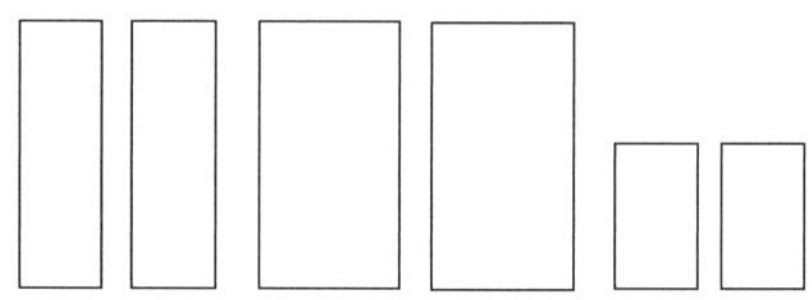

15. Write one thousand and fourteen as a numeral. ____
16. 8 000 + 200 + 70 + 5 ____
17. Hundreds in 7 523. ____
18. Round off 1 763 to the nearest thousand. ____
19. Use the short form to write 3 metres and 68 centimetres.

____ m ____ cm

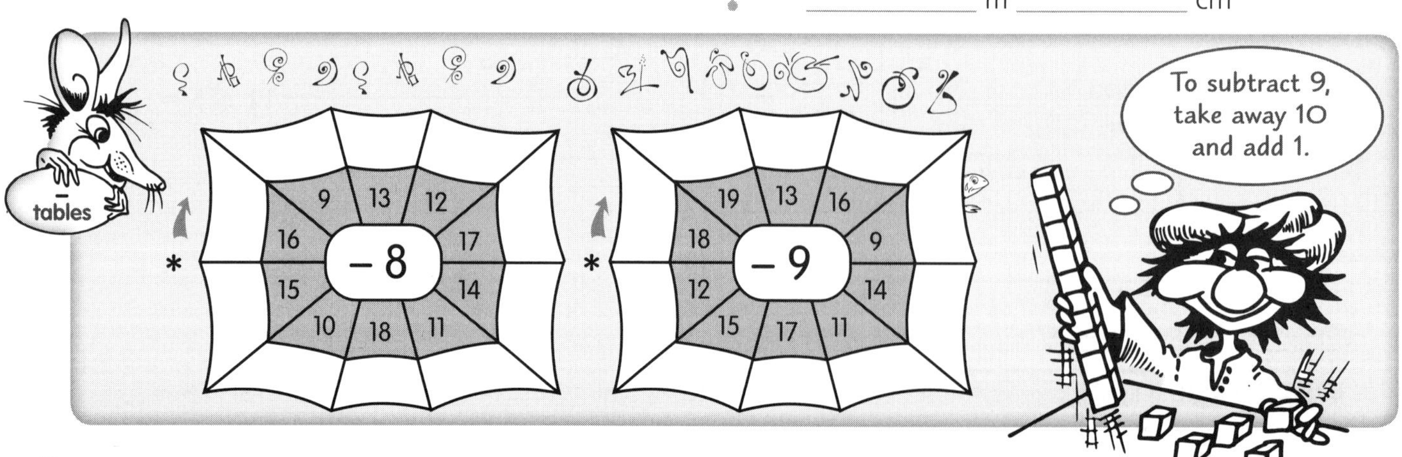

 • *AUSTRALIAN SIGNPOST MATHS 4 MENTALS* • ISBN 978 1 4886 2186 4

11:3
out of 8

❶

Hund.	Tens	Ones
1	4	2
+	5	3

❷

Hund.	Tens	Ones
	$8	7
+	$5	2

❸ 4000 + 600 + 40 + 3 ________

❹ What is the value of the 4 in 2340? ________

❺ 2652, 2653, 2654, ________ , ________

❻

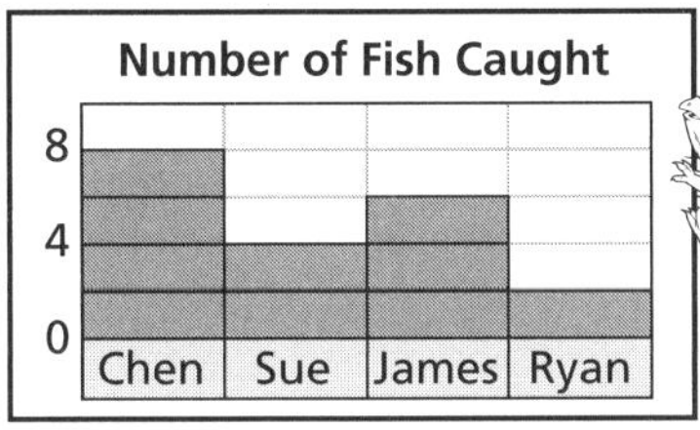

a Who caught the most fish? ________

b How many fish did Sue and Ryan catch altogether? ________

c How many more fish did Chen catch than Sue? ________

d How many fish were caught? ________

❼ Round 54479 to the nearest thousand. ________

❽ Write the numeral for the number shown. ________

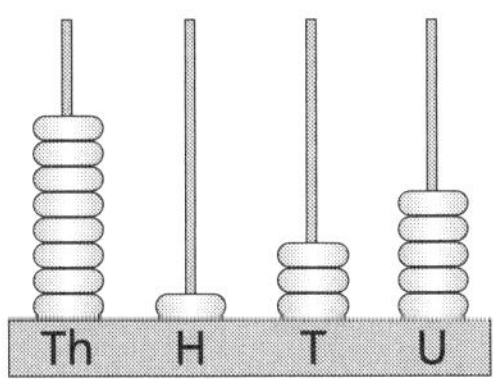

11:4
Extension

out of 6

❶ a The number of faces. ________

b The number of faces + corners − edges.

____ + ____ − ____ = ____

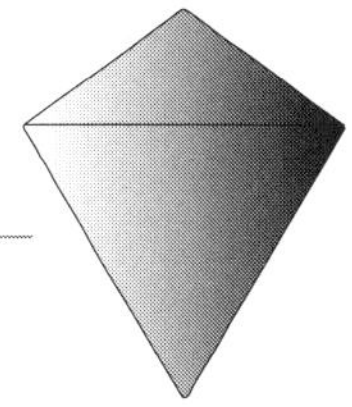

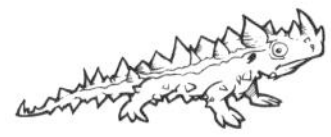

❷ Underline the word below, that is *not* the name of a quadrilateral.

diamond   trapezium   octagon

❸ How many lollies could I buy with $8 if each lolly cost 25c? ________

❹ a 31 + 31 + 31 + 31 ________

b 29 + 29 + 29 + 29 ________

❺ How many shoes are in 116 pairs? ________

❻ How many 60c stamps could I buy for $5? ________

Challenge

What facts are shown in this graph?

Name	Trips to the Shop
Greg	𝍸 𝍸 𝍸 I
Kate	𝍸 𝍸 IIII
Emily	𝍸 II
Sophie	III

____
____
____
____
____
____
____

What events have a 50–50 (or even) chance of happening? Write down as many as you can.

____
____
____
____
____

12:1 out of 15

1. 6 − 3 ______
2. 5 × 4 ______
3. 10 + 8 ______
4. 3 × 8 ______
5. $\begin{array}{r} 25 \\ -\ \ 2 \\ \hline \end{array}$
6. 7 + 4 ______
7. 9 − 2 ______
8. Six groups of 2. ______
9. 15c − 5c ______
10. $\begin{array}{r} 23 \\ +\ 10 \\ \hline \end{array}$

11. Round 507 to the nearest 10. ______
12. 800 + 30 + 6 ______
13. 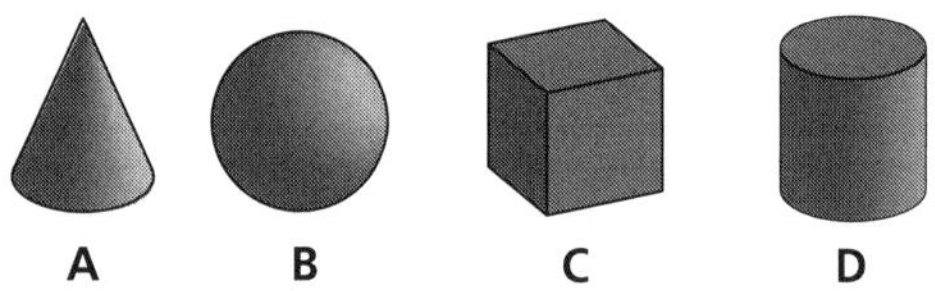

    a Which is a cylinder? ______

    b Which is a cone? ______
14. Which part is shaded? ______ sevenths.

15. What temperature is shown for each?

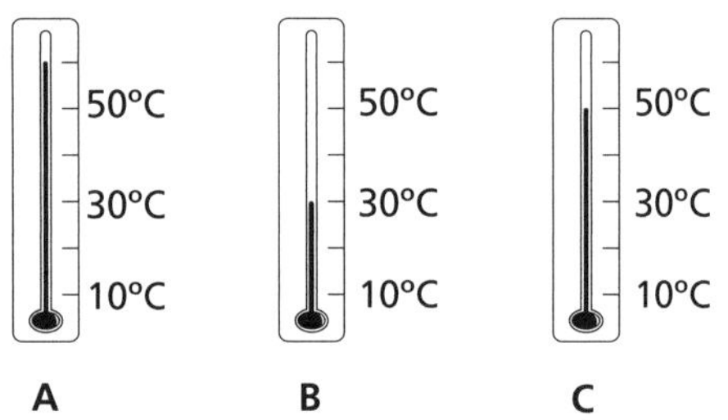

______ ______ ______

12:2 out of 19

1. 18 + 6 ______
2. 17 − 3 ______
3. 6 × 8 ______
4. 8 × 4 ______
5. $\begin{array}{r} 10 \\ \times\ \ 6 \\ \hline \end{array}$
6. 4 × 3 ______
7. 10 × 2 ______
8. 20 ÷ 2 ______
9. 6 × 4 ______
10. $\begin{array}{r} 8 \\ \times\ 9 \\ \hline \end{array}$
11. Round 2 399 to the nearest hundred. ______
12. The value of 7 in 175. ______
13. Write 1 389 in words. ______

    ______

    ______
14. The number 2 larger than 1 859. ______
15. Will this net make a pyramid, a prism or a cone? ______

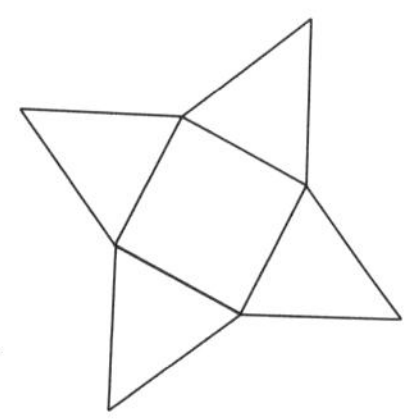

16. Does water freeze at 0°C? ______
17. Is a sphere a 3D object? ______
18. Write the numeral for the number shown. ______

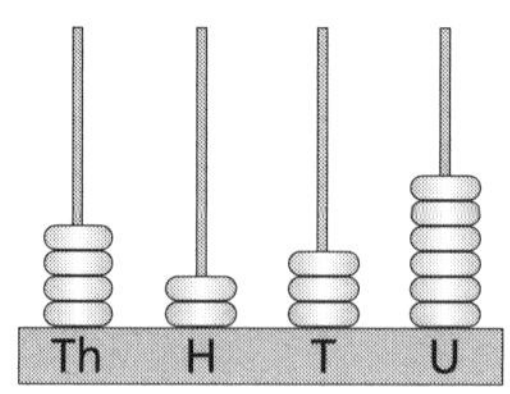

19. The value of 4 in 9 647. ______

×	5	10	4	0	2	6	1	3
2								
4								
8								
5								
10								

 • *AUSTRALIAN SIGNPOST MATHS 4 MENTALS* • ISBN 978 1 4886 2186 4

12:3 out of 10

1

Hund.	Tens	Ones
	1	2
6	2	5
+	7	3

2

Hund.	Tens	Ones
	1	2
	9	6
+	5	3

3 9 hundreds + 3 tens + 6 ones ________

4 Write fifty-three degrees Celsius in short form. ________

5

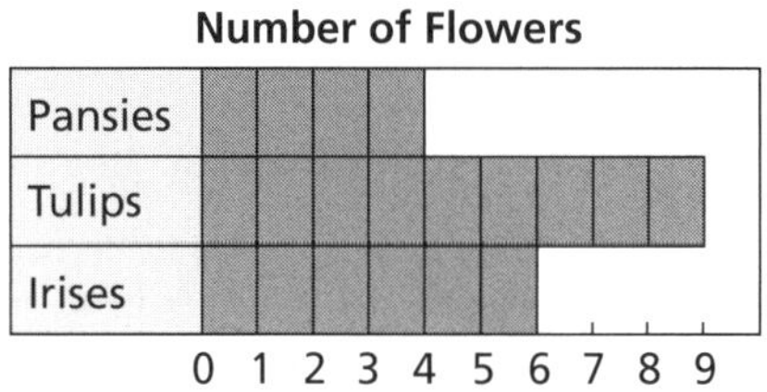

a Which was the smallest group? ________

b How many irises and tulips? ________

c How many more tulips than pansies? ________

6 The value of the 3 in 4830. ________

7 Add 3 hundreds, 5 tens and 7 ones. ________

8 Complete this pattern.

4343, 4344, ________, ________, ________

9 How many hundreds in 732? ________

10 Round 19234 to the nearest thousand. ________

12:4 out of 6

Extension

1 Which bowl has the:

a coolest water? ________

b warmest water? ________

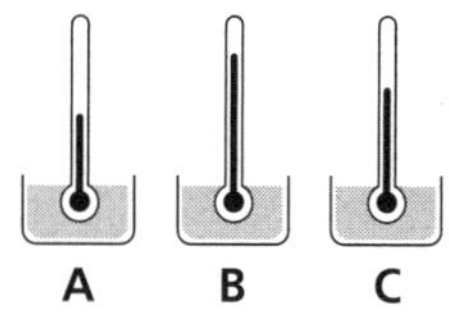

2 Am I a prism, a pyramid or neither if all my faces are triangles? ________

3 The Roman numeral for 5. ________

4 How many hours in a week? ________

5 (3 × 12) + (3 × 12) ________

6 If two slices of bread make 4 sandwiches, how many sandwiches can be made from a loaf of 24 slices?

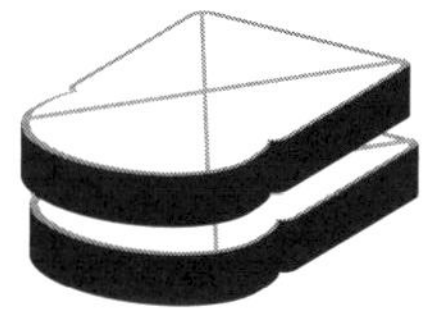

____

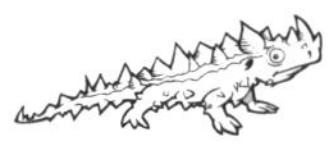

Challenge

Draw a pyramid. Label and describe its features.

____

____

____

____

____

What could this graph about living things represent?

____

Explain what you think each column could stand for.

____

____

____

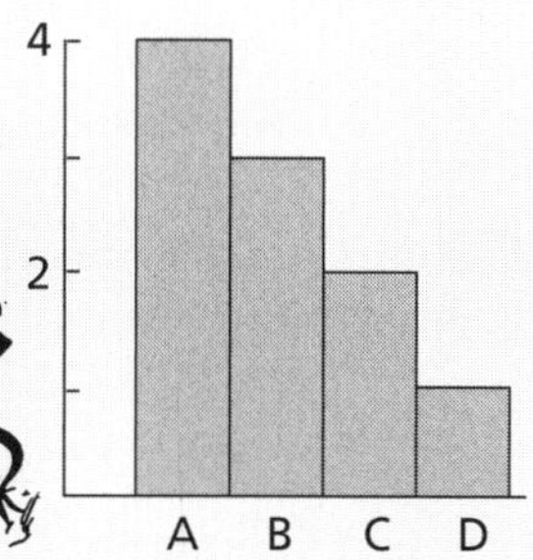

1. 17 − 15 ____
2. 8 × 2 ____
3. 15 + 3 ____
4. 18 − 3 ____
5. $\begin{array}{r} 20 \\ +\ \ 8 \\ \hline \end{array}$
6. 13 + 4 ____
7. 6 × 2 ____
8. Sum of 4 and 3. ____
9. Add $3 to $4. ____
10. $\begin{array}{r} 27 \\ -\ \ 6 \\ \hline \end{array}$
11. Write the numeral for 700 + 50 + 9. ____
12. Which of these is not a prism? ____

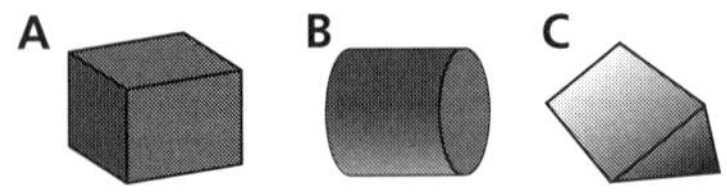

13. $\frac{1}{10}, \frac{2}{10}, \frac{3}{10}$, ____, ____, ____
14. Ely has 6 dolls, 3 bears and 7 trucks.

How many toys altogether? ____

15. Round off 278 to the nearest 10. ____
16. Write true (T) or false (F).
   a $\frac{3}{4} < \frac{1}{3}$ ____ b $\frac{3}{10} < \frac{7}{10}$ ____
   c $\frac{8}{8} = 1$ ____ d $\frac{1}{2} > \frac{2}{3}$ ____
17. Colour three quarters of this square.

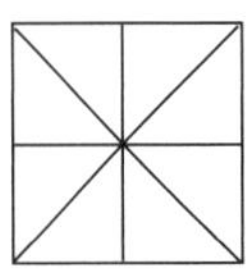

1. 15 − 5 ____
2. 50 − 10 ____
3. 27 + 9 ____
4. 21 + 7 ____
5. $\begin{array}{r} 31 \\ -\ \ 2 \\ \hline \end{array}$
6. 8 × 8 ____
7. 10 × 5 ____
8. 6 × 4 ____
9. 7 × 8 ____
10. $\begin{array}{r} 3 \\ \times\ \ 7 \\ \hline \end{array}$
11. Round 3 871 to the nearest hundred. ____
12. Colour the mercury to match the temperature.

a b c

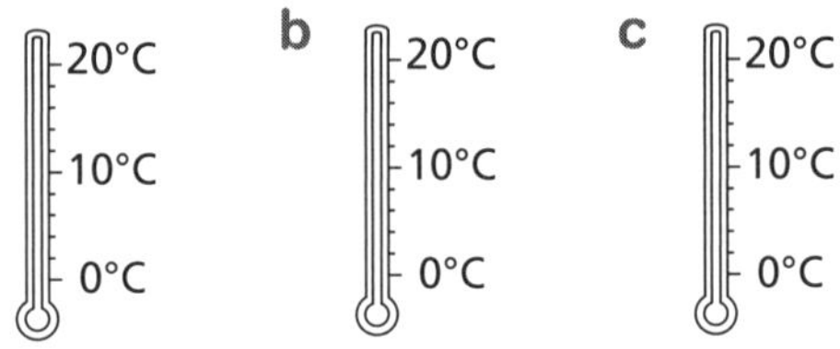

12°C **6°C** **19°C**

13. Which of these is a pyramid? ____

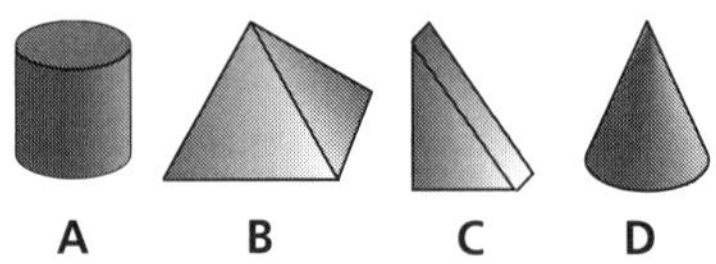

14. Write seventeen degrees Celsius in short form. ____
15. Write the numeral for six thousand two hundred and seventy-eight. ____
16. Put these numbers in order, from smallest to largest: 1 470, 165, 89, 932.

____

	2	4	6	8	10
× 4					

	1	2	3	4	5
× 8					

*

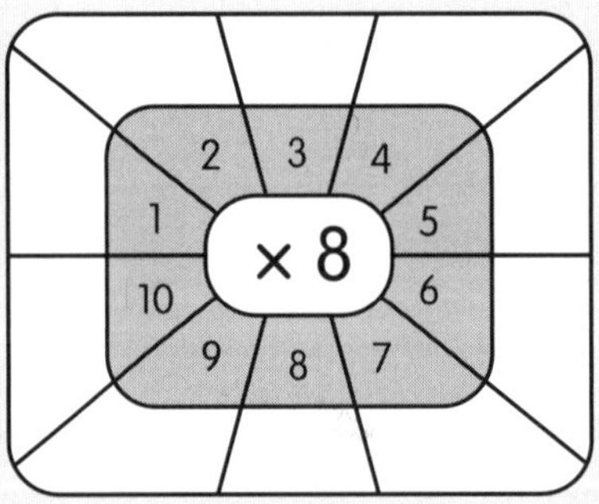

 • *AUSTRALIAN SIGNPOST MATHS 4 MENTALS* • ISBN 978 1 4886 2186 4

13:3 out of 12

1.

Tens	Ones
2	1
−	4

2.

Tens	Ones
4	3
−	5

3. Does water boil at 100°C? ______

4. What fraction of this shape is shaded? ______

5. Write an equivalent fraction for:
   a $\frac{1}{2}$ = ______ b $\frac{5}{5}$ = ______
   c $\frac{4}{5}$ = ______ d $\frac{4}{8}$ = ______

6. The value of the 4 in 4289. ______

7. Write the numeral six thousand four hundred and twenty. ______

8. Years in 3 centuries. ______

9. $\frac{1}{6}$, $\frac{2}{6}$, $\frac{3}{6}$, ______, ______, ______

10. On this triangular prism, how many:
    a faces? ______
    b edges? ______

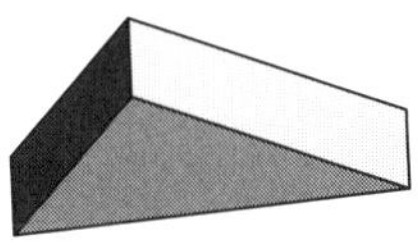

11. The number 10 more than 7. ______

12. Write in words 2006. ______

______

13:4 Extension out of 3

1. How many colours are needed to colour a cube if adjoining faces cannot have the same colour? ______

2.

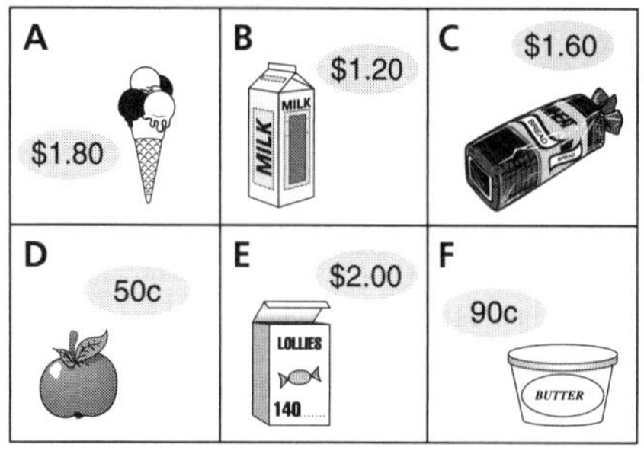

What is the cost of:
a two of B plus one of D? ______
b one of each item? ______
c four of D plus two of E? ______

3. 97 + 44 ______

Challenge

Complete each column as quickly as you can. Once finished, check your answers. Record your time.

3 × 2	______	6 × 10	______
5 × 4	______	5 × 5	______
2 × 10	______	8 × 5	______
2 × 5	______	4 × 8	______
3 × 8	______	1 × 10	______
5 × 8	______	9 × 8	______

Time = ______ seconds

To find the change from $2 when 15c is spent, start at 15c and count on as you give the change. (We say: 20c, 30c, 50c, $1, $2.)

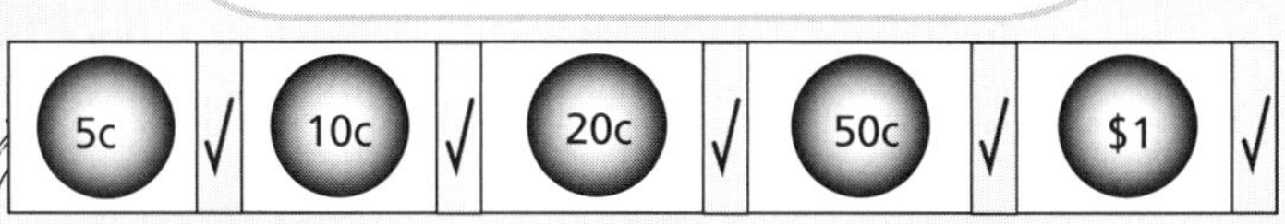

This shows you how to give change by counting on.

Find the change from $2 if you spend:
a $1.45 ______ **b** $0.90 ______
c $1.35 ______ **d** $0.75 ______
e $0.40 ______ **f** $1.05 ______

14:1 — out of 18

1. 19 − 6 ______
2. 4 × 4 ______
3. 13 + 4 ______
4. 17 + 3 ______
5. $\begin{array}{r} 26 \\ -\ \ 7 \\ \hline \end{array}$
6. 3 × 3 ______
7. 17 − 4 ______
8. Double 7. ______
9. 10c + 10c ______
10. $\begin{array}{r} 13c \\ +\ \ 5c \\ \hline \end{array}$
11. Which shape doesn't belong? ______

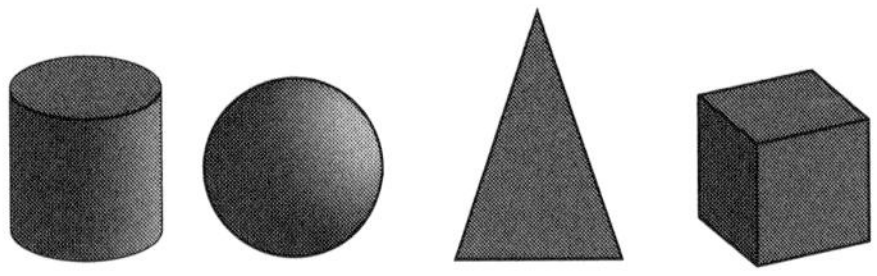

A B C D

12. $\frac{1}{7}$, $\frac{2}{7}$, $\frac{3}{7}$, ______, ______, ______
13. Colour five and a half balls.

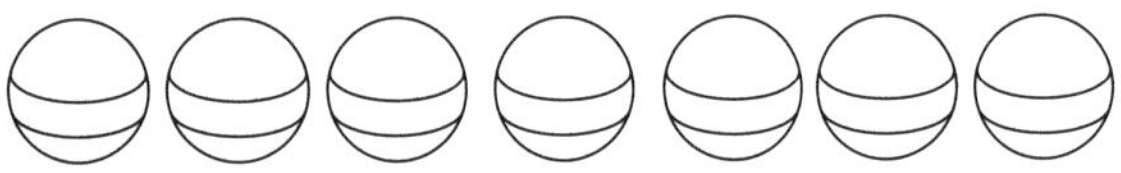

14. Write 754 in words. ______________________

____

15. Which number is larger, 9871 or 1789? ______
16. 6 rows of 4 boys is ______.
17. What day comes after Monday? ______
18. What fraction is shaded? ______

14:2 — out of 17

1. 16 + 4 ______
2. 15 − 5 ______
3. 8 × 3 ______
4. 6 × 6 ______
5. $\begin{array}{r} 19 \\ +\ \ 5 \\ \hline \end{array}$
6. 9 × 4 ______
7. 10 × 9 ______
8. 7 × 6 ______
9. 12 ÷ 4 ______
10. $\begin{array}{r} 5 \\ \times\ \ 8 \\ \hline \end{array}$
11. Shade $\frac{3}{4}$ of this rectangle.

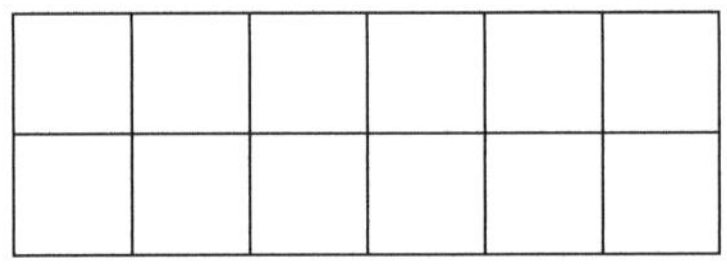

12. Use < or > in:
    - **a** 3214 ______ 3425
    - **b** 7029 ______ 6541
    - **c** 8132 ______ 8131

13. How many legs on 8 horses? ______
14. How many sides has a hexagon? ______

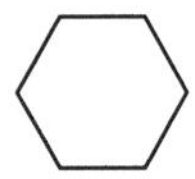

15. Is a square a quadrilateral? ______
16. True (T) or false (F)?
    - **a** $\frac{1}{4} = \frac{2}{8}$ ______
    - **b** $\frac{1}{4}$ is less than $\frac{1}{3}$. ______

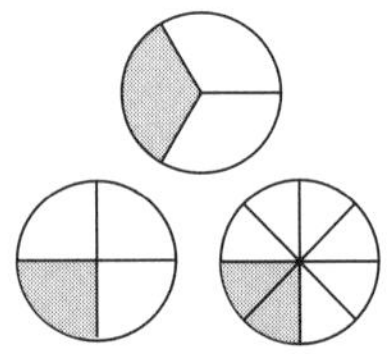

17. What two objects fit together to make this shape?

____

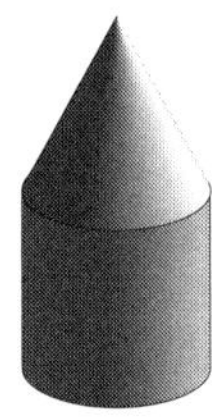

 ISBN 978 1 4886 2186 4

14:3 ☐ out of 8

1

Tens	Ones
4	0
−	7

2

Tens	Ones
5	0
− 3	4

3 Is this a prism or a pyramid or neither? ________

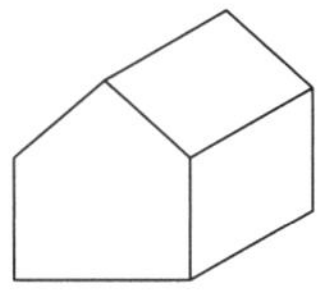

4 Write true (T) or false (F).

a $\frac{3}{3} = 1$ ________ **b** $\frac{1}{10} > \frac{4}{10}$ ________

c $\frac{1}{2} = \frac{5}{10}$ ________ **d** $\frac{4}{10} = \frac{2}{4}$ ________

5

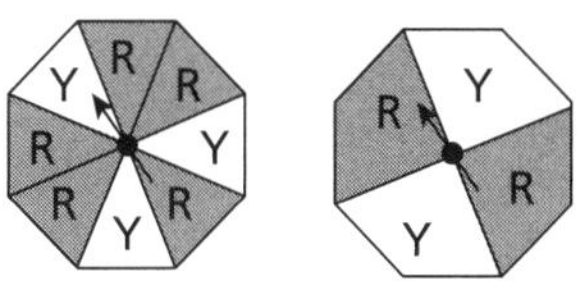

A **B**

red (R)
yellow (Y)

Which spinner is more likely to land on red than yellow? ________

6 How many bats? ________

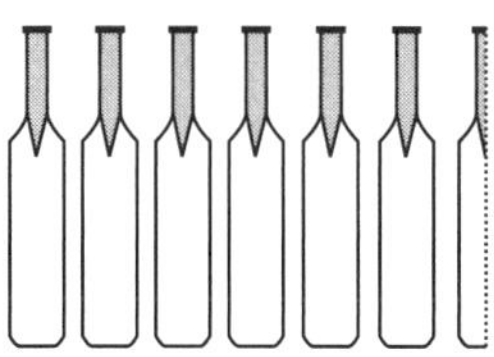

7 The value of 3 in 352. ________

8 Colour 3 tenths of the frogs green and 5 tenths red.

14:4 Extension ☐ out of 6

1 I have 2 surfaces, 1 edge and I can roll. What shape am I? ________

2 This pyramid is made of 50c coins.

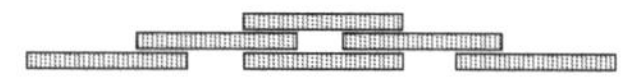

What is the total value if it is:

a 3 layers high? ________

b 4 layers high? ________

3 **a** How many days in autumn? ________

b How many days in winter? ________

4 **a** Our numeral for XXIV. ________

b Our numeral for XXXVII. ________

5 Su-Lin spent $1 and then found 5c. If she then had $6, how much did she have to start with? ________

6 **a** 32 + 32 + 32 + 32 ________

b 32 × 3 ________

Challenge

Draw and label fractions that are equivalent to $\frac{1}{2}$.

Turn to ID Card B on page 7.

Give the answers for these numbers.

(1) ________ line (2) ________ line

(3) ________ line (4) ________ line

(5) ________ line (6) ________ lines

(7) ________ lines (19) ________ line

  ISBN 978 1 4886 2186 4

15:1 out of 17

❶ 18 − 9 ______

❷ 3 × 6 ______

❸ 15 + 4 ______

❹ 17 − 3 ______

❺
$$\begin{array}{r} 21 \\ +\ 10 \\ \hline \end{array}$$

❻ 6 × 5 ______

❼ 8 + 7 ______

❽ 50c + 20c + 10c ______

❾ 8 less than 12. ______

❿
$$\begin{array}{r} 27 \\ -\ 19 \\ \hline \end{array}$$

⓫ Colour 4 and a half ice creams.

⓬ **a** Millilitres in 5 litres. ______

b Litres in 4000 mL. ______

⓭ Write 249 in words. ______

⓮ The value of the 6 in 671. ______

⓯ Is this a right angle? 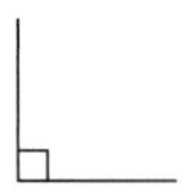 ______

⓰ I spent 20 cents, 10 cents and 50 cents.

How much did I spend? ______

⓱ What fraction of these animals is:

a black or grey? ______

b not black? ______

15:2 out of 14

❶ 60 + 10 ______

❷ 15 − 10 ______

❸ 8 × 4 ______

❹ 9 × 8 ______

❺
$$\begin{array}{r} 10 \\ \times\ 9 \\ \hline \end{array}$$

❻ 8 × 6 ______

❼ 6 × 6 ______

❽ 60 ÷ 6 ______

❾ 24 ÷ 3 ______

❿
$$\begin{array}{r} 8 \\ \times\ 7 \\ \hline \end{array}$$

⓫ Complete:

a $\frac{6}{8} = \frac{\square}{4}$ **b** $\frac{1}{3} = \frac{2}{\square}$

⓬ **A**

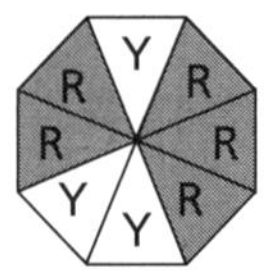

B

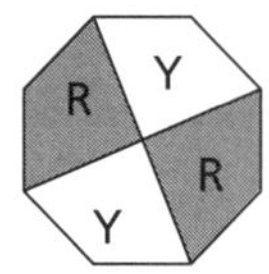

C

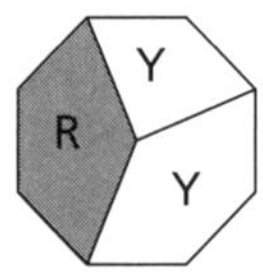

D

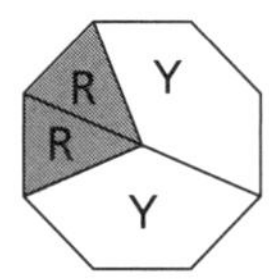

a Which spinner is more likely to land on R than Y? ______

b Which spinner is as likely to land on R than Y? ______

⓭ There are 40 golf balls. How many more are needed to make 90? ______

⓮ 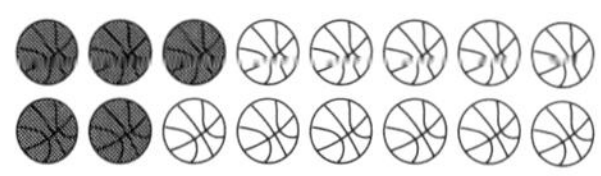 

What fraction of this group is:

a shaded? ______ **b** unshaded? ______

In each case, finish the given pattern.

a Add 4.

6					

b Multiply by 2.

2					

c Subtract 9.

90					

d Add 11.

11					

e Add 5.

4					

f Subtract 8.

90					

15:3 ☐ out of 9

1.

Tens	Ones
5	8
− 1	9

2.

Tens	Ones
$3	7
− $1	9

3. Arrange in order, from smallest to largest: 3096, 4123, 3127.

____

4. Hundreds in 5792. _______________

5. What must I add to 25 to make:

   a 30? __________ **b** 40? __________

6. Would it take about 1 L, 1800 mL, 500 mL or 20 L of water to fill 2 mugs?

____

7. If a right angle is a quarter turn, what is a straight angle? _______________

8. Use the short form to write:

   a 60 centimetres __________

   b 5 millimetres __________

   c 976 grams __________

   d 4·5 kilograms __________

9. $\frac{1}{8}$, $\frac{2}{8}$, $\frac{3}{8}$, ______, ______, ______, ______

15:4 Extension ☐ out of 5

1. Does each row, column and diagonal of this magic square, add up to 18? _______________

7	8	3
2	6	10
9	4	5

2. If # means "add 4" and ~ means "subtract 7", then 13 ##~~~ = __________

3. 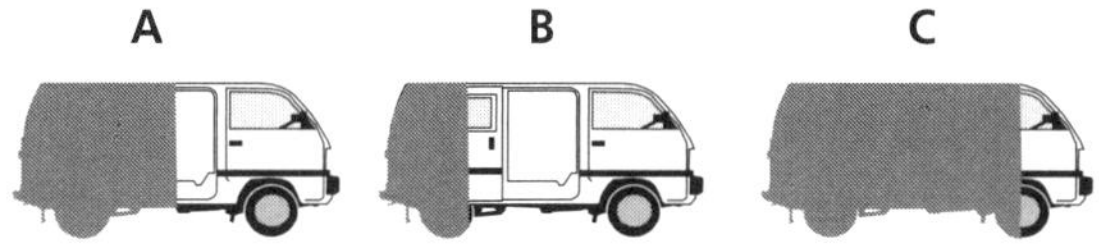

   Which van is about $\frac{3}{10}$ covered? __________

4. Eleven horses are in a stable. How many legs are there? __________

5. 99 + 32 __________

Challenge

List the name and capacity of containers in your kitchen or bathroom that are measured in L or mL.

____

____

____

____

Calculator Crossnumber Puzzle

Across		Down	
1	385 − 80	**1**	360 − 12
5	200 + 300	**2**	5224 + 20
6	8159 − 10	**3**	3 × 5
8	4 × 6	**4**	7040 + 1
9	761 − 50	**7**	1298 − 6
10	2012 + 6	**9**	700 + 8

16:1 out of 16

1. 7×3 ______
2. $10 + 9$ ______
3. $6 - 4$ ______
4. $10 - 8$ ______
5. $\begin{array}{r} 28 \\ -\ 10 \\ \hline \end{array}$
6. 8×6 ______
7. 0×5 ______
8. Increase 8 by 2. ______
9. Triple 4. ______
10. $\begin{array}{r} 0 \\ +\ 0 \\ \hline \end{array}$

11. The total number of days in April, June and November. ______
12. 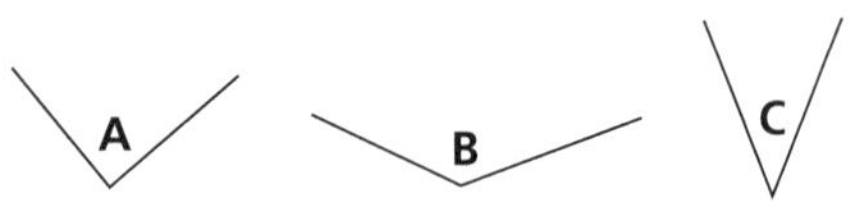

Which angle is the right angle? ______
13. The month before June. ______
14. Write the mixed number.
    a three and a half ______
    b one and three quarters ______
15. The area of this shape.
    ______ cm²
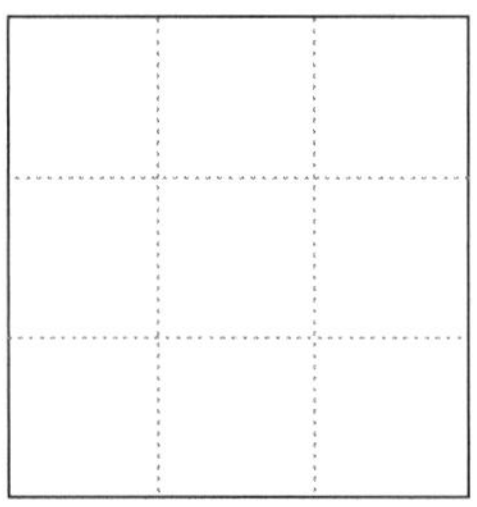
16. Show the level, if 700 mL of water is put into this container.
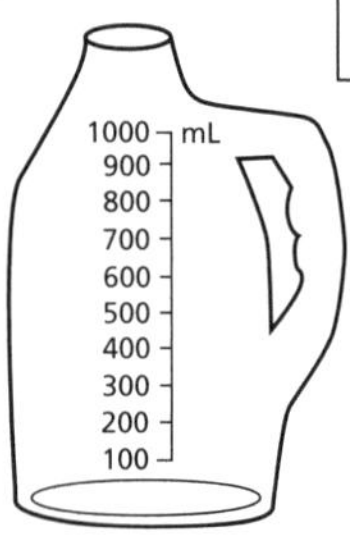

16:2 out of 17

1. $9 + 6$ ______
2. $18 - 9$ ______
3. 9×3 ______
4. 10×5 ______
5. $\begin{array}{r} 33 \\ -\ 4 \\ \hline \end{array}$
6. 4 times 6. ______
7. 6 groups of 8. ______
8. $20 \div 4$ ______
9. $50 \div 10$ ______
10. $\begin{array}{r} 5 \\ \times\ 8 \\ \hline \end{array}$
11. Which 3 consecutive months have the smallest total of days?
    ______
12. Would you use L or mL to measure the capacity of a:
    a bucket? ______
    b tablespoon? ______
    c bath tub? ______
13. Write the mixed numeral for the shaded part.
    a 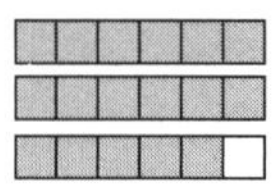
    b 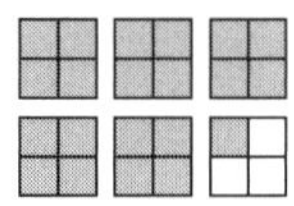
    ______ ______
14. Write the mixed number for:
    a $\frac{12}{5}$ ______ b $\frac{8}{3}$ ______
15. $5 \times 3 = 15$ so $5 \times 6 =$ ______
16. a Millilitres in 2 litres. ______
    b Centimetres in 5 metres. ______
17. $\frac{1}{9}, \frac{2}{9}, \frac{3}{9},$ ______, ______, ______, ______

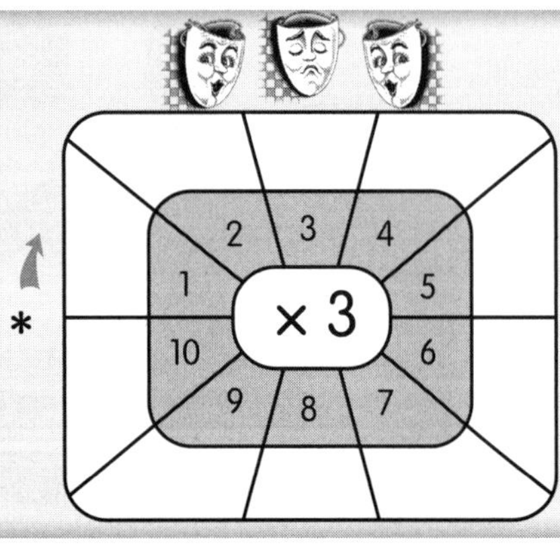

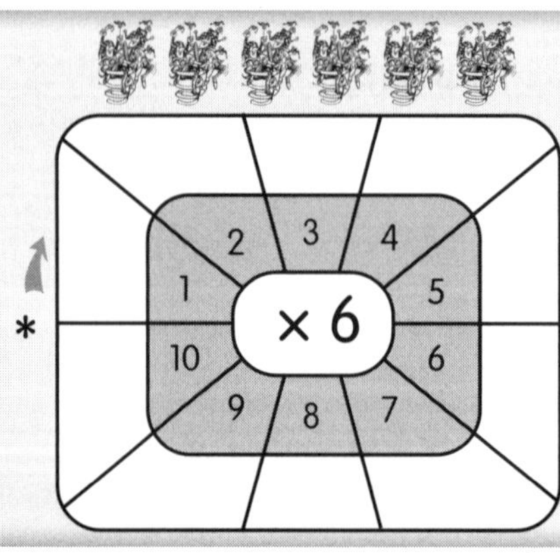

16:3 ☐ out of 12

1.

Tens	Ones
2	2
− 1	3

2.

Tens	Ones
$3	5
− $1	7

3. **m** is the abbreviation for ____________.
4. Our 23 turkeys hatched 64 chicks. How many birds altogether? ______
5. How many quarter turns make a full turn? ______
6. 

   60 mL 50 mL 75 mL

   How many mL altogether? ______
7. Write the mixed number for:

   a $\frac{15}{2}$ ______ **b** $\frac{11}{3}$ ______
8. $4 \times 3 = 12$ so $4 \times 6 =$ ______
9. Small areas can be measured in

   s__________ c__________.
10. 3 girls had 4 birds each. How many birds altogether? ______
11. 0, $\frac{1}{4}$, $\frac{2}{4}$, ______, 1, ______, ______
12. Use the short form to write:

    a 500 millilitres ______

    b 80 litres ______

    c 1·5 metres ______

16:4 Extension ☐ out of 6

1. In how many ways can you make 35 cents using 5c, 10c, and 20c coins? ______
2. How many hours in 3 days? ______
3. Shelby bought four 2 000 mL containers of milk. How many litres did she buy altogether? ______
4. 9 stamps fit on this square. How many stamps will fit on a square with side lengths twice as long? ______

   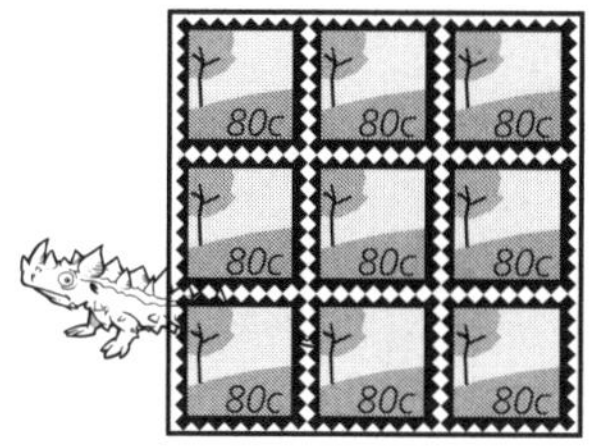

5. What fraction of $1 is:

   a 30c? ______

   b 75c? ______
6. **a** 53 + 12 + 21 + 12 ______

   b 23 + 12 + 42 + 11 ______

Challenge

Complete each column as quickly as you can. Once finished, check your answers and record your time.

2×6	______	8×2	______
2×3	______	4×2	______
5×3	______	3×3	______
0×6	______	3×6	______
5×6	______	10×6	______
1×6	______	4×3	______

Time = ______ seconds

Strategy Time

Friends are in a line holding hands.
How many hands are held if there are:

a 2 children? ______ **b** 3 children? ______

c 4 children? ______ **d** 7 children? ______

e 10 children? ______ **f** 20 children? ______

17:1 [ ] out of 14

1. 9 + 6 ______
2. 10 − 3 ______
3. 7 × 10 ______
4. 20 − 14 ______
5. 14 + 11 ______
6. 8 × 5 ______
7. 10 + 7 ______
8. 20c − 10c ______
9. 3 + 3 + 3 + 3 ______
10. 16 − 10 ______

11. **Comparing Area**

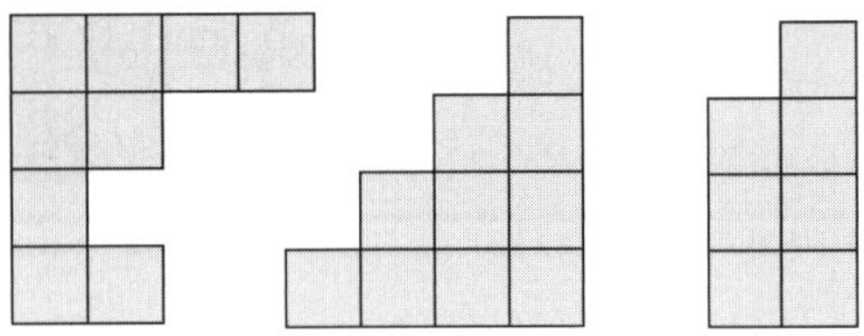

a Which shape has the greatest area? ______

b Which shape has the least area? ______

c What is the total area of the shapes A, B and C?

______ square units

12. 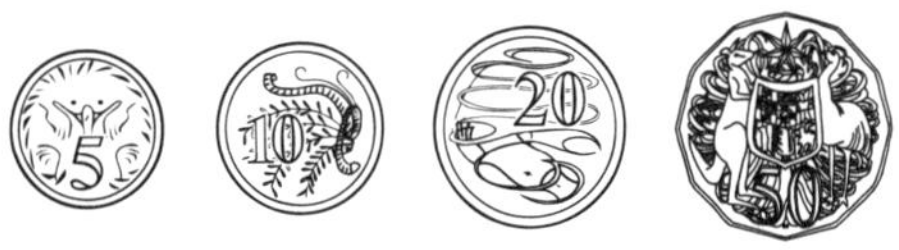

The total value of these coins in decimal form. ______

13. How many days in April? ______

14. $2\frac{1}{2}$, 3, ______, 4, ______, ______

17:2 [ ] out of 16

1. 14 + 7 ______
2. 20 − 7 ______
3. 2 × 6 ______
4. 3 × 4 ______
5. 30 + 15 ______
6. 5 groups of 6. ______
7. 7 × 8 ______
8. 10 ÷ 2 ______
9. 8 shared by 2. ______
10. 8 × 6 ______
11. Millilitres in 2 litres. ______
12. The abbreviation for **square centimetres**. ______
13. I did 30 minutes of homework each night for 4 nights. How much time did I spend on homework? ______
14. Natasha bought 3 rings. Each cost $2.00.

    How much did she pay? ______

15. 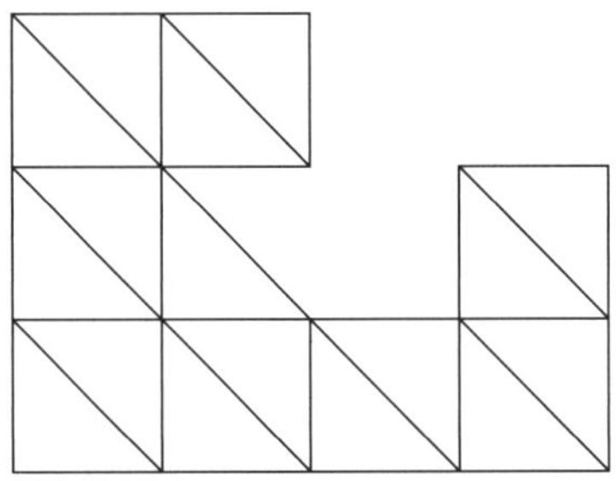

    How many small triangles cover this area? ______

16. Write the mixed number for:

    a $\frac{7}{3}$ ______ b $\frac{10}{4}$ ______

Place the letters in order, from *least likely* to *most likely*.
The first animal I see tomorrow will be a:

A	B	C	D	E	F
cat	rabbit	horse	cow	mouse	dog

least likely ______ most likely

Explain why you chose your order.

______

Answers

ID Card Answers

ID Card A

1 metres **2** centimetres **3** litres **4** grams **5** kilograms **6** minutes
7 square centimetres **8** square metres **9** degrees Celsius
10 freezing point of water **11** boiling point of water **12** before noon
13 after noon **14** 5 × 7 **15** is less than **16** is greater than **17** 20 ÷ 5
18 18 ÷ 6 **19** number sentence **20** numeral expander
21 counting numbers **22** even numbers **23** odd numbers
24 ordinal numbers **25** digits **26** factors **27** multiples
28 picture graph **29** tally **30** column graph

ID Card B

1 straight line **2** curved line **3** wavy line **4** zigzag line **5** dotted line
6 parallel lines **7** perpendicular lines **8** flip **9** slide **10** turn
11 acute angle **12** right angle **13** straight angle **14** obtuse angle
15 arm of an angle **16** vertex of an angle **17** axis of symmetry
18 tessellation **19** number line **20** five sixths shaded
21 24 hundredths shaded **22** three tenths shaded **23** 0·21 shaded
24 21 hundredths covered **25** abacus **26** calendar **27** compass
28 balance scales **29** metre ruler **30** 1 square metre

ID Card C

1 triangle **2** square **3** rectangle **4** rhombus **5** trapezium
6 parallelogram **7** quadrilaterals **8** pentagons **9** hexagons **10** octagon
11 circle **12** oval **13** regular shapes **14** irregular shapes **15** diagonals
16 face **17** corner **18** edge **19** base **20** flat surface **21** curved surface
22 cube **23** prism **24** pyramid **25** net of a cube **26** cylinder **27** cone
28 sphere **29** digital watch **30** analogue clock

1:1

1 4 **2** 9 **3** 4 **4** 6 **5** 19 **6** 10 **7** 15 **8** 13 **9** 5 **10** 3c

11 90, 100, 110 **12** 40 **13** one hundred **14** 73

15 2 out of 4 (or one half) **16** 15 (minutes) **17** tennis ball

18 15 (fish) **19** A figure with 5 sides will be drawn. 5 (sides)

1:2

1 20 **2** 20 **3** 11 **4** 20 **5** 18 **6** 0 **7** 6 **8** 2 **9** 5

10 15 **11** 3 metres **12** 73 **13** 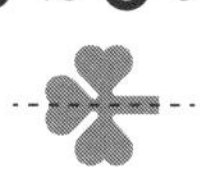 **14** A **15** A

Activity

10, 2, 6, 9, 4, 8, 12, 5, 11, 7
8, 11, 3, 6, 12, 5, 10, 13, 7, 9
9, 12, 4, 7, 13, 6, 11, 14, 8, 10

1:3

1 65 **2** 22 **3** **a** 45 (minutes) **b** 50 (minutes) **4** 40, 45, 50

5 prism **6** 4, 6, 8, 10 **7** 200 **8** 40 **9** irregular **10** odd

11 groups of, rows of, lots of, multiply or times **12** 13 (presents)

13 78 (stamps) **14** 612 **15** 30 (days)

1:4

1 pentagon will be underlined **2** $5.75 **3** 55 **4** 21 **5** yes

6 **a** 174 **b** 177 **7** true

Challenge

Answers will vary. One answer could be: A square has 4 equal sides and 4 right angles. It has 8 lines of symmetry.

Activity

Answers will vary.

2:1

1 5 **2** 11 **3** 4 **4** 3 **5** 7 **6** 8 **7** 25 **8** 11 **9** 5 **10** 7

11 60, 50, 40 **12** 70 **13** 3 out of 4 **14** 89 **15** 85c

16 $1 and $2 coins **17** 2 parts will be coloured. **18** yes

19 $5 **20** 7 (goals)

2:2

1 16 **2** 28 **3** 14 **4** 5 **5** 20 **6** 5 **7** 18 **8** 5 **9** 7

10 15 **11** B and C **12** 3 past 9 **13** 2 (mice) **14** 65c **15** 5

Activity

9, 11, 15, 12, 8, 7, 13, 10, 5, 14
14, 16, 20, 17, 13, 12, 18, 15, 10, 19
10, 13, 8, 15, 11, 6, 14, 9, 12, 16

2:3

1 96 **2** 20 **3** **a** 3:15 **b** 3:30 **4** 4 metres

5 **a** $1.65 **b** $1.30 **6** 77 **7** 1000 m

8 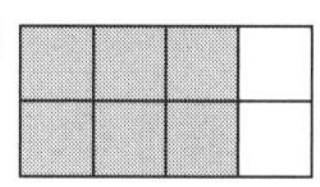 Any 6 out of 8 will be coloured.

9 **a** 4 (corners) **b** 6 (sides) **10** 3:17 **11** 30 (days) **12** 53 (stamps)

2:4

1 156 (weeks) **2** 40

3 6 boats will be coloured blue. 4 boats will be coloured red.

4 1000 mL or 1 L **5** 3 (stamps) **6** 61

Challenge

Answers will vary.

Activity

(4) rhombus (5) trapezium (6) parallelogram (7) quadrilaterals
(11) circle (12) oval (13) regular shapes (14) irregular shapes

3:1

1 12 **2** 14 **3** 2 **4** 4 **5** 18 **6** 0 **7** 3 **8** 9 **9** 5 **10** 12

11 53 **12** 19, 21, 23 **13** thirty-nine **14** 50c **15** 434 **16** 9:06

17 3 parts will be coloured.

3:2

1 15 **2** 20 **3** 17 **4** 11 **5** 38 **6** 8 **7** 10 **8** 12 **9** 2

10 45 **11** 9 tortoises will be coloured. **12** 50, 55, 60 **13** 6:53

14

Smiley Face	Circle	Square	Rhombus
Happy	3	5	2
Sad	5	1	2

15 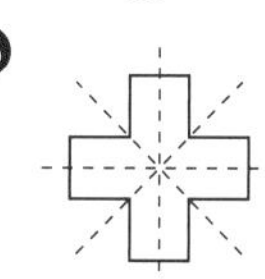

Activity

0, 30, 50, 70, 100, 80, 20, 60, 40, 90
0, 15, 25, 35, 50, 40, 10, 30, 20, 45

3:3

❶ \$88 ❷ \$44 ❸ a 28, 35, 42, 49 b 32, 40, 48, 56

❹  ❺ B

❻ Estimates will vary. Number = 78 (including each capital E)

❼ turn ❽ 3:30 ❾ a $\frac{3}{5}$ b $\frac{2}{5}$

3:4

❶ a 3500 mL b 450 cm ❷ a 48 b 52 ❸ a 16 b 36

❹ 3 (hours) ❺ a $1\frac{1}{2}$ b 3

Challenge

Answers will vary.

Activity

a 60 (minutes) b 30 (minutes) c 15 (minutes) d 45 (minutes)
e 50 (minutes) f 10 (minutes)

4:1

❶ 8 ❷ 10 ❸ 4 ❹ 2 ❺ 19 ❻ 40 ❼ 9 ❽ 10 ❾ 4 ❿ 11

⓫ 20, 25, 30 ⓬ flip ⓭ a B b C ⓮ 3 groups 6 ⓯ 60 (seconds)

⓰ 3 squares will be shaded. ⓱ 14 (years old)

4:2

❶ 24 ❷ 30 ❸ 7 ❹ 15 ❺ 58 ❻ 20 ❼ 18 ❽ 2 ❾ 6

❿ 40 ⓫ a 24, 30, 36 b 24, 27, 30 ⓬ 3 past 4

⓭ a 35 out of 100 or $\frac{35}{100}$ b 65 out of 100 or $\frac{65}{100}$ ⓮ a 4:50
b 5:20 ⓯ 12th ⓰ 8 ⓱ 6 objects should be drawn in each box.

Activity

13, 8, 16, 12, 14, 9, 17, 15, 11, 18
18, 13, 11, 9, 17, 12, 14, 19, 15, 16
12, 16, 10, 13, 7, 11, 15, 17, 9, 14

4:3

❶ \$95 ❷ 59 ❸ hundred square, 10 ❹ a 27 b 45 ❺ Tuesday

❻ yes ❼

Shapes	Rhombus	Pentagon	Rectangle
Shaded	3	3	2
Not Shaded	5	3	4

❽ a  b 

4:4

❶ 26 ❷ a 40 b 60 ❸ 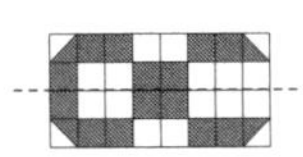 ❹ 20 (angles) ❺ 104

Challenge

Answers will vary.

Activity

a 60 (seconds) b 24 (hours) c 60 (minutes) d 7 (days)
e 30 (minutes) f 2 (weeks)

5:1

❶ 8 ❷ 8 ❸ 3 ❹ 5 ❺ 16 ❻ 12 ❼ 40 ❽ 9 ❾ 0 ❿ 10

⓫ 6 items will be drawn in each box. ⓬ turn ⓭ a 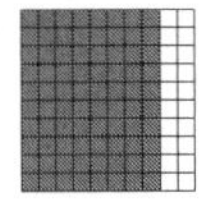
b 20 out of 100 or 0·2 ⓮ right angle ⓯ 4:16

5:2

❶ 17 ❷ 18 ❸ 7 ❹ 8 ❺ 64 ❻ 28 ❼ 20 ❽ 4 ❾ 2 ❿ 24

⓫ 9 hundredths or 0·09 ⓬ a  b triangle ⓭ 24 ⓮ 1

⓯ a 20 b 28

Activity

0, 6, 10, 14, 20, 16, 4, 12, 8, 18
0, 12, 20, 28, 40, 32, 8, 24, 16, 36

5:3

❶ 75 ❷ 43 ❸ 15 to 8, quarter to 8 or 7:45

❹ 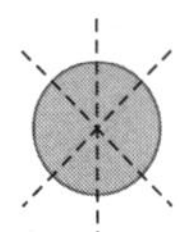 Other axes are possible. ❺ square or rhombus (diamond)

❻ 12 ❼ 101 ❽ \$18 ❾ 16 ❿ a B b A ⓫ 66

5:4

❶ 34 hundredths or 0·34 ❷ circle ❸ hexagon ❹ D ❺ 96 (mugs)

Challenge

Answers could include: 10 out of 100,ten out of one hundred, zero point one, 0·10 or 0·1

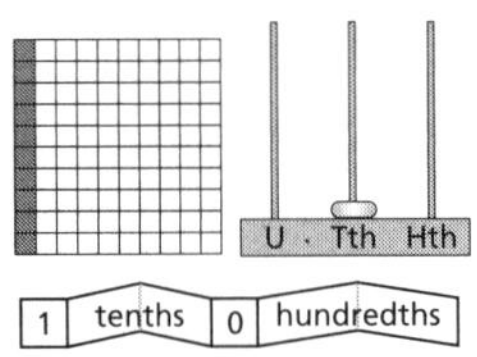

Activity

a 3 b 5 c 3 d 6 e 7 f 4

6:1

❶ 13 ❷ 10 ❸ 8 ❹ 6 ❺ 27 ❻ 8 ❼ 8 ❽ 80 ❾ 7 ❿ 11

⓫ a Friday b 4 c Monday d Tuesday (23rd) ⓬ 188

⓭ 36 out of 100 or 0·36 ⓮ no (heads and tails are equally likely.)

6:2

❶ 40 ❷ 19 ❸ 10 ❹ 2 ❺ 39 ❻ 20 ❼ 40 ❽ 9 ❾ 16

❿ 28 ⓫ 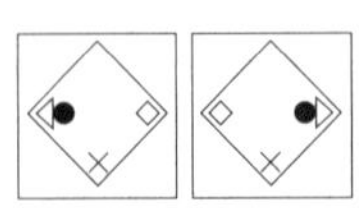 ⓬ C ⓭ autumn ⓮ 1009, 1010

Slide Flip

⓯ 526 ⓰ 34 out of 100 (or $\frac{34}{100}$), 0·34 ⓱ flip

Activity

10, 20, 30, 40, 50, 60, 70, 80, 90, 100
5, 10, 15, 20, 25, 30, 35, 40, 45, 50

6:3

1 \$39 **2** 21 **3** 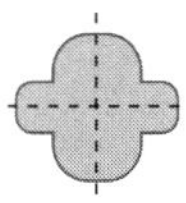 **4** a 0·35 b 0·83

5 2 heads, 2 tails, 1 head and 1 tail **6** 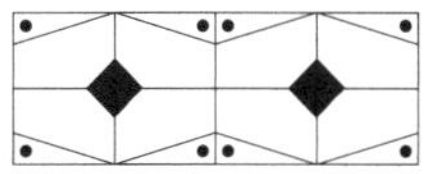

7 2 (lines of symmetry) **8** 48

6:4

1 92 (days) **2** a 4 b 6 **3** 6 **4** 84 (soldiers) **5** Wednesday

6 20 **7** 82

Challenge

Answers will vary. One example is that you may see a crocodile at school tomorrow.

Activity

12, 4, 24, 20, 32, 8, 36, 28, 16, 40

7:1

1 13 **2** 9 **3** 5 **4** 3 **5** 16 **6** 36 **7** 28 **8** 5 **9** 3 **10** 12

11 3 (digits) **12** 804 **13** a 43 mm b 79 mm **14** B, D, C, A

15 14 (days) **16** December **17** a 0·66 b 0·79

7:2

1 22 **2** 14 **3** 10 **4** 16 **5** 71 **6** 32 **7** 20 **8** 6 **9** 2

10 32 **11** 64 out of 100 **12** square **13** cm **14** 125 (cents) **15** 3 501

16 a (Friday) 18th b (Sunday) 13th **17** a 5 b 3

Activity

a 4, 8, 12, 16, 20 b 10, 20, 30, 40, 50 c 4, 8, 12, 16, 20

d 10, 20, 30, 40, 50 e 0, 0, 0, 0, 0 f 4, 7, 3, 9, 6

7:3

1 79 **2** 99 **3** 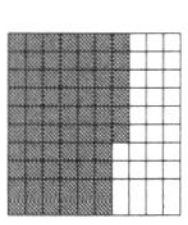 35 out of 100 is not shaded.

4 32 (mm) **5** a July b April

6 6 hundreds 4 tens 3 ones **7** a 15 b 14

8 a unlikely b even chance c very likely d certain

7:4

1 21 (days) **2** $\frac{2}{4}$ (or $\frac{1}{2}$) **3** 7 **4** 38 (hands) **5** a $\frac{1}{2}$ b $\frac{1}{4}$

Challenge

Answers will vary. One answer could be the angle made by two of your fingers or the angle at the top of the number 4.

Activity

(23) prism (24) pyramid (25) net of a cube (26) cylinder (27) cone (28) sphere (29) digital watch (30) analogue clock

8:1

1 7 **2** 15 **3** 4 **4** 5 **5** 25 **6** 6 **7** 32 **8** 10c **9** 11

10 22 **11** 749 **12** yes **13** 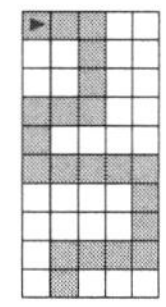 **14** A **15** 6 cm **16** 613

8:2

1 18 **2** 24 **3** 45 **4** 20 **5** 79 **6** 36 **7** 16 **8** 7 **9** 3

10 28 **11** 1 000 **12** \$0.90 **13** a 8 b 16 c 6 **14** C **15** 2 (days)

16 5 (angles) **17** a 5 (faces) b 5 (corners)

18 a 8 cm 4 mm b 5 cm 9 mm

Activity

a 52 (weeks) b 366 (days) c 12 (months) d 10 (years)

e 365 (days) f 100 (years)

8:3

1 \$77 **2** 90 **3** 1, 3, 5, 7 and 9 **4** one hundred and forty-three

5 999 **6** prism and pyramid **7** 3857 **8** 50 (toy cars) **9** sixth

10 80c **11** a 6 cm b 1 cm

8:4

1 a (rectangular) prism **2** \$47 **3** 6 (pairs) **4** 8 (squares)

5 a 365 b 366

Challenge

Answers will vary. One answer could be: This is a triangular pyramid. It has 4 flat faces, 4 corners, 6 edges. It has a triangular base. All of its faces are triangles.

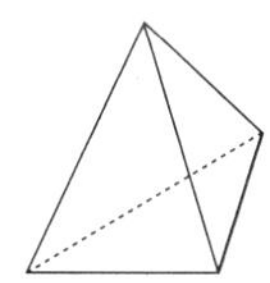

Activity

a \$1.35 b \$1.30 c \$2.50 d \$8.15 e \$6.00 f \$2.00

9:1

1 11 **2** 12 **3** 2 **4** 4 **5** 19 **6** 4 **7** 60 **8** \$5 **9** 8 **10** 12

11 A **12** 325 cm **13** 10 **14** 827 **15** 1 457 **16** 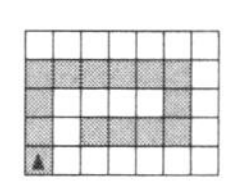

17 \$2.15 **18** 698 (tens) or 8

9:2

1 18 **2** 10 **3** 0 **4** 20 **5** 69 **6** 8 **7** 44 **8** 3 **9** 5 **10** 40

11 12 (edges) **12** 7 000 + 100 + 60 + 3 **13** 27 mm **14** a 9 b 15

c 30 (students) **15** 53 hundreds (or 3) **16** C

Activity

10, 2, 5, 1, 6, 9, 4, 8, 3, 7
8, 7, 6, 9, 1, 5, 10, 3, 0, 4
6, 3, 1, 5, 9, 7, 2, 10, 4, 8

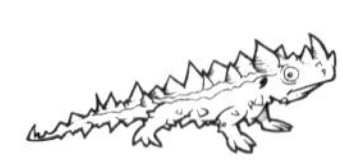

9:3

1 \$96 **2** \$72 **3** 9343

4 Estimates will vary. Measure = 6 cm or 60 mm

5 14 (kg) **6** eight thousand two hundred and forty **7** 26 (legs)

8 a 9 cm 3 mm b 7 cm 9 mm **9** a pyramid b prism

9:4

❶ **a** 4 **b** 4 ❷ **a** 37 **b** 100 ❸ 72 (sides) ❹ **a** 44 **b** 25

❺ **a** 48 **b** 96 ❻ 136

Challenge

Answers may include: It is an even number, has three digits and is palindromic (the same forwards and backwards). It is higher than 827 and lower than 850. It rounds to 840 (to the nearest 10) and 800 (to the nearest 100). It can be written as eight hundred and thirty-eight, 800 + 30 + 8 or (8 × 100) + (3 × 10) + 8. The number before is 837 and the number after is 839. It can be represented using 8 hundred blocks, 3 tens blocks and 8 ones blocks. It is in the pattern 808, 818, 828, 838. 838 − 38 = 800

Activity

yes

Answers will vary.

10:1

❶ 14 ❷ 14 ❸ 2 ❹ 5 ❺ 28 ❻ 50 ❼ 0 ❽ 4 ❾ 6 ❿ 24

⓫ **a** 4 m 59 cm **b** 3 m 27 cm ⓬ 631 ⓭ 77 ⓮ 28 (cm) ⓯ 20

⓰ three hundred and seventy-four ⓱ $2, $2 and $1 ⓲ 4 (sides)

⓳ **a** 95 mm **b** 42 mm

10:2

❶ 100 ❷ 10 ❸ 30 ❹ 40 ❺ 25 ❻ 60 ❼ 100 ❽ 3 ❾ 5

❿ 60 ⓫ 283 tens (or 3) ⓬ 6 (kg) ⓭ **a** Diane **b** 12 **c** 11

⓮ **a** 6 (faces) **b** 12 (edges)

Activity

7, 3, 10, 5, 6, 9, 1, 8, 2, 4
7, 2, 6, 3, 10, 4, 9, 5, 8, 0

10:3

❶ 93 ❷ 87 ❸ Estimates will vary. Measure = 5 cm, 50 mm

❹ 521 cm ❺ 3000 + 600 + 20 + 1 ❻ 60 (dots)

❼ **a** 14 (students) **b** 8 (students) ❽ 78 hundreds (or 8)

10:4

❶ 8 (corners) ❷ 1000, 10 000, 100 000 ❸ **a** 10 cm **b** 30 cm

❹ 96 (hours) ❺ 122 ❻ **a** 17 **b** 60

Challenge

Answers may include:

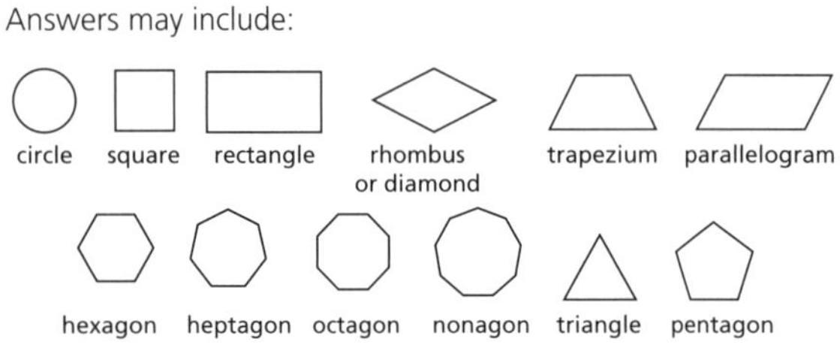

Activity

a	5 + 6 = **11**	11 − 5 = **6** 11 − 6 = **5**	b	5 + 7 = **12**	12 − 5 = **7** 12 − 7 = **5**
c	6 + 8 = **14**	14 − 6 = **8** 14 − 8 = **6**	d	8 + 7 = **15**	15 − 8 = **7** 15 − 7 = **8**
e	8 + 5 = **13**	13 − 8 = **5** 13 − 5 = **8**	f	7 + 6 = **13**	13 − 7 = **6** 13 − 6 = **7**

11:1

❶ 6 ❷ 3 ❸ 11 ❹ 2 ❺ 25 ❻ 7 ❼ 11 ❽ 9 ❾ 14 ❿ 12

⓫ 824 ⓬ $1.75 ⓭ 60 (minutes) ⓮ $25 ⓯ 2927, 2972, 2982

⓰ 3030 ⓱ pyramid ⓲ **a** 790 **b** 800 ⓳ 2 418 ⓴ 500

11:2

❶ 20 ❷ 6 ❸ 70 ❹ 45 ❺ 27 ❻ 70 ❼ 80 ❽ 7 ❾ 3 ❿ 18

⓫ 7 (thousands) ⓬ 6107 ⓭ prism ⓮ yes ⓯ 1014 ⓰ 8275

⓱ 75 hundreds (or 5) ⓲ 2000 ⓳ 3 m 68 cm

Activity

8, 1, 5, 4, 9, 6, 3, 10, 2, 7
9, 10, 4, 7, 0, 5, 2, 8, 6, 3

11:3

❶ 195 ❷ $139 ❸ 4643 ❹ 40 ❺ 2655, 2656 ❻ **a** Chen **b** 6 **c** 4 **d** 20 (fish) ❼ 54 000 ❽ 8135

11:4

❶ **a** 4 (faces) **b** 4 + 4 − 6 = 2 ❷ octagon will be underlined.

❸ 32 (lollies) ❹ **a** 124 **b** 116 ❺ 232 (shoes) ❻ 8 (stamps)

Challenge

Answers may include: "Greg went to the shops 16 times. Greg went to the shops the most and Sophie went to the shops the least. Kate went to the shops 11 more times than Sophie. Altogether there were 40 trips to the shops. Emily and Sophie went to the shops 10 times altogether. It could be that Greg and Kate are adults because they went to the shops a lot more than Emily and Sophie who could be children. Alternatively Emily and Sophie may not live near the shops."

Activity

Answers could include tossing heads or rolling an even number on a dice.

12:1

❶ 3 ❷ 20 ❸ 18 ❹ 24 ❺ 23 ❻ 11 ❼ 7 ❽ 12 ❾ 10c

❿ 33 ⓫ 510 ⓬ 836 ⓭ **a** D **b** A ⓮ 4 out of 7 or 4 sevenths

⓯ A 60°C B 30°C C 50°C

12:2

❶ 24 ❷ 14 ❸ 48 ❹ 32 ❺ 60 ❻ 12 ❼ 20 ❽ 10

❾ 24 ❿ 72 ⓫ 2400 ⓬ 70

⓭ one thousand three hundred and eighty-nine ⓮ 1 861

⓯ pyramid ⓰ yes ⓱ yes ⓲ 4 236 ⓳ 40

Activity

×	5	10	4	0	2	6	1	3
2	10	20	8	0	4	12	2	6
4	20	40	16	0	8	24	4	12
8	40	80	32	0	16	48	8	24
5	25	50	20	0	10	30	5	15
10	50	100	40	0	20	60	10	30

12:3

❶ 710 ❷ 161 ❸ 936 ❹ 53°C ❺ **a** pansies **b** 15 **c** 5 ❻ 30
❼ 357 ❽ 4345, 4346, 4347 ❾ 7 ❿ 19000

12:4

❶ **a** A **b** B ❷ pyramid ❸ V ❹ 168 (hours) ❺ 72 ❻ 48

Challenge

Answers will vary. One answer could be:
"This is a pyramid. It has a square base. It has 5 flat faces. It has 5 corners. It has 8 edges. It is the shape of an Egyptian pyramid. It can slide. It cannot roll."

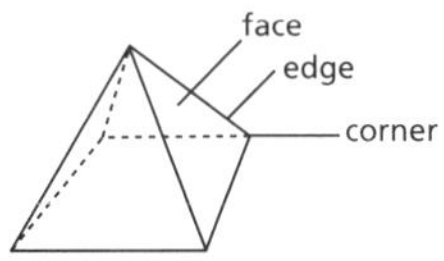

Activity

Answers will vary. One answer is "It could represent the height in metres of the living things shown in the picture."

13:1

❶ 2 ❷ 16 ❸ 18 ❹ 15 ❺ 28 ❻ 17 ❼ 12 ❽ 7 ❾ $7
❿ 21 ⓫ 759 ⓬ B ⓭ $\frac{4}{10}, \frac{5}{10}, \frac{6}{10}$ ⓮ 16 (toys) ⓯ 280
⓰ **a** F **b** T **c** T **d** F ⓱ 6 triangle parts will be coloured.

13:2

❶ 10 ❷ 40 ❸ 36 ❹ 28 ❺ 29 ❻ 64 ❼ 50 ❽ 24 ❾ 56
❿ 21 ⓫ 3900 ⓬ **a** **b** **c**

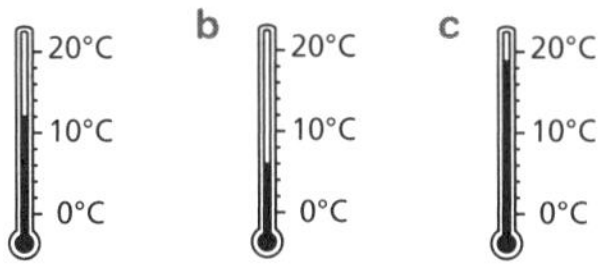

⓭ B ⓮ 17°C ⓯ 6278 ⓰ 89, 165, 932, 1470

Activity

8, 16, 24, 32, 40
8, 16, 24, 32, 40
8, 16, 24, 32, 40, 48, 56, 64, 72, 80

13:3

❶ 17 ❷ 38 ❸ yes ❹ 2 out of 9 or $\frac{2}{9}$
❺ Answers will vary. One answer could be: **a** $\frac{2}{4}$ **b** $\frac{1}{1}$ **c** $\frac{8}{10}$ **d** $\frac{1}{2}$
❻ 4000 ❼ 6420 ❽ 300 (years) ❾ $\frac{4}{6}, \frac{5}{6}, \frac{6}{6}$
❿ **a** 5 (faces) **b** 9 (edges) ⓫ 17 ⓬ two thousand and six

13:4

❶ 3 ❷ **a** $2.90 **b** $8.00 **c** $6.00 ❸ 141

Challenge

6, 20, 20, 10, 24, 40
60, 25, 40, 32, 10, 72

Activity

a 55c **b** $1.10 **c** 65c **d** $1.25 **e** $1.60 **f** 95c

14:1

❶ 13 ❷ 16 ❸ 17 ❹ 20 ❺ 19 ❻ 9 ❼ 13 ❽ 14 ❾ 20c
❿ 18c ⓫ C ⓬ $\frac{4}{7}, \frac{5}{7}, \frac{6}{7}$ ⓭

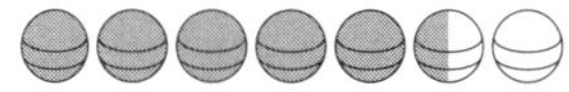

⓮ seven hundred and fifty-four ⓯ 9871 ⓰ 24 (boys) ⓱ Tuesday
⓲ $\frac{5}{9}$ or 5 out of 9

14:2

❶ 20 ❷ 10 ❸ 24 ❹ 36 ❺ 24 ❻ 36 ❼ 90 ❽ 42 ❾ 3
❿ 40 ⓫ 9 squares will be coloured. ⓬ **a** $<$ **b** $>$ **c** $>$ ⓭ 32 (legs)
⓮ 6 (sides) ⓯ yes ⓰ **a** true **b** true ⓱ cone and cylinder

Activity

4, 28, 20, 8, 32, 0, 12, 24, 36, 16
8, 56, 40, 16, 64, 0, 24, 48, 72, 32

14:3

❶ 33 ❷ 16 ❸ prism ❹ **a** T **b** F **c** T **d** F ❺ A ❻ $6\frac{1}{2}$ (bats)
❼ 300 ❽ 3 frogs will be coloured green. 5 frogs will be coloured red.

14:4

❶ cone ❷ **a** $3 **b** $5 ❸ **a** 92 (days) **b** 92 (days) ❹ **a** 24 **b** 37
❺ $6.95 ❻ **a** 128 **b** 96

Challenge

Answers will vary. Some answers are:

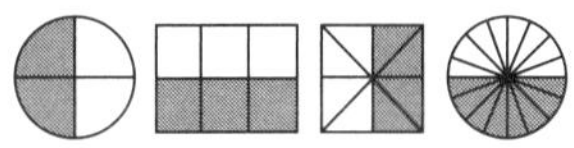

$\frac{2}{4}$ $\frac{3}{6}$ $\frac{4}{8}$ $\frac{8}{16}$

Activity

(1) straight line (2) curved line (3) wavy line (4) zigzag line
(5) dotted line (6) parallel lines (7) perpendicular lines (19) number line

15:1

❶ 9 ❷ 18 ❸ 19 ❹ 14 ❺ 31 ❻ 30 ❼ 15 ❽ 80c ❾ 4
❿ 8 ⓫

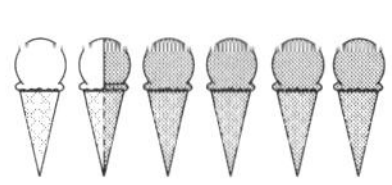

⓬ **a** 5 000 (mL) **b** 4 (L)

⓭ two hundred and forty-nine ⓮ 600 ⓯ yes ⓰ 80 cents
⓱ **a** 6 out of 8, $\frac{6}{8}$, 3 out of 4 or $\frac{3}{4}$ **b** 7 out of 8 or $\frac{7}{8}$

15:2

❶ 70 ❷ 5 ❸ 32 ❹ 72 ❺ 90 ❻ 48 ❼ 36 ❽ 10 ❾ 8
❿ 56 ⓫ **a** $\frac{3}{4}$ **b** $\frac{2}{6}$ ⓬ **a** A **b** B ⓭ 50 ⓮ **a** $\frac{5}{16}$ **b** $\frac{11}{16}$

Activity

a 10, 14, 18, 22, 26 **b** 4, 8, 16, 32, 64 **c** 81, 72, 63, 54, 45
d 22, 33, 44, 55, 66 **e** 9, 14, 19, 24, 29 **f** 82, 74, 66, 58, 50

15:3

1 39 **2** $18 **3** 3096, 3127, 4123 **4** 57 (hundreds) **5** **a** 5 **b** 15
6 500 mL **7** a half turn **8** **a** 60 cm **b** 5 mm **c** 976 g **d** 4·5 kg
9 $\frac{4}{8}, \frac{5}{8}, \frac{6}{8}, \frac{7}{8}$

15:4

1 yes **2** 0 **3** B **4** 44 (legs) **5** 131

Challenge

Answers will vary. Answers could include: milk (1 L), juice (2·4 L), soft drink (2 L), face cream (200 mL), shampoo (500 mL), soap (250 mL)

Activity

[1]3	0	[2]5		[3]1		[4]7
4		2		[5]5	0	0
[6]8	[7]1	4	9			4
	[8]2	4		[9]7	1	1
	9			0		
	[10]2	0	1	8		

16:1

1 21 **2** 19 **3** 2 **4** 2 **5** 18 **6** 48 **7** 0 **8** 10 **9** 12 **10** 0
11 90 (days) **12** A **13** May **14** **a** $3\frac{1}{2}$ **b** $1\frac{3}{4}$ **15** 9 (cm^2)
16

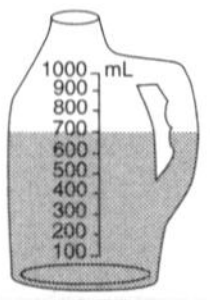

16:2

1 15 **2** 9 **3** 27 **4** 50 **5** 29 **6** 24 **7** 48 **8** 5 **9** 5
10 40 **11** February, March, April **12** **a** L **b** mL **c** L **13** **a** $2\frac{5}{6}$ **b** $5\frac{1}{4}$
14 **a** $2\frac{2}{5}$ **b** $2\frac{2}{3}$ **15** 30 **16** **a** 2 000 (mL) **b** 500 (cm) **17** $\frac{4}{9}, \frac{5}{9}, \frac{6}{9}, \frac{7}{9}$

Activity

3, 6, 9, 12, 15, 18, 21, 24, 27, 30
6, 12, 18, 24, 30, 36, 42, 48, 54, 60

16:3

1 9 **2** $18 **3** metres **4** 87 **5** 4 **6** 185 (mL) **7** **a** $7\frac{1}{2}$ **b** $3\frac{2}{3}$
8 24 **9** square centimetres **10** 12 (birds) **11** $\frac{3}{4}, 1\frac{1}{4}, 1\frac{2}{4}$
12 **a** 500 mL **b** 80 L **c** 1·5 m

16:4

1 6 **2** 72 (hours) **3** 8 (L) **4** 36 **5** **a** $\frac{3}{10}$ (or $\frac{30}{100}$) **b** $\frac{3}{4}$ (or $\frac{75}{100}$)
6 **a** 98 **b** 88

Challenge

12, 6, 15, 0, 30, 6
16, 8, 9, 18, 60, 12

Activity

a 2 **b** 4 **c** 6 **d** 12 **e** 18 **f** 38

17:1

1 15 **2** 7 **3** 70 **4** 6 **5** 25 **6** 40 **7** 17 **8** 10c **9** 12
10 6 **11** **a** B **b** C **c** 26 (square units) **12** $0.85 **13** 30 (days)
14 $3\frac{1}{2}, 4\frac{1}{2}, 5$

17:2

1 21 **2** 13 **3** 12 **4** 12 **5** 45 **6** 30 **7** 56 **8** 5 **9** 4
10 48 **11** 2000 (mL) **12** cm^2 **13** 120 minutes or 2 hours **14** $6 **15** 17
16 **a** $2\frac{1}{3}$ **b** $2\frac{2}{4}$ or $2\frac{1}{2}$

Activity

Answers will vary. One answer would be: B, E, D, C, A, F

17:3

1 $125 **2** 31 **3** $6\frac{1}{2}$ **4** yes **5** **a** < **b** > **c** < **6** 200c or $2
7 summer **8** square metres **9** 48 **10** mL **11** 225 mL

17:4

1 8, $9\frac{1}{2}$, 11 **2** 4 **3** 144 (hours) **4** 10 × 8 × 1 = 80
5 27 **6** 145

Challenge

Answers will vary. Each shape will have 5 squares.

Activity

6, 12, 18, 24, 30
21, 15, 27, 9, 3
6, 12, 18, 24, 30
48, 60, 42, 54, 36

18:1

1 24 **2** 24 **3** 12 **4** 10 **5** 31 **6** 5 **7** 12 **8** 60c **9** 13
10 12 **11**

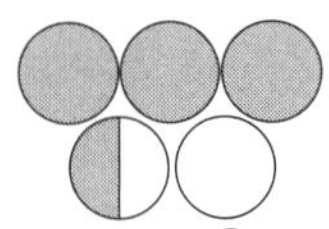

12 4 **13** Wednesday **14** winter
15

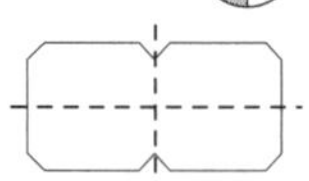

16 **a** 15 (books) **b** 35 (books) **17** iron

18:2

1 16 **2** 12 **3** 48 **4** 90 **5** 46 **6** 60 **7** 28 **8** 9 **9** 4
10 45 **11** 30 g **12** true **13** 48 (books) **14** 45c **15** 8:50
16 September **17** 24 (hours) **18** C (washing powder) **19** 30 (days)

Activity

9, 18, 27, 36, 45, 54, 63, 72, 81, 90
9, 45, 72, 18, 63, 81, 27, 54, 90, 36

18:3

1 27 **2** 17 **3** **a** Sarah **b** Lachlan
4

❺ The letter A will be circled.

❻ 18 (sides) ❼ 70 cm ❽ **a** 18th **b** 21st ❾ $3.00 ❿ 1400 (g)

18:4

❶ 72 ❷ 40 (5c coins) ❸ 55 (blocks) ❹ $2.80 or 280c

❺ 100 (10c coins) ❻ 3 ❼ 242 ❽ 240

Challenge

Answers will vary. One answer could be: 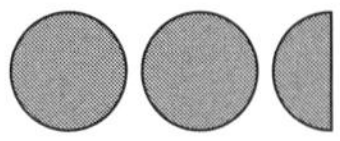 $2\frac{1}{2}$ or $\frac{5}{2}$

Activity

a 8 **b** 6 **c** 4 **d** 12 **e** 2 **f** 3 **g** 4 (with 4 left over)

19:1

❶ 12 ❷ 11 ❸ 14 ❹ 15 ❺ 27 ❻ 16 ❼ 35 ❽ 10c ❾ 8

❿ 20 ⓫  ⓬ 400 g

⓭ 73 808 ⓮ spring ⓯ Saturday ⓰ $1.95 ⓱ 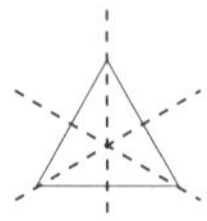

19:2

❶ 20 ❷ 5 ❸ 81 ❹ 42 ❺ 45 ❻ 35 ❼ 56 ❽ 27 ❾ 4

❿ 72 ⓫ mass ⓬ g ⓭ **a** 6 (sides) **b** 9 (diagonals) ⓮ 55 (children)

⓯ **a** grapes, ham, melon **b** 12 kg

Activity

1 × 9 = [0][9], [0] + [9] = 9	6 × 9 = [5][4], [5] + [4] = 9
2 × 9 = [1][8], [1] + [8] = 9	7 × 9 = [6][3], [6] + [3] = 9
3 × 9 = [2][7], [2] + [7] = 9	8 × 9 = [7][2], [7] + [2] = 9
4 × 9 = [3][6], [3] + [6] = 9	9 × 9 = [8][1], [8] + [1] = 9
5 × 9 = [4][5], [4] + [5] = 9	10 × 9 = [9][0], [9] + [0] = 9

The digits in each answer always add up to 9.

19:3

❶ 18 ❷ $82 ❸ 70 000 ❹ 23 430 ❺ **a** 4 (faces) **b** 6 (edges)

❻ 59 249 ❼ **a** (regular) hexagon **b** 6 **c** 6

❽ 27, 63, 36, 45, 18, 90, 54, 81 ❾ 6·5 or $6\frac{1}{2}$ (kg) ❿ 5 (kg)

⓫ 

19:4

❶ 36 (chairs) ❷ 78 (branches) ❸ 36 (wheels) ❹ 72 (wheels)

❺ **a** 7 (matchsticks) **b** 13 (matchsticks) **c** 19 (matchsticks) **d** 25 (matchsticks) **e** 31 (matchsticks)

Challenge

Answers will vary. 21 312 is a palindrome. It can be read the same way in either direction. It has 5 digits. The number before it is 21 311. It is even. It is larger than 20 000. It rounds to 21 000 (to the nearest thousand).

Activity

a 7 (cm^2) **b** 5 (cm^2) **c** 11 (cm^2)

20:1

❶ 12 ❷ 9 ❸ 23 ❹ 7 ❺ 13 ❻ 20 ❼ 49 ❽ 20c ❾ 20c

❿ 24c ⓫ no ⓬ 3658 ⓭ 171 will be circled.

⓮ **a** 160c **b** $1.60 ⓯ 25 401 ⓰ $\frac{4}{10}, \frac{5}{10}, \frac{6}{10}$ ⓱ 5 (sides)

20:2

❶ 21 ❷ 17 ❸ 42 ❹ 30 ❺ 30 ❻ 72 ❼ 70 ❽ 6 ❾ 21

❿ 36 ⓫ 1 000 (g) ⓬ $35 ⓭ B will be circled.

⓮ sixteen thousand one hundred and ninety-four ⓯ Answers will vary.

⓰ no ($\frac{18}{18}$ is equal to 1.) ⓱ 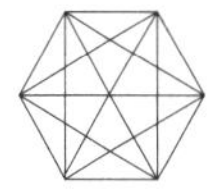 ⓲ 1 (kg)

Activity

7, 14, 21, 28, 35, 42, 49, 56, 63, 70

20:3

❶ 401 ❷ $68 ❸ 39 141 ❹ 500 ❺ 5c ❻ 13 ❼ $10

❽ **a** true **b** true **c** false **d** true ❾ 1924 ❿ yes ⓫ yes

⓬ 2 000 (g) ⓭ yes

20:4

❶ 35 cm ❷ 36 and 37 ❸ 8 ❹ **a** 233 **b** 180 ❺ 210

❻ 13 (9 + 3 + 1 triangles)

Challenge

Answers will vary.

Activity

18, 0, 36, 24, 6, 30, 12, 42
24, 0, 48, 32, 8, 40, 16, 56

21:1

❶ 11 ❷ 5 ❸ 54 ❹ 13 ❺ 12 ❻ 9 ❼ 24 ❽ 9 ❾ 12

❿ 24 ⓫ 10th (or tenth) ⓬ **a** 6 **b** emu **c** 4 ⓭ 34 641

⓮ 4 ⓯ 25 849 ⓰ triangle

21:2

❶ 50 ❷ 20 ❸ 9 ❹ 45 ❺ 77 ❻ 10 ❼ 49 ❽ 28 ❾ 5

❿ 35 ⓫ 30 ⓬ 445 cm or 4 45 m ⓭ 3 ⓮ 23 512

⓯ 20 000 + 7 000 + 200 + 5 ⓰ **a** $2\frac{1}{3}$ **b** $3\frac{2}{5}$

⓱ 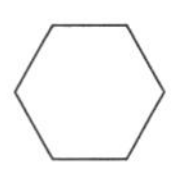 ⓲ diagonal

Activity

35, 63, 42, 21, 56, 14, 49, 70, 28, 0
40, 72, 48, 24, 64, 16, 56, 80, 32, 0

21:3

❶ 200 ❷ 568 ❸ 10 (years) ❹ **a** 2 km **b** 7 km **c** Red St **d** the shop ❺ **a** true **b** true **c** true **d** false ❻  ❼ 48

21:4

1 70 (shells) **2** 8 m 98 cm (or 898 cm) **3** 20 **4** 6 (outfits)
5 181 **6** **a** 96 **b** 92

Challenge
Answers will vary.

Activity
a 8 ÷ 2 **b** 27 ÷ 3 **c** 4 **d** 9 **e** 6 **f** 6 **g** 9 **h** 7

22:1

1 60 **2** 16 **3** 14 **4** 12 **5** 39 **6** 14 **7** 11 **8** 35c **9** 13
10 19 **11** 9 cm^2
12

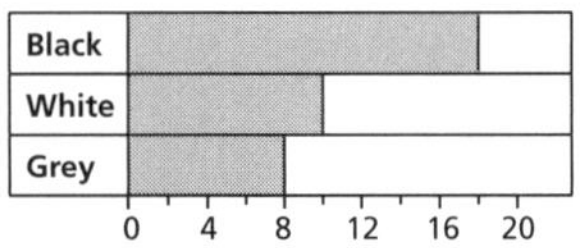

13 45 653 **14** 6 (angles)

22:2

1 20 **2** 15 **3** 50 **4** 63 **5** 13 **6** 64 **7** 27 **8** 2 **9** 5
10 56 **11** $1.35 **12** cm^2 **13** Answers will vary, e.g. ball, orange and marble. **14** **a** town hall **b** fire station **c** 1 cm = 100 m
d about 200 m **15** + **16**

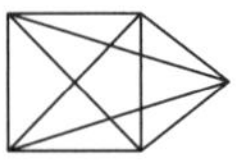

Activity
12, 42, 18, 48, 60, 36, 24, 54, 30, 48
16, 56, 24, 64, 80, 48, 32, 72, 40, 64

22:3

1 18 **2** 615 **3** 24th **4** 28 **5**

6 10
7 **a** no **b** yes **c** A, D, H **d** B, E, G, I

22:4

1 80 **2** 36 (cakes) **3** 8 **4** 44 **5** 116 (stars)
6 14 (9 + 4 + 1 squares)

Challenge
Note: the letter 'p' features in the footer, too.

		Total
p	||||/ ||||/ ||	12
b	||||/ ||||/	10

Activity
a 7 (cm^2) **b** 6 (cm^2) **c** 11 (cm^2)

23:1

1 0 **2** 6 **3** 17 **4** 9 **5** 12 **6** 18 **7** 27 **8** 80 **9** 54
10 39 **11** **a** 53c **b** $7.00 **12** m^2 **13** **a** 27 (hundredths) **b** 0·27
14 cylinder **15** **a** 2 **b** 3 **16** 58 254

23:2

1 20 **2** 11 **3** 30 **4** 80 **5** 83 **6** 72 **7** 15 **8** 6 **9** 5
10 54 **11** $2.00 **12** 0·30 (or 0·3), 0·31 **13** **a** true **b** true
14 [1·54] — [$1\frac{54}{100}$] [0·54] — [$\frac{54}{100}$] **15** Shape C **16** 5 (cm^2) **17** 42 (angles)

Activity
0, 15, 24, 9, 30, 18, 27, 6, 21, 12
0, 30, 48, 18, 60, 36, 54, 12, 42, 24

23:3

1 513 **2** 712 **3** yes **4** **a** The "Total" column is: 22, 8, 19, 28
b possum **5** 1·3 **6** 0·7 **7** **a** true **b** Answers will vary. **8** 0·46
9 30 (cm) **10** yes

23:4

1 42 **2** 12 and 17
3 3 (hundreds), 4 (tens), 1 (unit), 8 (tenths) and 2 (hundredths)
4 63·21 **5** cm^2

Challenge
Answers will vary.

Activity
a 3 **b** 11 **c** 51 **d** 65

24:1

1 13 **2** 8 **3** 20 **4** 60 **5** 18 **6** 5 **7** 21 **8** 15 **9** 8
10 66 **11** cylinder, cone, sphere **12** 8 **13** square metres **14** 0·48
15 0·43 **16** 30 315

24:2

1 20 **2** 14 **3** 14 **4** 81 **5** 503 **6** 30 **7** 24 **8** 1 **9** 3
10 28 **11** square centimetres **12** 1·4 **13** A, C, B
14 Answers will vary. **15** **a**

b yes **16** 0·32

Activity
a always **b** probably **c** likely **d** probably **e** never

24:3

1 324 **2** 388 **3** 0·75, 0·76 **4** **a** Spinner B **b** Spinner A
5 **a** m^2 **b** cm^2 **6** 23 **7** **a** 0·27 **b** 0·73 **8** **a** 0·07 **b** 0·37
9 28 (days)

24:4

1 0 or 1 **2**

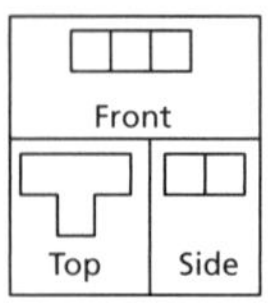

3 11 **4** VIII **5** **a** true **b** true

© PEARSON AUSTRALIA 2018 • *AUSTRALIAN SIGNPOST MATHS 4 MENTALS* • ISBN 978 1 4886 2186 4

Challenge

Answers will vary. Some answers include: 0·7 is the same as 7 tenths ($\frac{7}{10}$). It is less than one and greater than a half. 0·7 is equal to 0·70 or 70 hundredths.

Activity

a IV **b** V **c** IX **d** X **e** XI **f** XII **g** II **h** VIII **i** 9 **j** 11 **k** 6 **l** 4

25:1

1 12 **2** 17 **3** 24 **4** 21 **5** 96 **6** 30 **7** 13 **8** 55c **9** 18
10 327 **11** $4.68 **12** m **13** blue **14** 20 hundredths **15** 6
16 40, 50 **17** no **18** **a** 0·72 **b** 0·61 **c** 0·83 **d** 0·11

25:2

1 25 **2** 12 **3** 45 **4** 16 **5** 37 **6** 30 **7** 24 **8** 7 **9** 8
10 32 **11** 864 (cents) **12** **a** 49 (hundredths) **b** 0.49
13 **a** Pa **b** Nanna **c** Alan **d** Diane **e** Lyn

Activity

6, 42, 30, 12, 48, 0, 18, 36, 54, 24
7, 49, 35, 14, 56, 0, 21, 42, 63, 28

25:3

1 654 **2** 744 **3** 26 **4** $0.06 **5** $6.15 **6** $21 **7** 48 (cubes)
8 7 (ones) **9** 9000 mL **10** **a** false **b** true

25:4

1 13 **2** **a** 27 **b** 64 **3** 6 **4** **a** IX **b** XIII **5** 221

Challenge

Answers will vary.

Activity

(15) diagonals (16) face (17) corner (18) edge (19) base
(20) flat surface (21) curved surface (22) cube

26:1

1 24 **2** 12 **3** 20 **4** 50 **5** 21 **6** 8 **7** 10 **8** 42 **9** 8
10 68 **11** flip **12** 21 (days) **13** **a** 4:02 **b** 8:51 **14** 39857 **15** 0·76

26:2

1 26 **2** 8 **3** 36 **4** 60 **5** 42 **6** 40 **7** 16 **8** 8 **9** 4
10 24 **11** 18 hundredths **12** 53 (minutes) **13** 3 (years) **14** 49012
15 **a** Spinner C **b** Spinner A **16** 1·3

Activity

a 5 **b** 15 **c** 60 **d** 151 **e** 165 **f** 166 **g** XXV **h** CX **i** CCXXI
j CCVII **k** LXVII **l** CCCXXXIII

26:3

1 88 **2** 229 **3** $3\frac{1}{2}$ (hours) **4** **a** $40 **b** $920 **c** $230 **d** $580
5 eighty-nine thousand and twenty-five **6** 82315
7 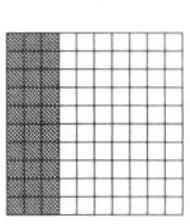 0·3 **8** 0·9

26:4

1 5 **2** **a** 2:40 **b** 1:56 **3** **a** V **b** X **4** **a** 197 **b** 803 **5** 12
6 Sunday

Challenge

Answers will vary. Answers may include: 49 is a 2-digit odd number. Its factors are 1, 49 and 7. The number after it is 50. 49 rounds to 50 (to the nearest 10).

Activity

4 throws

27:1

1 0 **2** 21 **3** 14 **4** 35 **5** 99 **6** 8 **7** 20 **8** 2 **9** 68 kg
10 23 **11** 14773 **12** **a** 6:25 am (or 6:25) **b** 25 past 6 **13** 24 (months)
14 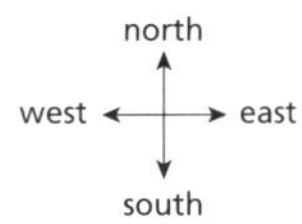

15 3 lollies; 3 **16** 27th **17** $7.85 **18** 2 (weeks)

27:2

1 20 **2** 15 **3** 20 **4** 21 **5** 76 **6** 15 **7** 60 **8** 4 **9** 5
10 36 **11** **a**  **b**  **12** Saturday **13** 18 **14** division
15 30214 **16** 30621 **17** **a** 2 (tenths) **b** 20 (hundredths)

Activity

a 2 m **b** 5 m **c** 30 cm **d** 3 cm **e** 10 cm **f** 12 m **g** 12 m
h $1\frac{1}{2}$ m (or 2 m)

27:3

1 143 **2** 676 **3** Saturday **4** 18 past 11 **5** 100 (weeks) **6** 10
7 **a** east **b** west **8** forty-one thousand six hundred and eight
9 1·5 **10** **a** 20 **b** 28 **11** 7

27:4

1 **a** 3 **b** 7 **2** **a** 8:30 **b** 8:00 **3** 6 km north **4** 9 (pairs)
5 **a** IX **b** XII **6** 200

Challenge

Answers will vary. 20 ÷ 5 = 4

Activity

a WA **b** WA, NT, Qld **c** Qld, NSW, Vic, Tas **d** WA, SA, Vic, Tas

28:1

1 17 **2** 45 **3** 16 **4** 40 **5** 34 **6** 12 **7** 18 **8** 5 **9** 10
10 123 **11** **a** 4:05 **b** 5 past 4 **12** 8 crayons **13** 14 (cm^2) **14** divide
15 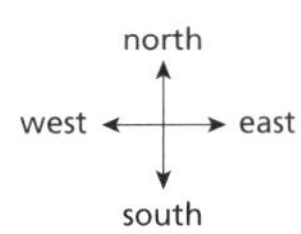

28:2

1 20 **2** 15 **3** 56 **4** 30 **5** 74 **6** 56 **7** 12 **8** 4 **9** 2
10 45 **11** 7 **12** 180 (minutes) **13** 6 tops; 6 **14** 9 **15** 8:50
16 **a** 18 **b** 24 **17** **a** $\frac{18}{24}$ (or $\frac{3}{4}$) **b** $\frac{6}{24}$ (or $\frac{1}{4}$) **18** 8

Activity

×	3	7	6	9	8	4
4	12	28	24	36	32	16
6	18	42	36	54	48	24
7	21	49	42	63	56	28
8	24	56	48	72	64	32
9	27	63	54	81	72	36

28:3

1 366 + 1 = 367 **2** 707 + 1 = 708 **3** 5:00 **4** **a** 16 **b** 40
5 **a** 3 × 6 **b** 7 × 3 **6** \$5 **7** \$26 **8** 90 (degrees) **9** 95c

28:4

1 1 **2** **a** 9:00 or 9 o'clock **b** no **3** **a** 12 **b** 1

Challenge

14, 30, 40, 63, 28, 36, 48, 49
16, 21, 70, 42, 24, 56, 56, 35

Activity

(20) 5 sixths shaded (21) 24 hundredths shaded (22) 3 tenths shaded
(23) 0·21 shaded (24) 21 hundredths covered (25) abacus
(26) calendar (27) compass

29:1

1 14 **2** 20 **3** 28 **4** 2 **5** 97 **6** 16 **7** 72 **8** 15 **9** 9
10 52 **11** 6 past 7 **12** 4000 **13** 14 **14** 5 (marbles) **15** 6, 3
16 2 (cakes)

29:2

1 30 **2** 20 **3** 25 **4** 28 **5** 67 **6** 90 **7** 36 **8** 2 **9** 6
10 35 **11** 5 **12** 72 492 **13** 10 000 + 4000 + 800 + 70 + 4
14 8, 8 **15** 91 (days) **16** \$190 **17** 12, 4

Activity

(1) metres (2) centimetres (3) litres (4) grams (5) kilograms
(6) minutes (7) square centimetres (8) square metres

29:3

1 853 + 1 = 854 **2** 430 + 1 = 431 **3** 9 **4** 3 **5** 2 **6** 4, 4
7 10 (cm^3) **8** 20 (years) **9** 10 (lollies) **10** false
11 **a** 9:25 **b** 25 past 9 **12** **a** C, B, A **b** B

29:4

1 **a** 15, 19 **b** 27, 18 **2** 8 km west **3** 6 **4** 6 ties (with \$7 left)
5 hexagon

Challenge

Answers will vary. Some answers include: 20 000 + 1000 + 300 + 20 and 21 000 + 320.

Activity

a 2 **b** 5 **c** 7 **d** 9

30:1

1 13 **2** 4 **3** 7 **4** 3 **5** 98 **6** 5 kg **7** 35c **8** 15 **9** 21
10 24 **11** 26 197 **12** 8, 4 **13** 0·2 **14** 5 **15** 9 **16** 32
17 **a** 49 past 3 **b** 8 past 5

30:2

1 20 **2** 30 **3** 45 **4** 42 **5** 48 **6** 40 **7** 54 **8** 2 **9** 6
10 49 **11** 8 **12** true **13** 8 **14** 12 **15** 18, 6
16 **a** 30 (minutes) **b** 45 (minutes)

Activity

35, 63, 42, 21, 56, 14, 49, 70, 28, 0
40, 72, 48, 24, 64, 16, 56, 80, 32, 0

30:3

1 578 **2** 644 **3** 2 **4** 4 **5** 6 **6** 5, 5 **7** **a** ÷ **b**  **c** 2B
d 1B **8** 74·96 **9** 11 **10** 75 355

30:4

1 **a** 6 cm^3 **b** 12 cm **2** yes **3** **a** IV **b** VII **4** Wednesday
5 **a** 2, 6 and 8 **b** 5 **6** 184

Challenge

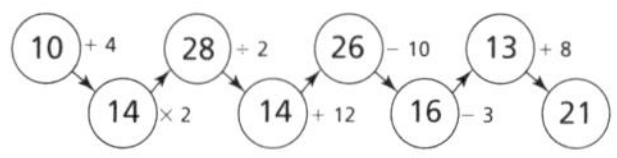

Answers will vary.

Activity

a 3 **b** 6 **c** 2 **d** 4 **e** 10 **f** 2 **g** 5 **h** 3 **i** 7 **j** 7

31:1

1 10 **2** 10 **3** 12 **4** 17 **5** 151 **6** \$17 **7** 35 **8** 2 **9** 200 g
10 68 **11** 60 (seconds) **12** **a** grapes **b** plums **c** bananas **d** 2
e 2 out of 6 **13** 3 (pencils)

31:2

1 20 **2** 14 **3** 40 **4** 18 **5** 52 **6** 100 **7** 72 **8** 5 **9** 9
10 42 **11** 4 (triangles) **12** 8·25 **13** 22 **14** 6 cm^2 **15** 15, 5
16  **17** 9731

Activity

a 6 **b** 7 **c** 7 **d** 9

31:3

1 98 **2** 115 **3** 8 **4** 2 **5** 4 **6** 3·49 **7** \$50, \$2, \$1, 10c
(Answers may vary.) **8** \$5.10 **9** **a** 5A or A5 **b** 3D or D3
c 4B or B4 **d** 1C or C1 **10** 8, 8

 ISBN 978 1 4886 2186 4

31:4

1 7 (semi-trailers) **2** 24 **a** 32 **b** 40 **3** 6 **4** 7

Challenge

Answers may include: It has 6 tens. It is larger than 260. It rounds to 262 (to the nearest whole).

Activity

3, 6, 1, 9, 5, 8, 0, 7, 4, 10
3, 1, 7, 5, 2, 8, 6, 10, 4, 9

32:1

1 24 **2** 18 **3** 3 **4** 13 **5** 52 **6** 6 **7** 15 **8** 27 **9** 12

10 98 **11** 14 (days) **12** 20 **13** **a** 6 (months) **b** 30 (months)

14 300 039 **15** **a** biscuits **b** second from the left, on the bottom row

16 10 cm^2

32:2

1 20 **2** 13 **3** 70 **4** 12 **5** 55 **6** 48 **7** 35 **8** 3 **9** 8

10 36 **11** 31 (days) **12** **a** cube **b** square **c** 4A **d** 1B

13 Answers will vary. Between 16 and 21.

14 \$100, \$100, \$20, \$10, \$1, 20c, 5c **15** 0·5 **16** 4

Activity

30, 54, 36, 18, 48, 12, 42, 60, 24, 0
45, 81, 54, 27, 72, 18, 63, 90, 36, 0

32:3

1 515 **2** 1020 **3** 912 **4** 6 **5** 7 **6** 5 **7** B will be circled.

8 Answers will vary. **9** 930 609 **10** 10 (players)

11 **a** 8 min **b** 12 min **c** 6 min **12** \$44.70

32:4

1 14 (dolls) **2** 19 (houses) **3** 9 (pizzas) **4** 324

5 9 + 8 − 6 = 11 **6** 243

Challenge

Answers may include: It is even, has 4 thousands, is a whole number and rounds to 35 000 (nearest thousand). It is larger than 34 000.

Activity

1, 4, 7, 2, 9, 6, 3, 8, 5, 10
7, 4, 9, 0, 8, 2, 5, 10, 3, 6

33:1

1 2 **2** 11 **3** 15 **4** 30 **5** 56 **6** 56 **7** 18 **8** 8 **9** 15

10 99 **11** 437 809 **12** right angle **13** Jon **14** 1, 24, 2, 12, 3, 8, 4, 6

15 12 **16** litres or millilitres **17** 50c, 10c, 10c and 5c **18** 70

33:2

1 20 **2** 19 **3** 20 **4** 16 **5** 49 **6** 42 **7** 48 **8** 40 **9** 7

10 40 **11** 31 (days) **12** **a** Monday **b** Tuesday **13** D, C, A, B

14 **a** obtuse **b** acute **15** **a** 1, 8, 2, 4 **b** 5, 10, 15, 20, 25, 30

16 30 (minutes) **17** 10 **18** \$18.25 **19** 5

Activity

a 7 × 6 = **42**: 42 ÷ 7 = **6**, 42 ÷ 6 = **7**

b 4 × 7 = **28**: 28 ÷ 4 = **7**, 28 ÷ 7 = **4**

c 6 × 8 = **48**: 48 ÷ 6 = **8**, 48 ÷ 8 = **6**

d 9 × 6 = **54**: 54 ÷ 9 = **6**, 54 ÷ 6 = **9**

e 8 × 9 = **72**: 72 ÷ 8 = **9**, 72 ÷ 9 = **8**

f 8 × 7 = **56**: 56 ÷ 8 = **7**, 56 ÷ 7 = **8**

33:3

1 977 **2** 502 **3** 405 **4** \$6.89 **5** 635 **6** ÷ **7** autumn

8 4 cards **9** factors **10** 207 106 **11** 4 (mice)

12 Answers may vary. \$50, \$20, \$10, \$2, \$2, 50c, 10c, 5c **13** 5 (cards)

33:4

1 200 mL **2** 4 will be circled. **3** 8 **4** 332

Challenge

Answers will vary.

Activity

0, 6, 3, 9, 1, 5, 7, 2, 8, 4
2, 5, 1, 9, 7, 4, 10, 8, 3, 6

34:1

1 19 **2** 14 **3** 11 **4** 3 **5** 79 **6** 15 **7** 54 **8** 4 **9** 16

10 37 **11** 5 out of 9 **12** after midday **13** 15 **14** L

15 DVDs, camera, TV **16** 7 **17** 31 (days)

34:2

1 23 **2** 12 **3** 80 **4** 18 **5** 37 **6** 36 **7** 50 **8** 9 **9** 7

10 27 **11** 185 **12** **a** C **b** A **13** 32 **14** 16 **15** 70 mL **16** \$52.20

17 10 (shells)

Activity

0, 9, 4, 8, 1, 6, 3, 10, 7, 5
2, 8, 5, 3, 7, 4, 1, 6, 0, 9

34:3

1 1028 **2** 601 **3** 489 **4** 45 − 27 = 18 **5** 25 past 9 **6** am

7 **a** E, F, C, G and A **b** B and D **c** H and I **d** B, D, H and I

8 **a** 1, 39, 3 and 13 **b** 1, 77, 7 and 11 **9** yes **10** 7 flowers

34:4

1 \$10.50 **2** \$20 000 **3** 16 **4** **a** 10 and 3 **b** 12 and 2

5 **a** 279 **b** 1 252 **6** **a** VIII **b** IX

Challenge

Answers will vary. One answer could be: 18 ÷ 2 = 9.
There were 18 legs. How many people?

Activity

(18) 18 ÷ 6 (19) number sentence (20) numeral expander
(21) counting numbers (22) even numbers (23) odd numbers
(24) ordinal numbers (25) digits (26) factors (27) multiples

35:1

1 11 **2** 4 **3** 15 **4** 19 **5** 35 **6** 18 **7** 10 **8** 10 **9** 18
10 55 **11** 7 (candles) **12** 971 000 **13** 700 mL **14** 804 654
15 700 000 **16** 95 (mm) **17** pm **18** 4

35:2

1 20 **2** 12 **3** 90 **4** 21 **5** 71 **6** 35 **7** 54 **8** 49 **9** 7
10 63 **11** yes **12** 41 mm **13** Estimates will vary. Measure = 45 (mm)
14 post meridiem **15** **a** right **b** acute **c** obtuse **16** vertical
17 56 **18** 60c

Activity

2, 7, 3, 8, 9, 5, 1, 4, 6, 10

	4	1	9	0	7	5	2	11	6	3	8	10
× 4	16	4	36	0	28	20	8	44	24	12	32	40

	8	4	7	1	11	0	5	10	2	3	6	9
× 7	56	28	49	7	77	0	35	70	14	21	42	63

	3	0	4	8	5	10	7	1	6	11	2	9
× 9	27	0	36	72	45	90	63	9	54	99	18	81

35:3

1 8 **2** 5 **3** 4 **4** 4 **5** 8 **6** 8 **7** **a** Monday **b** 25 (dolls)
c 100 (dolls) **8** **a** 45 (minutes) **b** 15 (minutes) **9** 4 **10** 6

35:4

1 \$16 **2** 11 (birds) **3** 98 **4** 11 (fives) **5** **a** 56 **b** 49

Challenge

Answers will vary. Another answer could be 2 × 5 = 10 so 4 × 5 = 20.

Activity

a 1, 15, 3, 5 **b** 1, 21, 3, 7 **c** 1, 16, 2, 8, 4 **d** 1, 12, 2, 6, 3, 4

36:1

1 13 **2** 18 **3** 17 **4** 9 **5** 71 **6** 15 **7** \$3 **8** 24 **9** 9
10 33 **11** 4, 8, 16 **12** 24 (hours) **13** 8 **14** **a** 12 (books)
b 2 (books read) **c** 30 (books) **15** 20 minutes past 2

36:2

1 30 **2** 15 **3** 24 **4** 63 **5** 57 **6** 24 **7** 70 **8** 64 **9** 8
10 70 **11** F **12** 24 **13** 4, 8, 16 **14** 658 000
15 quarter past 10 or 10:15 **16** yes **17** 10

Activity

(9) degrees Celsius (10) freezing point of water
(11) boiling point of water (12) before noon
(13) after noon (14) 5 × 7 (15) less than (16) greater than

36:3

1 1015 **2** 602 **3** 783 **4** 119 cm **5** B **6** 36 **7** 111 (marbles)
8 five hundred and six thousand four hundred **9** yes
10 Estimates will vary. Measure = 50 mm **11** 75 mm
12 **a** 7 pm **b** 9 am **13** obtuse

36:4

1 24 **2** 400 **3** \$70 000 **4** 16, 32, 64, 128 **5** **a** VII **b** IV
6 72 (chocolates) **7** 100 (eels) **8** 11

Challenge

Answers will vary. One answer could be 5##~~~ = 5.

Activity

11, 22, 33, 44, 55, 66, 77, 88, 99, 110
33, 77, 55, 22, 88, 11, 66, 99, 44, 110

37:1

1 9 **2** 19 **3** 7 **4** 54 **5** 32 **6** \$9 **7** 5 **8** 25 **9** 70
10 77 **11** zero **12** morning **13** 20, 25, 30, 35
14

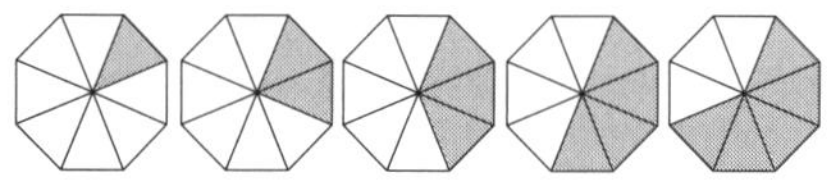

15 **a** $2\frac{3}{10}$ **b** $6\frac{3}{4}$
16

17 200 **18** evening

37:2

1 19 **2** 11 **3** 28 **4** 72 **5** 61 **6** 32 **7** 81 **8** 9 **9** 8
10 27 **11** 28 (days) **12** \$1.25 **13** 1, 16, 2, 8, 4 **14** even
15 25, 23, 21, 19 **16** $\frac{4}{5}, \frac{5}{5}, \frac{6}{5}$ **17** **a** $2\frac{5}{6}$ **b** $5\frac{1}{4}$
18 **a** 35 (mm) **b** $3\frac{1}{2}$ (cm)

Activity

(11) acute angle (12) right angle (13) straight angle (14) obtuse angle
(15) arm of an angle (17) axis of symmetry
(16) vertex of an angle (18) tessellation

37:3

1 1358 **2** 382 **3** 943 **4** **a** 229 **b** 1010 **5** **a** 12 (months)
b 120 (months) **c** 40 (years) **6** odd **7** 12, 15, 24 **8** **a** $1\frac{3}{4}$ **b** $1\frac{2}{3}$
9 **a** $\frac{5}{4}$ **b** $\frac{23}{10}$
10 four hundred and three thousand seven hundred and twenty
11 **a** 4 cm 5 mm **b** 8 cm 7 mm **12** am

37:4

1 1, 2, 3, 4, 6 and 12 **2** **a** 14 **b** 104 **3** 92 (sandwiches) **4** odd
5 30 **6** 5 **7** **a** 512, 614 **b** Add 102.

Challenge

Answers will vary.

Activity

Answers will vary.

 ISBN 978 1 4886 2186 4

17:3 ☐ out of 11

1.

Tens	Ones
\$5	7
+ \$6	8

2.

Tens	Ones
5	6
− 2	5

3. Which is larger $3\frac{9}{10}$ or $6\frac{1}{2}$? ____________

4. If I toss a dice, is there an even chance of getting an odd number? ____________

5. Use < or > in:

a 4506 ____________ 4617

b 5981 ____________ 5807

c 6753 ____________ 6754

6. One pen costs 50c. How much will it cost for 4 pens? ____________

7. December, January and February are in what season? ____________

8. Larger areas can be measured in

s____________ m____________.

9. $8 \times 3 = 24$ so $8 \times 6 =$ ____________

10. What unit of measurement has been left off this label?

____

11. What is the total quantity held?

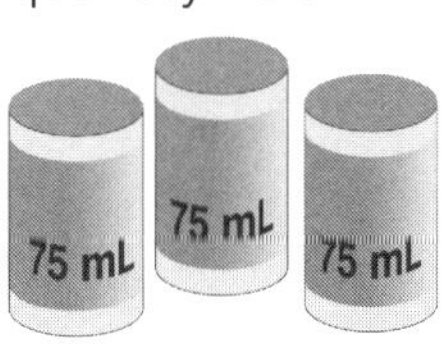

____

17:4 Extension ☐ out of 6

1. $3\frac{1}{2}$, 5, $6\frac{1}{2}$, ________, ________, ________

2.

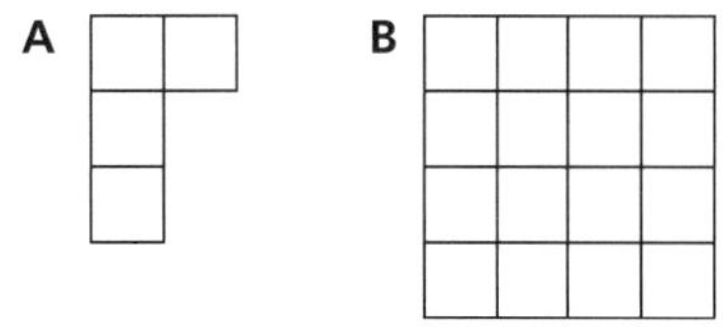

How many of shape A could be cut from shape B? ____________

3. How many hours in 6 days? ____________

4. If $6 + \square = 16$, $4 + \triangle = 12$ and $12 - \diamond = 11$, find $\square \times \triangle \times \diamond$. ____________

5. $3 \times 3 \times 3$ ____________

6. $118 + 27$ ____________

Challenge

Use different colours to make shapes with an area of 5 cm².

	2	4	6	8	10
× 3					

	1	2	3	4	5
× 6					

	7	5	9	3	1
× 3					

	8	10	7	9	6
× 6					

Why are these the same?

Practise your tables until you know them.

18:1 ☐ out of 17

1. 4 × 6 ______
2. 8 × 3 ______
3. 4 + 8 ______
4. 10 − 0 ______
5. 25 + 6 = ______
6. 6 − 1 ______
7. 7 + 5 ______
8. 10c + 50c ______
9. Add 5 and 8. ______
10. 19 − 7 = ______
11. Colour 3 and a half circles.

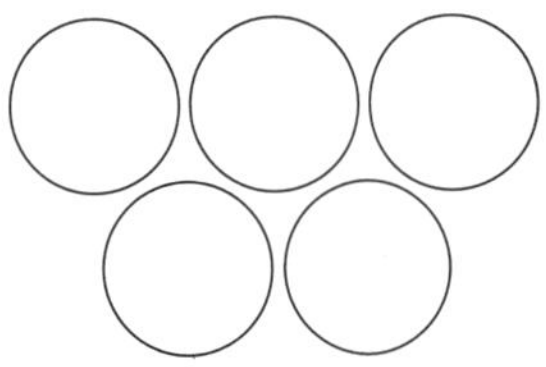

12. The difference between 9 and 5. ______
13. The day after Tuesday. ______
14. What season is made up of June, July and August? ______
15. Draw all the axes of symmetry.

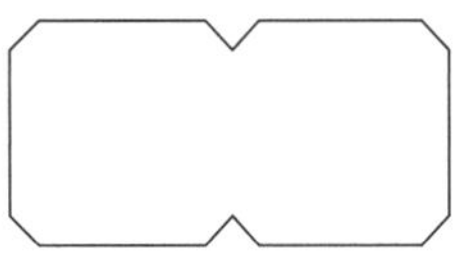

16. **a** 5 students read 3 books each. How many books were read? ______

    b 20 more books were then read. How many books were read altogether? ______
17. Which has the greater mass, a light globe or an iron? ______

18:2 ☐ out of 19

1. 10 + 6 ______
2. 20 − 8 ______
3. 8 × 6 ______
4. 10 × 9 ______
5. 15 + 31 = ______
6. 6 groups of 10. ______
7. 7 × 4 ______
8. 45 ÷ 5 ______
9. 12 ÷ 3 ______
10. 5 × 9 = ______
11. Write thirty grams in short form. ______
12. A brick is heavier than 1 kg.

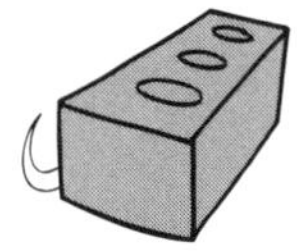

    True or false? ______
13. I can read 8 books a month. How many books can I read in 6 months? ______

14. The change from $1.00 if I spend 55 cents. ______
15. The time 5 minutes after 8:45. ______
16. The ninth month of the year. ______
17. Hours in 1 day. ______
18. Which measured in kg? ______

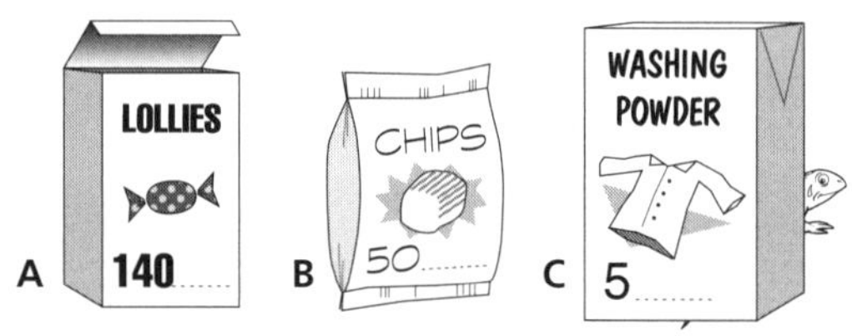

19. Days in June. ______

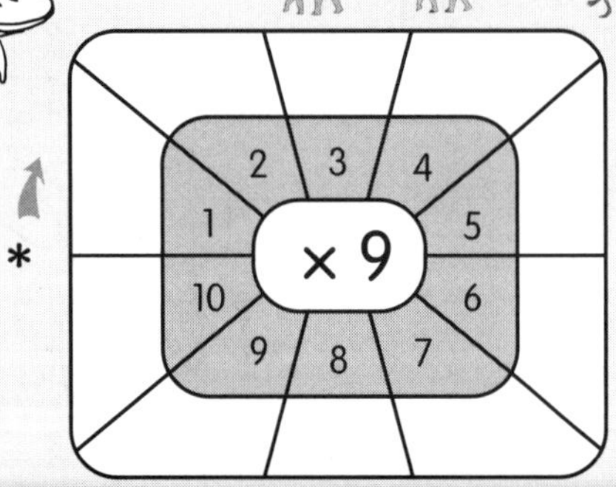

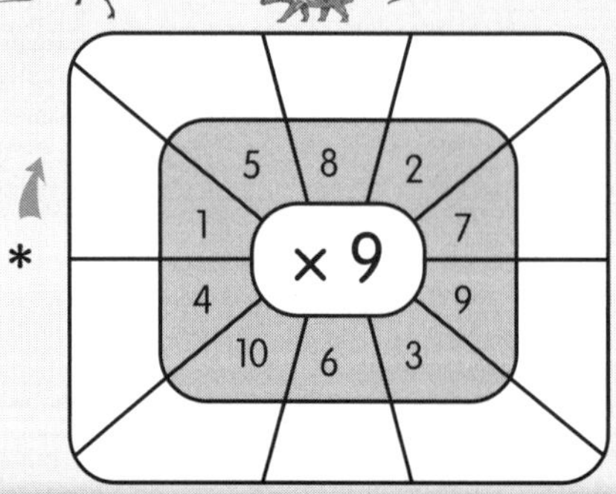

You can count nine at a time.

 • *AUSTRALIAN SIGNPOST MATHS 4 MENTALS* • ISBN 978 1 4886 2186 4

18:3 ☐ out of 10

1.

Tens	Ones
4	3
− 1	6

2.

Tens	Ones
6	5
− 4	8

3. A dice is rolled. Sarah wins if an odd number is rolled. Josh wins if a 2 or 4 are rolled. Lachlan wins if a 6 is rolled. Who is:

   a most likely to win? ____________

   b least likely to win? ____________

4. 

   Colour $3\frac{1}{2}$ of this group.

5. Circle the correctly written measure.

   A 9 kg **B** 9 KG **C** 9 Kg **D** 9 kgs

6. Sides in 6 triangles. ____________

7. A ribbon is 1 metre long.
   If I cut off 30 centimetres,
   how much is left? ____________

8. The ordinal number after:

   a 17th ____________ **b** 20th ____________

9. 5 bananas cost $1.00.
   Find the cost of 15 bananas.

   ____

10. Grams in 1 kg 400 g. ____________

18:4 Extension ☐ out of 8

1. How many sides on 24 triangles? ____________

2. How many 5 cent coins have the same value as $2? ____________

3. How many blocks are needed to make a staircase of ten steps?

   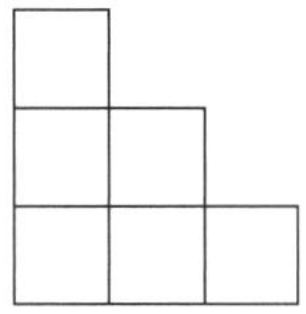

   ____

4. The total value of sixteen 5c coins and ten 20c coins. ____________

5. How many 10c coins have the same value as two hundred 5c coins? ____________

6. If $\square - 8 = 4$, and $30 - \triangle = 26$, find the answer to: $\square \div \triangle$. ____________

7. If $23 \times 11 = 253$, what does 22×11 equal? ____________

8. $4 \times 3 \times 20$ ____________

Challenge

Draw and label mixed numbers.
Write the improper fraction for each.

Division and Repeated Subtraction

How many groups of 4 shoes in 22?

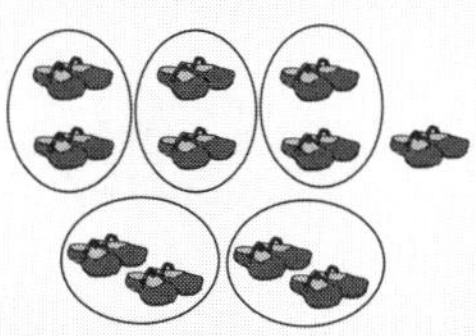

Answer:
5 groups, with 2 left.

There are 24 notes. How many:

a groups of 3? ______ **b** groups of 4? ______
c groups of 6? ______ **d** groups of 2? ______
e groups of 12? ______ **f** groups of 8? ______
g groups of 5? ______ with ____ left over.

19:1 ☐ out of 17

1. 16 − 4 ______
2. 18 − 7 ______
3. 9 + 5 ______
4. 7 + 8 ______
5. $\begin{array}{r} 17 \\ +\ 10 \\ \hline \end{array}$
6. 2 × 8 ______
7. 5 × 7 ______
8. Half of 20c. ______
9. 2 groups of 4. ______
10. $\begin{array}{r} 13 \\ +\ 7 \\ \hline \end{array}$

11. Colour $2\frac{1}{2}$ of these pentagons.

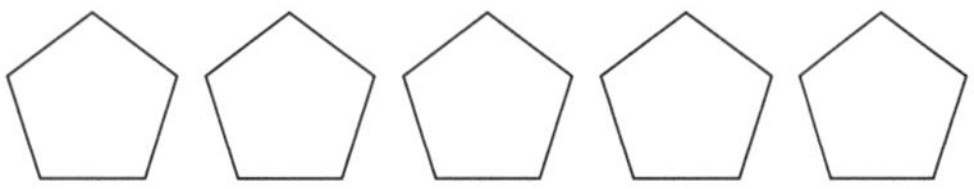

12. Write four hundred grams in short form. ______
13. Write the numeral shown.

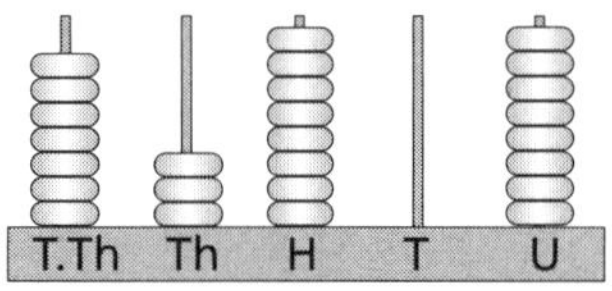

______

14. The season made up of September, October and November. ______
15. The day after Friday. ______
16. Write the total value of these coins in decimal form. ______

17. Draw three axes of symmetry for this shape.

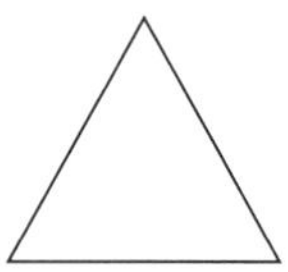

19:2 ☐ out of 15

1. 12 + 8 ______
2. 10 − 5 ______
3. 9 × 9 ______
4. 6 × 7 ______
5. $\begin{array}{r} 33 \\ +\ 12 \\ \hline \end{array}$
6. 5 groups of 7. ______
7. 7 rows of 8. ______
8. 3 × 9 ______
9. 16 shared by 4. ______
10. $\begin{array}{r} 9 \\ \times\ 8 \\ \hline \end{array}$

11. The bottle and the stones have the same:

    m______________.

12. The abbreviation for **gram**. ______
13. For this hexagon:
    a how many sides? ______
    b how many diagonals? ______

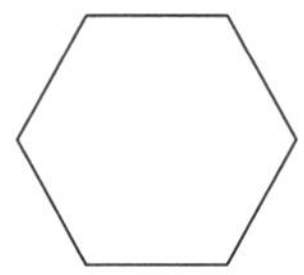

14. There are 11 children in each row.

    How many children would there be in 5 rows? ______

15. **Ham** 4 kg **Grapes** 2 kg **Melon** 6 kg

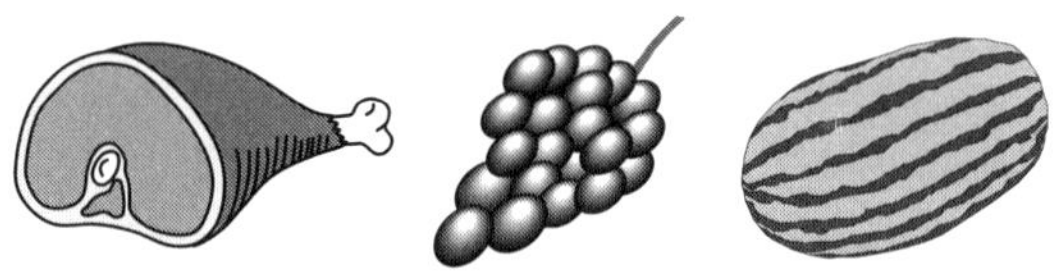

a Put these items in order of mass, from least to most.

____

b The total mass. ______

Finish these to find the pattern.

1 × 9 = [0][9], [0] + [9] = ______	6 × 9 = [ ][ ], [ ] + [ ] = ______
2 × 9 = [1][8], [1] + [8] = ______	7 × 9 = [ ][ ], [ ] + [ ] = ______
3 × 9 = [2][7], [2] + [7] = ______	8 × 9 = [ ][ ], [ ] + [ ] = ______
4 × 9 = [ ][ ], [ ] + [ ] = ______	9 × 9 = [ ][ ], [ ] + [ ] = ______
5 × 9 = [ ][ ], [ ] + [ ] = ______	10 × 9 = [ ][ ], [ ] + [ ] = ______

Nine times tables:
The digits in each answer always add up to ______.

 ISBN 978 1 4886 2186 4

19:3 ☐ out of 11

1.

Tens	Ones
4	6
− 2	8

2.

Tens	Ones
$3	9
+ $4	3

3. The value of the 7 in 70 392. ________

4. 20 000 + 3 000 + 400 + 30 = ________

5. On this shape, how many:

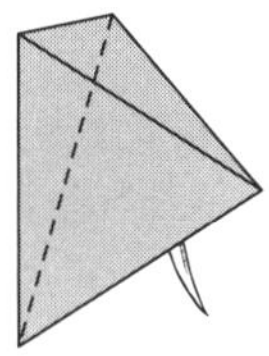

   a faces? ________

   b edges? ________

6. Write the numeral fifty-nine thousand two hundred and forty-nine. ________

7. a Name this shape. ________

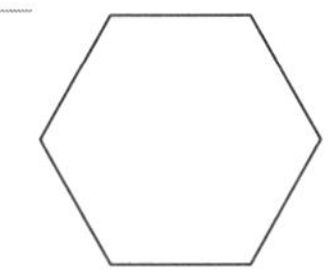

   In this shape, how many:

   b sides? ________

   c angles? ________

8.

	3	7	4	5	2	10	6	9
× 9								

9. 6 500 g = ________ kg

10. Kilograms in 5 000 g. ________

11. Colour $4\frac{1}{2}$ of these shapes.

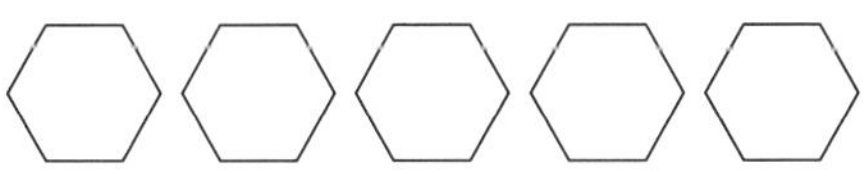

19:4 Extension ☐ out of 5

1. A desk weighs the same as 12 chairs. How many chairs weigh the same as 3 desks? ________

2. Yuan drew 3 trees. On each he drew 26 branches. How many branches did he draw altogether? ________

3. Number of wheels on 9 trucks. ________

4. Number of wheels on 18 trucks. ________

5. What is the smallest number of matchsticks needed to make:

   a 2 squares? ________

   b 4 squares? ________

   c 6 squares? ________

   d 8 squares? ________

   e 10 squares? ________

Challenge

What do you know about the number 21 312?

Find the area of each shape.

a

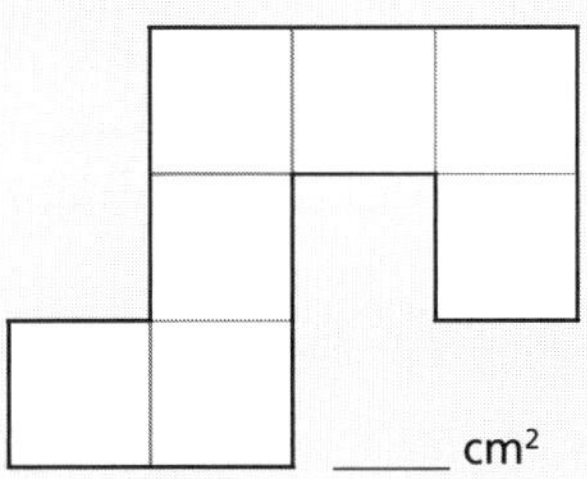

____ cm²

b

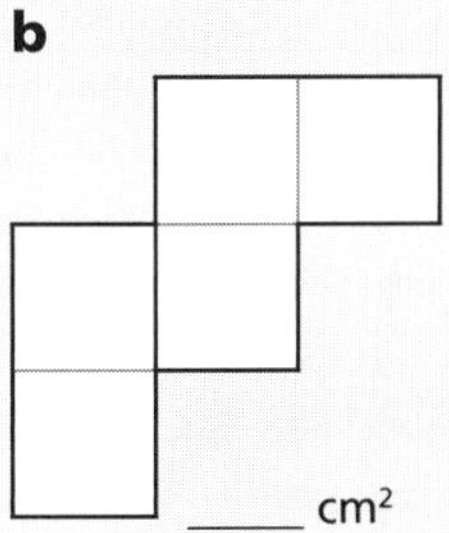

____ cm²

c

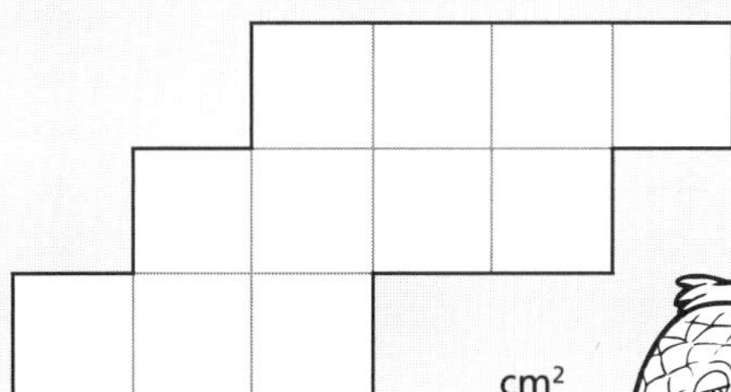

____ cm²

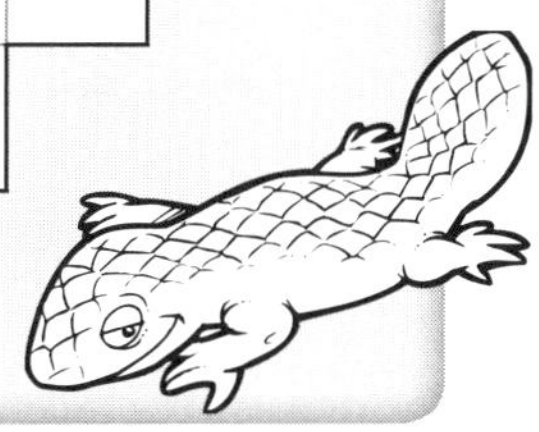

 • *AUSTRALIAN SIGNPOST MATHS 4 MENTALS* • ISBN 978 1 4886 2186 4

20:1 out of 17

1. 19 − 7 ____
2. 6 + 3 ____
3. 18 + 5 ____
4. 15 − 8 ____
5. 17 − 4 = ____
6. 16 + 4 ____
7. 7 × 7 ____
8. 15c + 5c ____
9. 30c − 10c ____
10. 15c + 9c = ____

11. Is this book heavier than a kilogram? ____
12. What number is shown on the abacus? ____

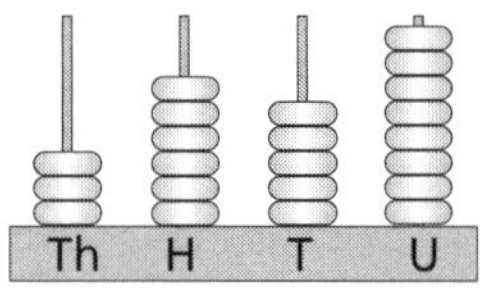

13. Circle the largest number.

71 17 171 117

14. 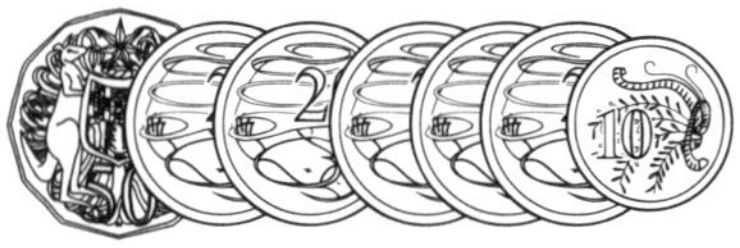

Write the value of these coins in:

a cents ____

b decimal form ____

15. Write the numeral twenty-five thousand four hundred and one. ____
16. $\frac{1}{10}$, $\frac{2}{10}$, $\frac{3}{10}$, ☐, ☐, ☐
17. The number of sides on a pentagon. ____

20:2 out of 18

1. 18 + 3 ____
2. 17 − 0 ____
3. 7 × 6 ____
4. 3 × 10 ____
5. 37 − 7 = ____
6. 9 rows of 8. ____
7. 10 times 7. ____
8. 12 ÷ 2 ____
9. 3 × 7 ____
10. 4 × 9 = ____

11. How many grams in 1 kilogram? ____
12. A book costs $5. There are seven books in a set. How much would the set cost? ____
13. Circle the shape below that can be made from these three triangles.

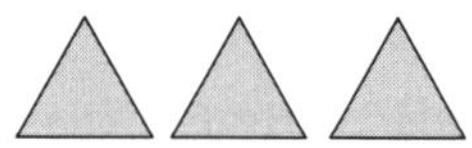

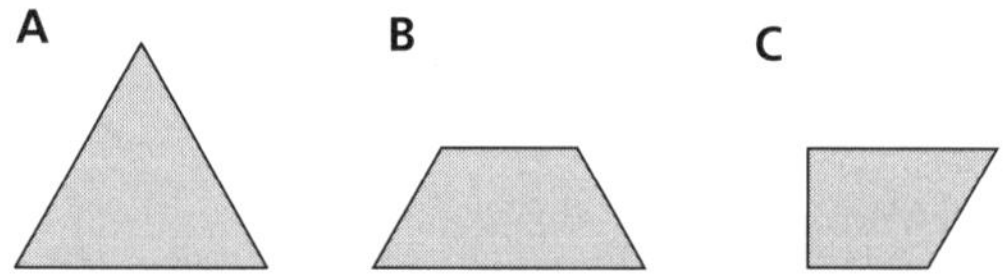

14. Write 16 194 in words. ____
15. What is your age now?

____ years ____ months

16. Is $\frac{18}{18}$ equal to 18? ____
17. Draw in all the diagonals for this hexagon.

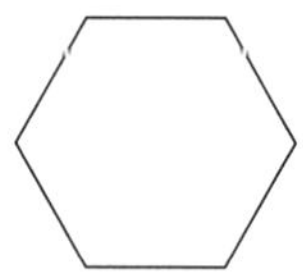

18. 1 000 g = ____ kg

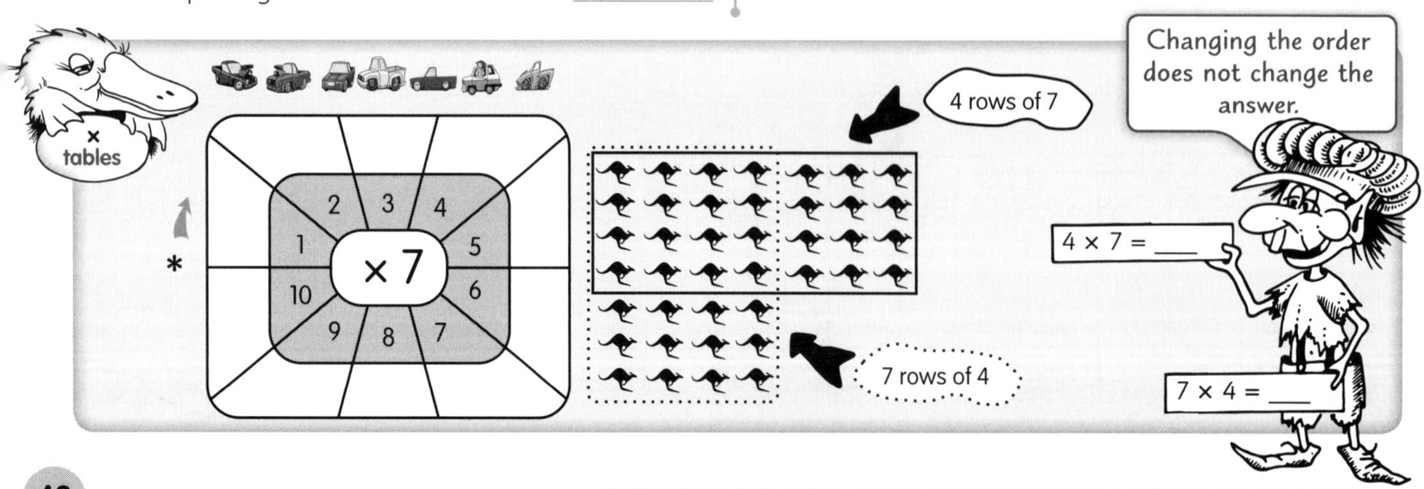

20:3 ☐ out of 13

1.

Hund.	Tens	Ones
2	0	8
+ 1	9	3

2.

Tens	Ones
$5	0
+ $1	8

3. 30 000 + 9 000 + 100 + 40 + 1 = ________
4. The value of 5 in 34 531. ________
5. Half of 10c. ________
6. The numeral for thirteen. ________
7. Which amount is larger, $10 or 100c? ________
8. 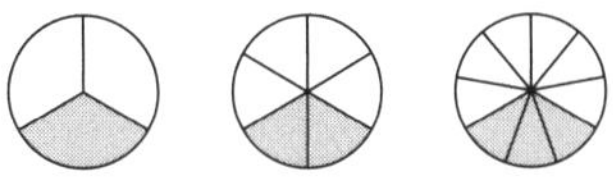

True (T) or false (F)?

a $\frac{2}{6} = \frac{1}{3}$ ________   b $\frac{2}{6} = \frac{3}{9}$ ________

c $\frac{2}{3} = \frac{2}{6}$ ________   d $\frac{1}{3} = \frac{3}{9}$ ________

9. What is the year 100 years before 2024? ________
10. Do the diagonals of a rectangle have the same length? ________

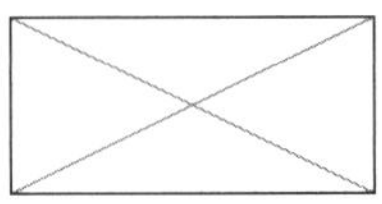

11. Do the diagonals above cut each other in half (bisect each other)? ________
12. Grams in 2 kilograms. ________
13. Would watermelons be weighed in kilograms? ________

20:4 ☐ out of 6

Extension

1. Is the length of the diagonal of this page closest to: 30 mm, 30 cm, 35 mm, 35 cm, 40 mm or 40 cm? ________
2. I opened a book. The sum of the two page numbers I saw was 73. What were the numbers?

   ________ and ________
3. The smallest number of coins that would total $12.60. ________
4. **a** 180 + 53 ________

   b 156 + 24 ________
5. If 14 × 14 = 196, what does 15 × 14 equal? ________
6. This figure has triangles of different size. How many triangles altogether? ________

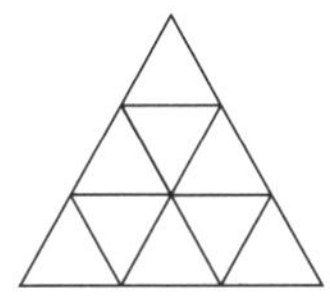

Challenge

Draw as many different composite shapes as you can using two squares and two triangles.

Example:

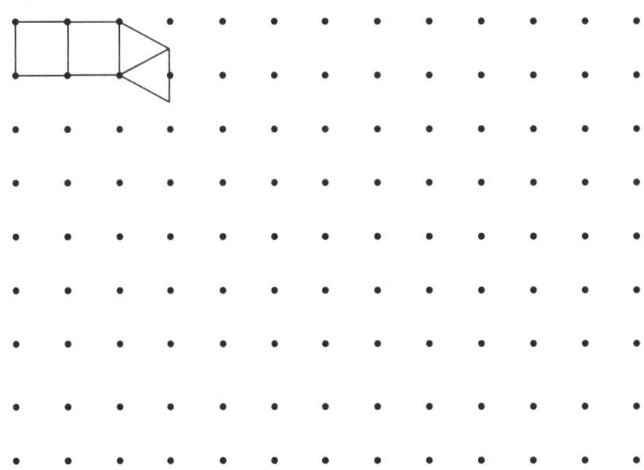

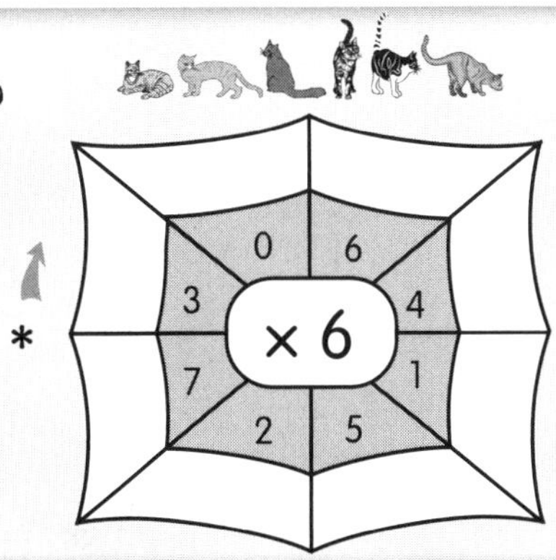

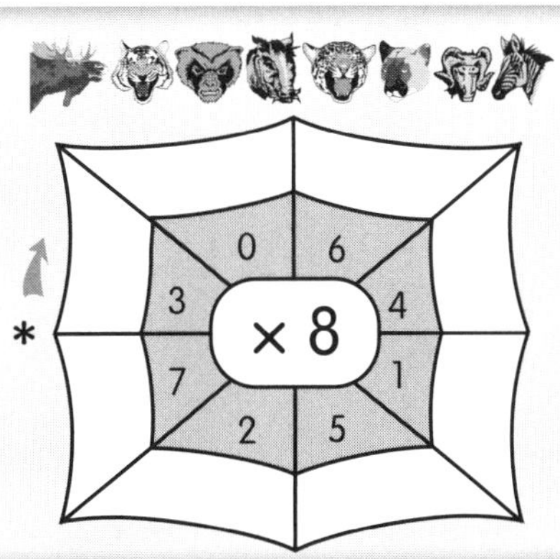

21:1

out of 16

1. 5 + 6 ____
2. 16 − 11 ____
3. 9 × 6 ____
4. 8 + 5 ____
5. 28 − 16 ____
6. 18 − 9 ____
7. 3 × 8 ____
8. Triple 3. ____
9. Increase 6 by 6. ____
10. 7 + 17 ____
11. The ordinal number after ninth is ____.
12.

Animals Seen			
Koala	IIII	Emu	𝍸 𝍸
Bilby	𝍸 I	Echidna	𝍸 III

a How many bilbies were seen? ____

b Which animal was seen most often? ____

c How many more echidnas than koalas were seen? ____

13. Write the number thirty-four thousand six hundred and forty-one. ____
14. 9 × ☐ = 36 ☐ = ____
15. The number shown on this abacus. ____

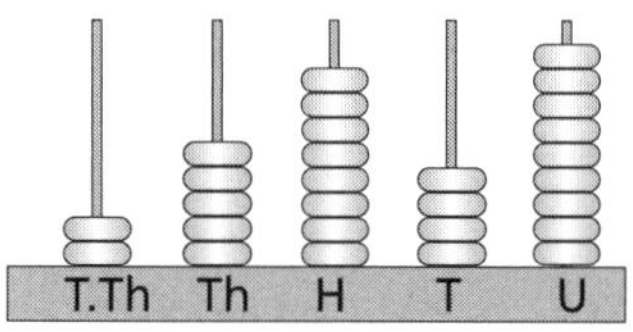

16. What shape has 3 sides, 3 corners and 3 angles? ____

21:2

out of 18

1. 20 + 30 ____
2. 40 − 20 ____
3. 9 × 1 ____
4. 5 × 9 ____
5. 62 + 15 ____
6. 10 lots of 1. ____
7. 7 × 7 ____
8. 4 × 7 ____
9. 15 shared by 3. ____
10. 7 × 5 ____

11. Days in September. ____
12. Two pieces of wood are joined together. What is the total length if one piece is 185 cm and the other piece is 260 cm? ____
13. 6 + 3 + ☐ = 12 ☐ = ____
14. 20 000 + 3 000 + 500 + 10 + 2 ____
15. Write 27 205 in expanded form. ____
16. Write the mixed number for:

a $\frac{7}{3}$ ____ b $\frac{17}{5}$ ____

17. Draw a hexagon in this space.
18. A line drawn from one corner of a polygon to another is called a ____.

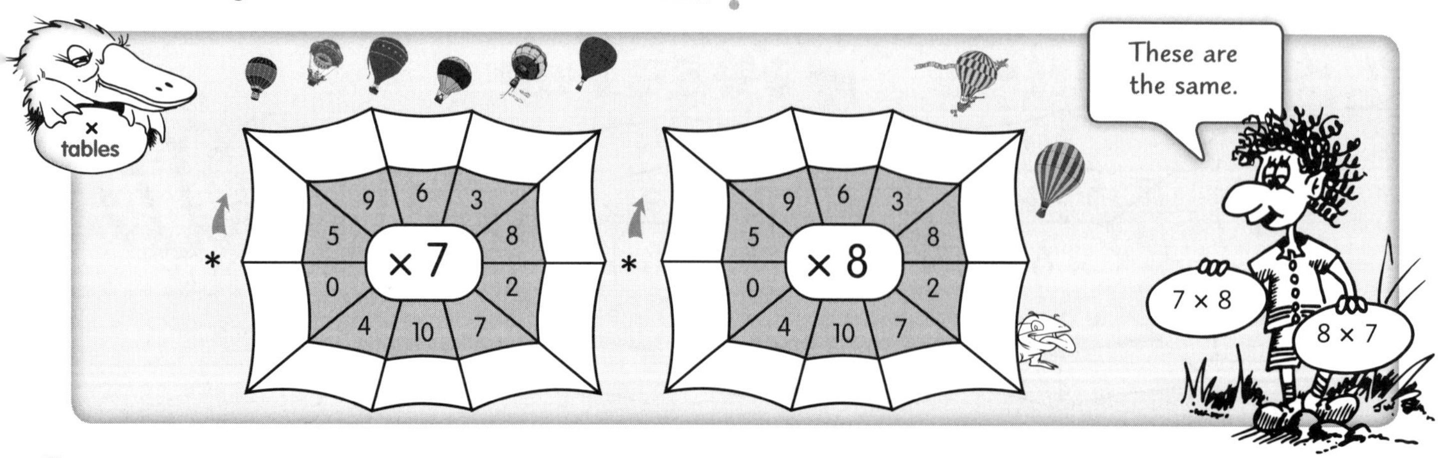

 ISBN 978 1 4886 2186 4

21:3 ☐ out of 7

1

Hund.	Tens	Ones
	3	4
+ 1	6	6

2

Hund.	Tens	Ones
	4	7
+ 5	2	1

3 Years in a decade. ______

4

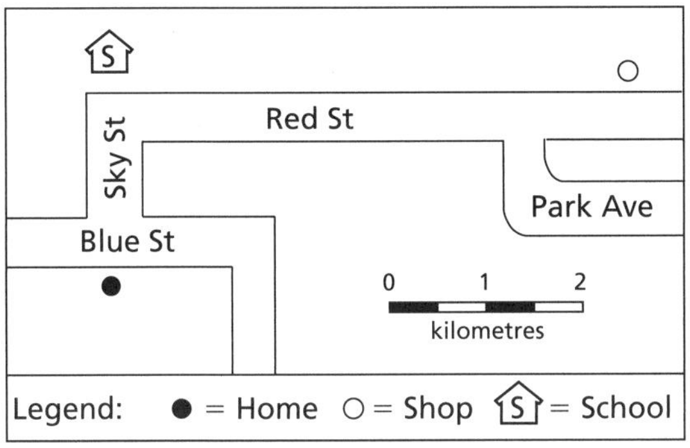

Use the scale to find the distance from home to:

a school ______ **b** the shop ______

c On which street is the shop? ______

d What special feature is 5 km from the school? ______

5

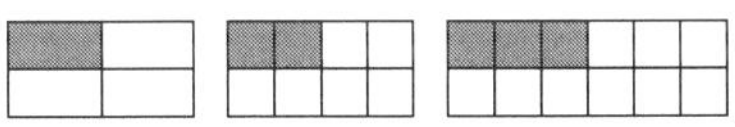

Use the above to write true (T) or false (F).

a $\frac{1}{4} = \frac{2}{8}$ ______ **b** $\frac{1}{4} = \frac{3}{12}$ ______

c $\frac{2}{8} = \frac{3}{12}$ ______ **d** $\frac{3}{4} = \frac{3}{12}$ ______

6 Draw all of the diagonals for this rectangle.

7 If one dozen is 12, how many in 4 dozen? ______

21:4 ☐ out of 6

Extension

1 If 3 boys collected 10 shells each and 5 girls collected 8 shells each, how many shells were collected? ______

2 What is the total length of four pieces of ribbon of lengths 5 m, 2 m 36 cm, 134 cm, and 28 cm? ______

3 If 8 + △ = 13 and 4 × □ = 16, what is △ × □ equal to? ______

4 How many different outfits can you make from 3 shirts and 2 pants? ______

5 139 + 42 ______

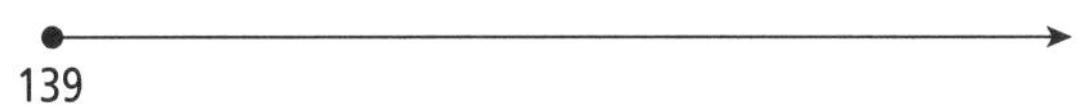

6 **a** 24 + 24 + 24 + 24 ______

b 23 + 23 + 23 + 23 ______

Challenge

Ask at least 4 people what time they went to bed last night. Record their answers and compare your results with your classmates'.

before 8 pm	
between 8 pm and 9 pm	
between 9 pm and 10 pm	
between 10 pm and 11 pm	
after 11 pm	

$\frac{12}{4} = 12 \div 4$

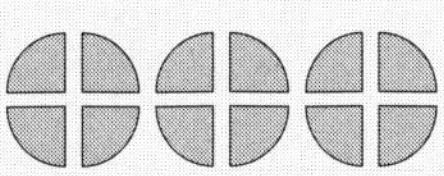

Twelve quarters = 3

Write each fraction as a division.

a $\frac{8}{2}$ = ______ ÷ ______ **b** $\frac{27}{3}$ = ______ ÷ ______

In each case, find the answer.

c $\frac{8}{2}$ ______ **d** $\frac{27}{3}$ ______ **e** $\frac{24}{4}$ ______

f $\frac{30}{5}$ ______ **g** $\frac{90}{10}$ ______ **h** $\frac{28}{4}$ ______

 • • ISBN 978 1 4886 2186 4

22:1 ☐ out of 14

1. 10 × 6 ______
2. 8 + 8 ______
3. 7 × 2 ______
4. 17 − 5 ______
5.
$$\begin{array}{r} 15 \\ +\ 24 \\ \hline \end{array}$$
6. 8 + 6 ______
7. 18 − 7 ______
8. 20c + 5c + 10c ______
9. 9 more than 4. ______
10.
$$\begin{array}{r} 29 \\ -\ 10 \\ \hline \end{array}$$

11. 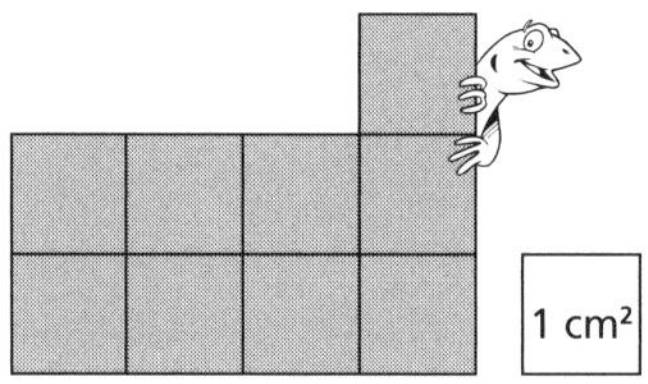

What is the area? ______

12. Complete the bar graph for this group of marbles.

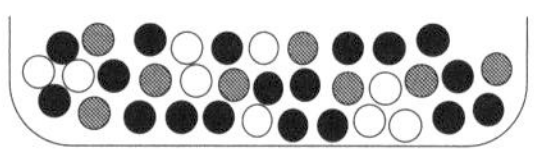

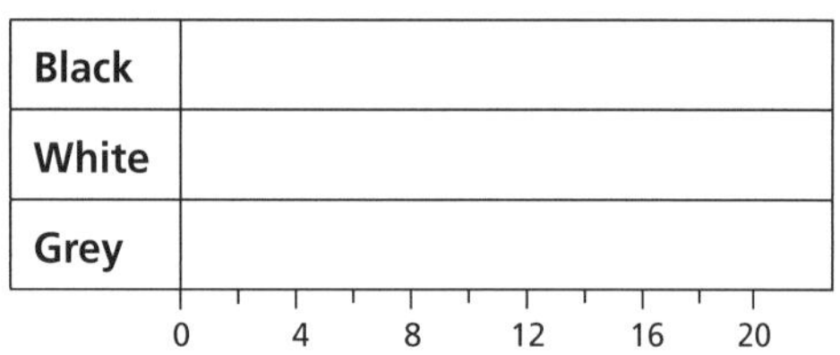

13. Write the numeral shown.

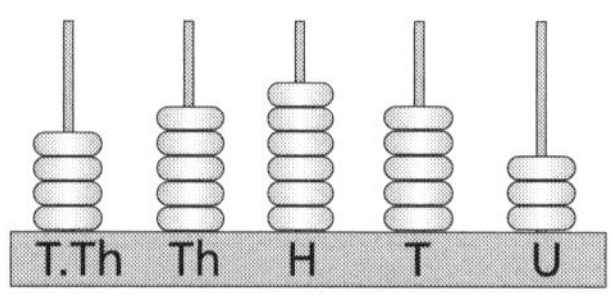

______

14. How many angles has a hexagon? ______

22:2 ☐ out of 16

1. 14 + 6 ______
2. 20 − 5 ______
3. 5 × 10 ______
4. 9 × 7 ______
5.
$$\begin{array}{r} 20 \\ -\ 7 \\ \hline \end{array}$$
6. 8 × 8 ______
7. 9 × 3 ______
8. 4 shared by 2. ______
9. 20 ÷ 4 ______
10.
$$\begin{array}{r} 8 \\ \times\ 7 \\ \hline \end{array}$$

45 cents each

11. The cost of 3 bananas. ______
12. The abbreviation for **square centimetres**. ______
13. Name an object that has the shape of a sphere. ______
14. 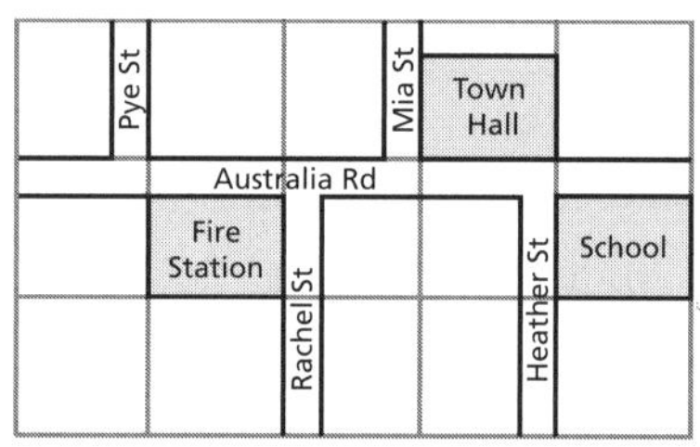

   a What is on Mia St? ______
   b What is on Rachel St? ______
   c The scale is: 1 cm = ______
   d How far is it from the fire station to the school? ______
15. 7 ☐ 7 = 14
    The operation for ☐ is: ______
16. Draw in all the diagonals of this polygon.

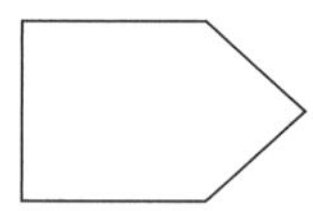

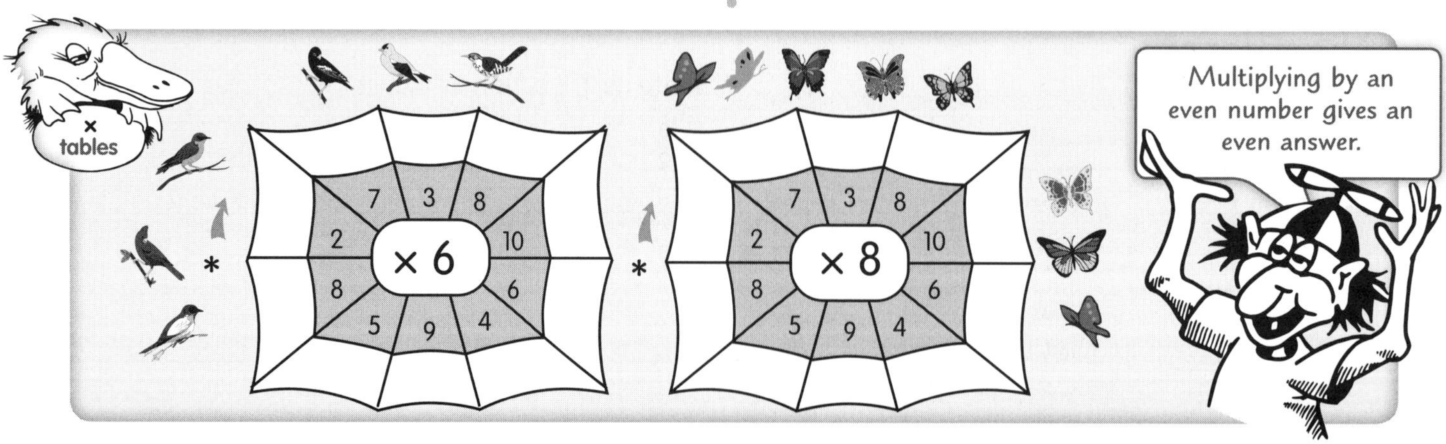

 ISBN 978 1 4886 2186 4

❶

Tens	Ones
6	1
− 4	3

❷

Hund.	Tens	Ones
2	8	1
+ 3	3	4

❸ Write the ordinal number for twenty-fourth. ______

❹ 卌 卌 卌 卌 卌 III

This tally stands for ______.

❺ Draw a cylinder in this space.

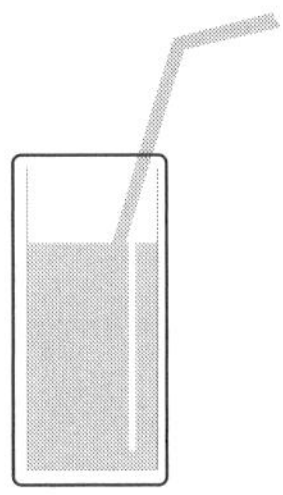

❻ 30 ÷ ☐ = 3 ☐ = ______

❼

A 	B 6 x 4	C 3 x 4
D 3 x 3	E 4 x 6	F 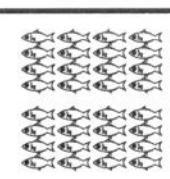
G 6 lots of 4	H 3 lots of 3	I 6 x 4

a Is D equal to E? ______

b Is B equal to E? ______

Which of the above are equal to:

c 3 rows of 3? ______

d 6 groups of 4? ______

❶ 10 octagons have ______ sides.

❷ If 5 students in 4M had 3 cakes each and 7 students in 4D had 3 cakes each, how many cakes were there altogether? ______

❸ 6 × ☐ + 4 = 52 ☐ = ______

❹  represents 14.

 represents 24.

What is represented by:

? ______

❺ How many stars would be in the 116th row?

______

❻ This figure has squares of different size. How many squares altogether?

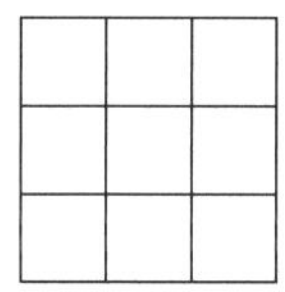

______

Challenge

Use tally marks to record how many times the letters "p" and "b" appear on this page.

		Total
p		
b		

Find the area of each shape.

a

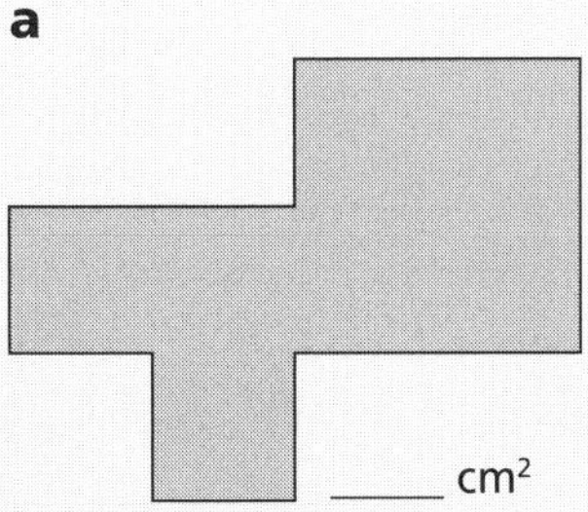

______ cm^2

b

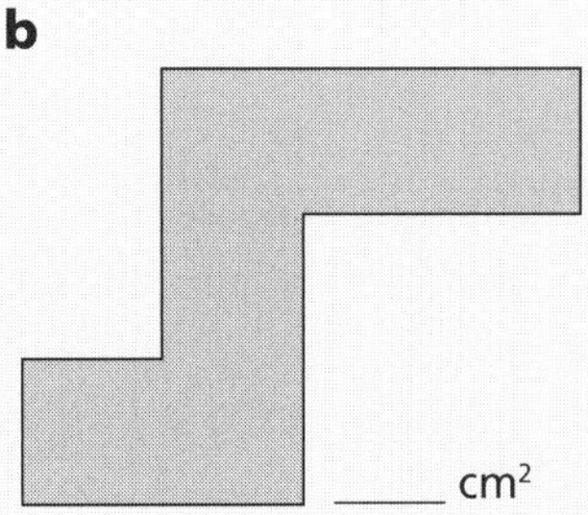

______ cm^2

c

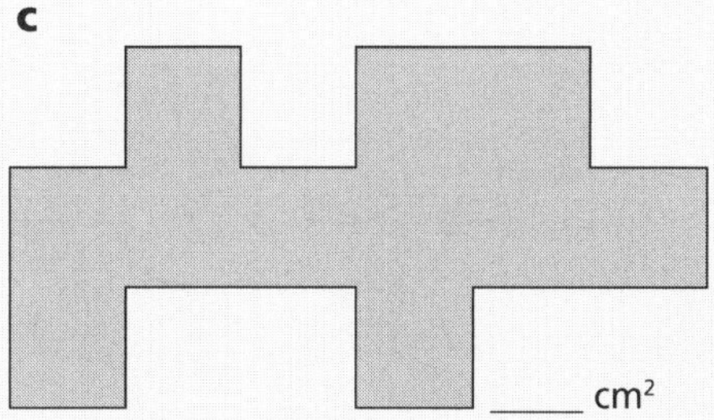

______ cm^2

23:1   ☐ out of 16

1. 0 × 9 ______
2. 11 − 5 ______
3. 10 + 7 ______
4. 13 − 4 ______
5. $\begin{array}{r} 23 \\ -\ 11 \\ \hline \end{array}$
6. 9 + 9 ______
7. 9 × 3 ______
8. 8 rows of 10. ______
9. Multiply 9 × 6. ______
10. $\begin{array}{r} 25 \\ +\ 14 \\ \hline \end{array}$
11. **a** Write $0.53 as cents. ______
    b Write 700 cents as dollars. ______
12. The abbreviation for **square metre**. ______
13. What fraction is shaded?

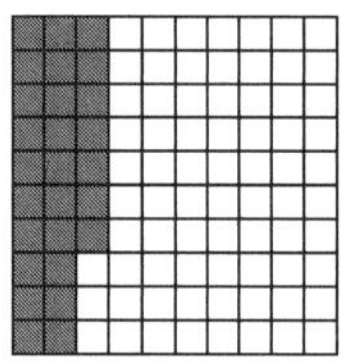

    a ______ hundredths
    b As a decimal this is: ______.
14. Name the shape below. ______

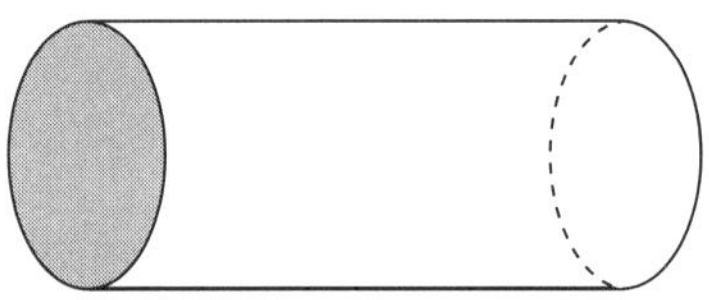

15. On the shape above, how many:
    a faces? ______
    b surfaces? ______
16. Write the numeral shown.

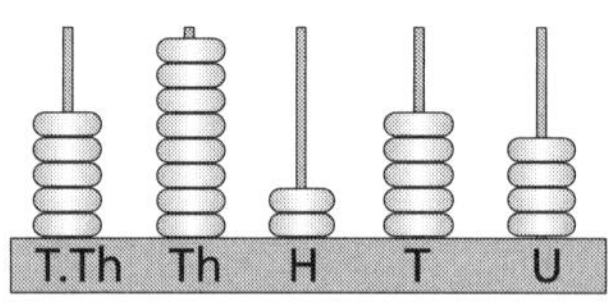

______

23:2   ☐ out of 17

1. 17 + 3 ______
2. 20 − 9 ______
3. 5 × 6 ______
4. 10 × 8 ______
5. $\begin{array}{r} 79 \\ +\ \ 4 \\ \hline \end{array}$
6. 8 × 9 ______
7. 5 × 3 ______
8. 42 ÷ 7 ______
9. 25 ÷ 5 ______
10. $\begin{array}{r} 9 \\ \times\ 6 \\ \hline \end{array}$
11. The cost of 10 pencils at 20 cents each. ______
12. 0·27, 0·28, 0·29, ______, ______
13. True (T) or false (F)?
    a 13 hundredths = 0·13 ______
    b 5 hundredths = 0·05 ______
14. Match equal numbers.

1·54	$1\frac{54}{100}$	0·54	$\frac{54}{100}$

15. 

    Which shape can the boy see? ______
16. The area of these squares is:

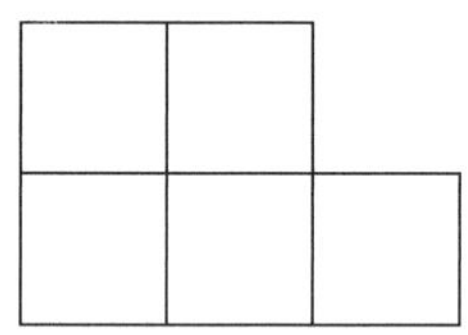

    ______ cm²
17. 7 hexagons have ______ angles.

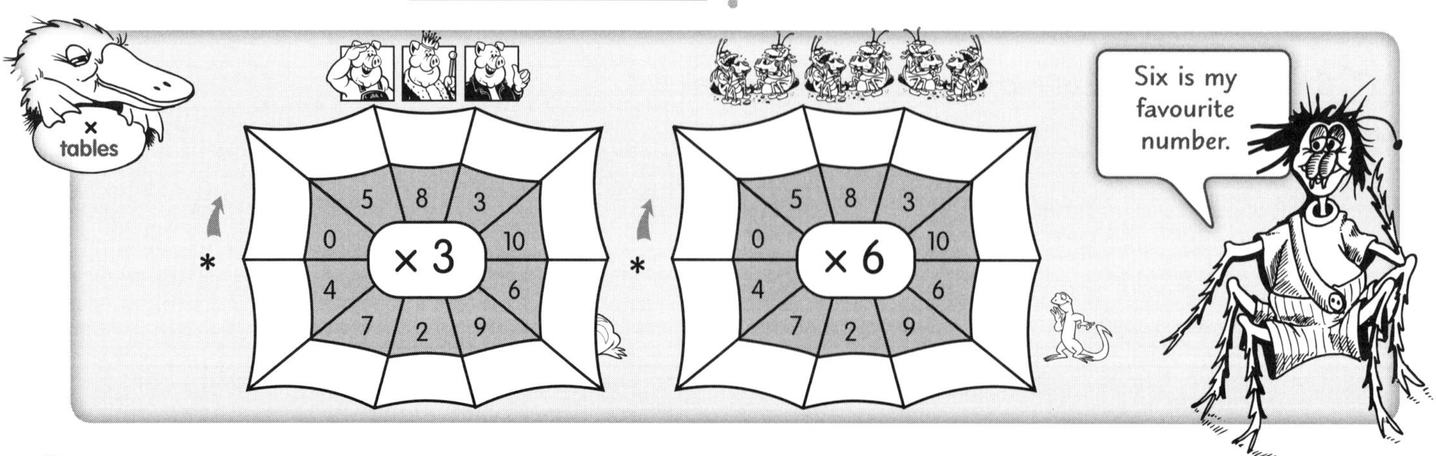

© PEARSON AUSTRALIA 2018 • *AUSTRALIAN SIGNPOST MATHS 4 MENTALS* • ISBN 978 1 4886 2186 4

23:3

out of 10

❶

Hund.	Tens	Ones
4	6	5
+	4	8

❷

Hund.	Tens	Ones
2	9	3
+ 4	1	9

❸ Is a cylinder a 3D object? ________

❹

Name	Tally	Total
Koala	~~IIII~~ ~~IIII~~ ~~IIII~~ ~~IIII~~ II	
Bilby	~~IIII~~ III	
Emu	~~IIII~~ ~~IIII~~ ~~IIII~~ IIII	
Possum	~~IIII~~ ~~IIII~~ ~~IIII~~ ~~IIII~~ ~~IIII~~ III	

a Fill in the last column of the tally above.

b Which animal was most common? ________

❺ Write $1\frac{3}{10}$ as a decimal. ________

❻ Write 7 tenths as a decimal. ________

❼ True (T) or false (F)? One square metre is less than the area of:

a one side of a door. ________

b the top of your desk. ________

❽ Write the decimal modelled.

Ones	Tens	Hundredths
0 •		

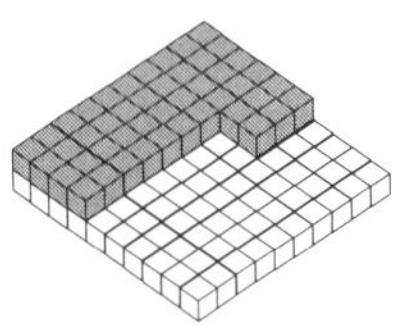

❾ A ruler is about ______ cm long.

❿ Will a cone roll? ________

23:4

Extension

out of 5

❶ I have four boxes of matches. 2 boxes have 9 matches left in each. The other boxes have 12 matches in each.

How many matches do I have? ________

❷ Which of the numbers 12, 14, 17 and 25, go in the square and triangle below?

$\eta + \nu = 29$ ________

❸ Complete the following:

341·82 = ________ hundreds
________ tens
________ unit
________ tenths
________ hundredths

❹ Use numerals to write sixty-three point two one. ________

❺ Is the area of a footprint measured in mm², cm² or m²? ________

Challenge

Choose an object.

Draw and label the top, front and side view.

Find the number of pages in a chapter if the chapter:

a starts on page 1 and ends on page 3. ________

b starts on page 4 and ends on page 14. ________

c starts on page 15 and ends on page 65. ________

How many pages are in these three chapters altogether? ________

24:1 ☐ out of 16

1. 16 − 3 ______
2. 2 × 4 ______
3. 15 + 5 ______
4. 6 × 10 ______
5. $\begin{array}{r} 37 \\ -\ 19 \\ \hline \end{array}$
6. 13 − 8 ______
7. 17 + 4 ______
8. Total of 7 and 8. ______
9. Sum of 5 and 3. ______
10. $\begin{array}{r} 33 \\ +\ 33 \\ \hline \end{array}$
11. What shapes have been used in this picture?

____

____

12. How many blocks have been used?

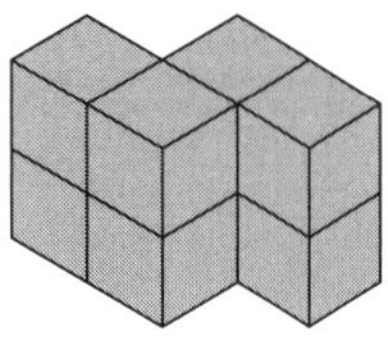

______

13. The area of a classroom floor is measured in

s__________ m__________.

14. Write the decimal shown by this model.

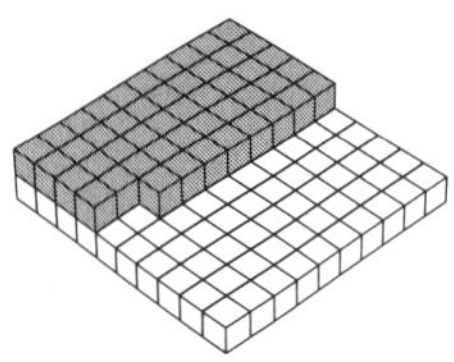

____

15. Write $\frac{43}{100}$ as a decimal. ______

16. 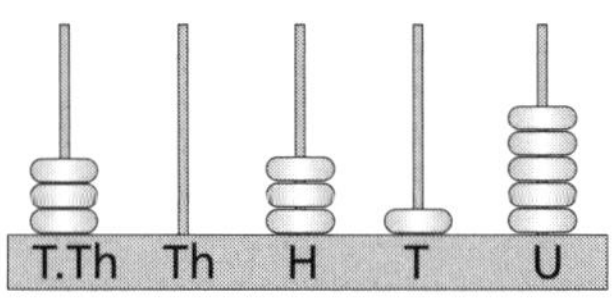

The number shown above. __________

24:2 ☐ out of 16

1. 19 + 1 ______
2. 18 − 4 ______
3. 2 × 7 ______
4. 9 × 9 ______
5. $\begin{array}{r} 551 \\ -\ 48 \\ \hline \end{array}$
6. 10 groups of 3. ______
7. 3 × 8 ______
8. 6 ÷ 6 ______
9. 6 shared by 2. ______
10. $\begin{array}{r} 7 \\ \times\ 4 \\ \hline \end{array}$
11. **cm²** is the abbreviation for:

____

12. Write $1\frac{4}{10}$ as a decimal. ______

13. 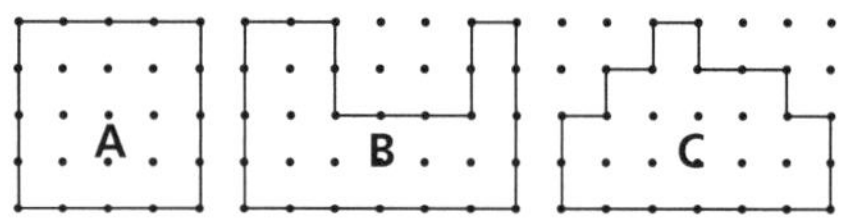

List these areas from smallest to largest.

______, ______, ______

14. Estimate how many desks like yours could be covered with one square metre of paper. ______

15. 20 out of 100 people chose red.

a Show this fraction on the square.

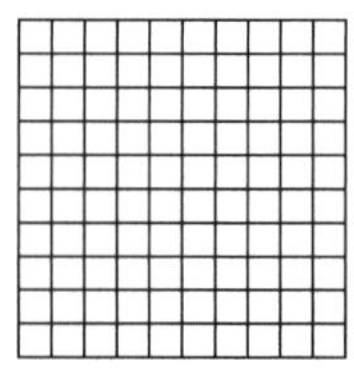

b Is $\frac{20}{100}$ the same as $\frac{2}{10}$?

____

16. Write the decimal shown here.

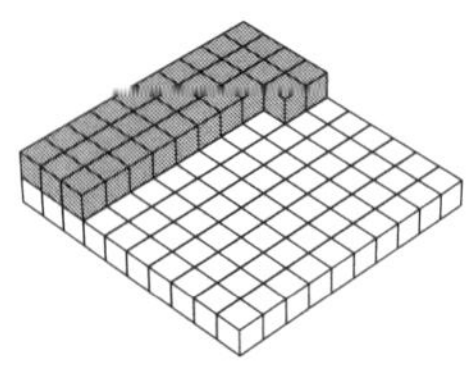

____

Complete the meaning of each chance card.

a | **certain** | means "It will __________ happen."

b | **likely** | means "It will __________ happen."

c | **fifty-fifty** | means "It is as __________ to happen as not."

d | **unlikely** | means "It will __________ not happen."

e | **impossible** | means "It will __________ happen."

 ISBN 978 1 4886 2186 4

24:3 ☐ out of 9

1

H	T	U
6	0	3
− 2	7	9

2

H	T	U
5	2	4
− 1	3	6

3 0·72, 0·73, 0·74, _______, _______

4 A B

a Which spinner is more likely to stop on red (R)? _______

b Which spinner has an equal chance of stopping on red (R) and yellow (Y)? _______

5 Would you use cm², m² or kg to measure the area of:

a the classroom floor? _______

b the cover of your book? _______

6 What number is represented by this tally?

卌 卌 卌 卌 III _______

7 **a** Decimal shaded. _______

b Decimal not shaded. _______

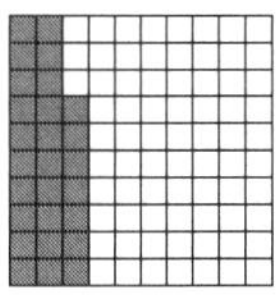

8 Write as a decimal:

a 7 hundredths _______

b 37 hundredths _______

9 Days in 4 weeks. _______

24:4 Extension ☐ out of 5

1 The same number must go in each of the three boxes. ☐ × ☐ = ☐

Give two possible answers. _____ or _____

2 Draw the different views of this shape.

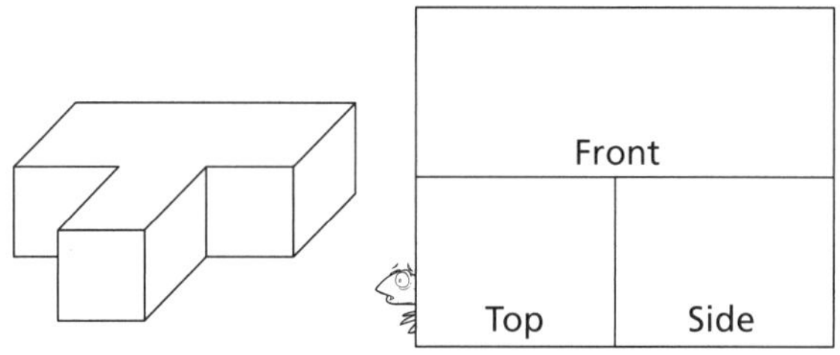

3 In this solid symmetrical shape, how many blocks cannot be seen from this angle? _______

4 The Roman numeral for 8. _______

5 True (T) or false (F)?

a 19 × 12 = 12 × 19 _______

b 19 + 12 = 12 + 19 _______

Challenge

What do you know about the decimal 0·7?

____

____

____

____

____

Roman Numerals

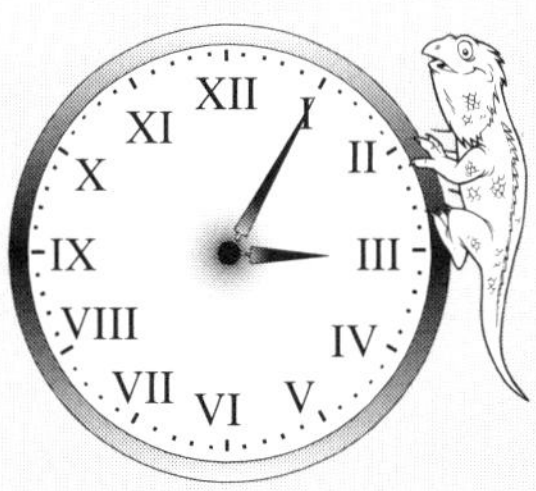

Use this clock to give the Roman numeral for:

a 4 _______ **b** 5 _______ **c** 9 _______ **d** 10 _______

e 11 _______ **f** 12 _______ **g** 2 _______ **h** 8 _______

Write our numeral for:

i IX _______ **j** XI _______ **k** VI _______ **l** IV _______

25:1 out of 18

1. 17 − 5 ______
2. 17 + 0 ______
3. 6 × 4 ______
4. 18 + 3 ______
5. $\begin{array}{r} 74 \\ +\ 22 \\ \hline \end{array}$
6. 3 × 10 ______
7. 19 − 6 ______
8. 35c + 20c ______
9. Double 9. ______
10. $\begin{array}{r} 692 \\ -\ 365 \\ \hline \end{array}$

11. Write 468c in the decimal form. ______
12. The abbreviation for **metres**. ______
13. R = Red, B = Blue, Y = Yellow.
    Which colour is the spinner least likely to land on? ______

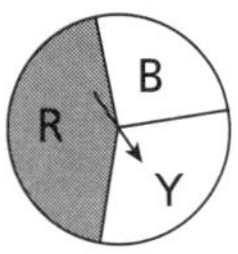

14. Complete the pattern:
    14 hundredths, 16 hundredths, 18 hundredths, ______
15. How many cubes are used in this model? ______

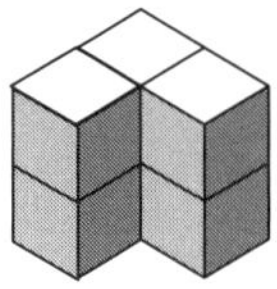

16. 10, 20, 30, ______, ______
17. Could 80 people stand on a school desk at the same time? ______
18. Write as a decimal:
    a $\frac{72}{100}$ ______ b $\frac{61}{100}$ ______
    c $\frac{83}{100}$ ______ d $\frac{11}{100}$ ______

25:2 out of 13

1. 15 + 10 ______
2. 18 − 6 ______
3. 9 × 5 ______
4. 4 × 4 ______
5. $\begin{array}{r} 25 \\ +\ 12 \\ \hline \end{array}$
6. 10 × 3 ______
7. 8 rows of 3. ______
8. 7 ÷ 1 ______
9. 64 ÷ 8 ______
10. $\begin{array}{r} 8 \\ \times\ 4 \\ \hline \end{array}$
11. Cents in $8.64. ______
12. a As a fraction, this is ______ hundredths.
    b As a decimal, this is ______.

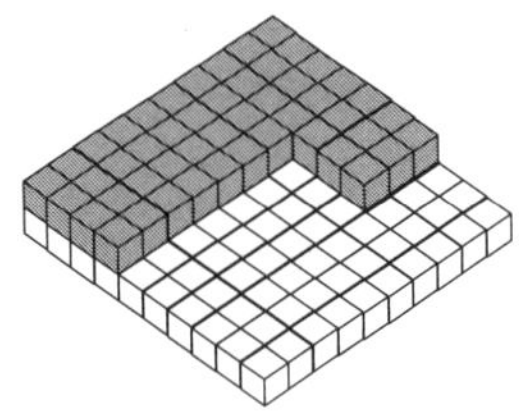

13.

Whose photo is:
a in the middle? ______
b at the bottom left? ______
c at the top right? ______
d above Nanna's photo? ______
e below Alan's photo? ______

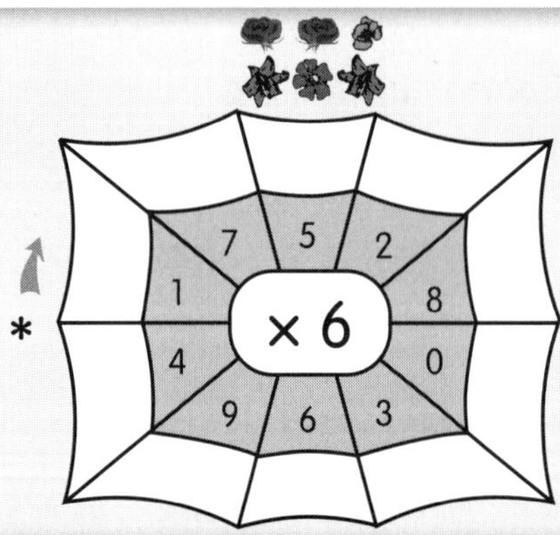

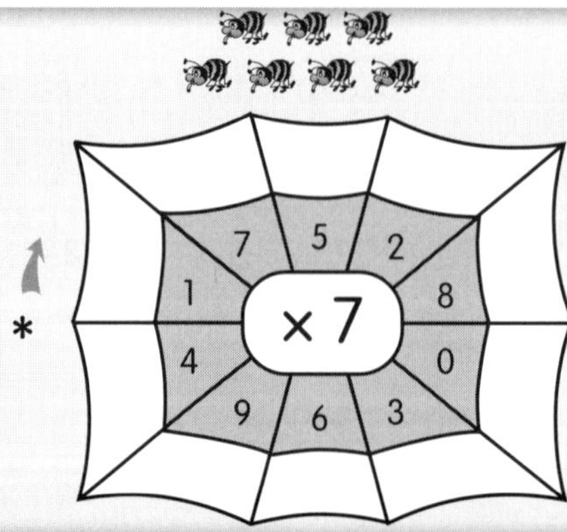

25:3 ☐ out of 10

1.

H	T	U
6	9	2
−	3	8

2.

H	T	U
7	8	0
−	3	6

3. 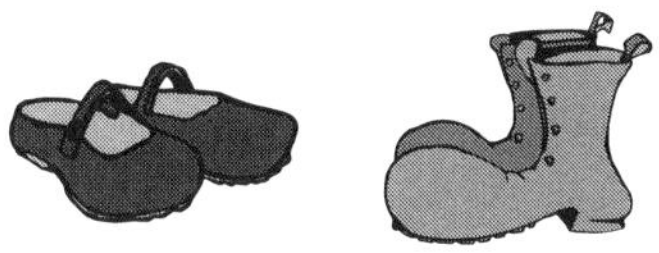 

How many shoes in 13 pairs? ______

4. Write 6c in decimal form. ______
5. If a loaf of bread costs \$2.05, how much will 3 loaves cost? ______
6. I am paid \$3 an hour. How much do I earn if I work 7 hours? ______
7. How many cubes are needed to make this shape?

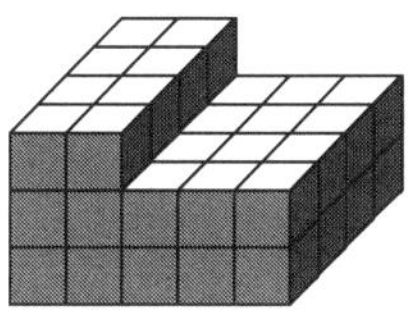

______

8. How many place-value ones do you need to cover this area?

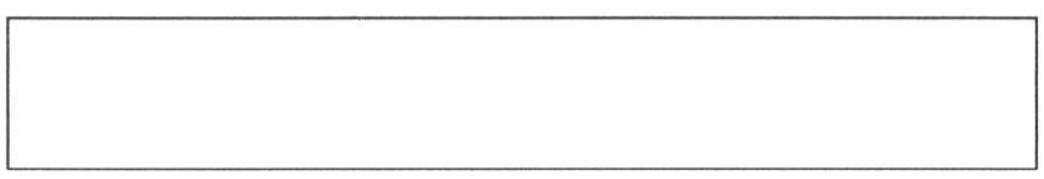

Area = ______ blocks

9. Millilitres in 9 L. ______
10. True (T) or false (F) ?
    a 8 hundredths = 0·80 ______
    b 8 hundredths = 0·08 ______

25:4 Extension ☐ out of 5

1. 6 × □ = 24, △ × 3 = 27
   The answer to □ + △. ______
2. I need 8 cubes to make a 2 × 2 × 2 stack like this. How many cubes do I need to make a:

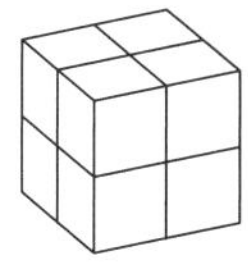

   a 3 × 3 × 3 cube? ______
   b 4 × 4 × 4 cube? ______
3. In how many ways can 30c be paid using 5c, 10c and 20c coins? ______
4. a The Roman numeral for 9. ______
   b The Roman numeral for 13. ______
5. 185 + 36 ______

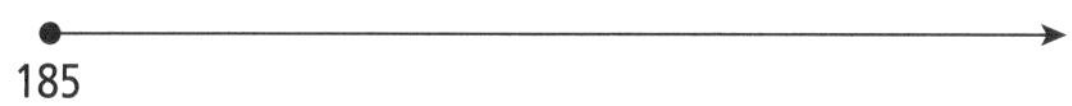

Challenge

List small areas, and estimate the area in cm² (e.g. the top of an eraser, mobile phone, CD case or DVD cover).

______
______
______
______
______
______
______

Turn to ID Card C on page 8.
Give the answers for these numbers.

(15) ______ (16) ______
(17) ______ (18) ______
(19) ______ (20) ______ surface
(21) ______ surface (22) ______

26:1   ☐ out of 15

1. 19 + 5 ______
2. 16 − 4 ______
3. 17 + 3 ______
4. 5 × 10 ______
5. 81 − 60 ______
6. 8 × 1 ______
7. 18 − 8 ______
8. 7 groups of 6. ______
9. Take 8 from 16. ______
10. 42 + 26 ______

11. Does this show a flip, a slide or a turn?

______

12. 3 weeks = ______ days.
13. What is the digital time?

a

b

______ ______

14. Write the numeral for thirty-nine thousand eight hundred and fifty-seven.

______

15. Write the decimal shown by this model.

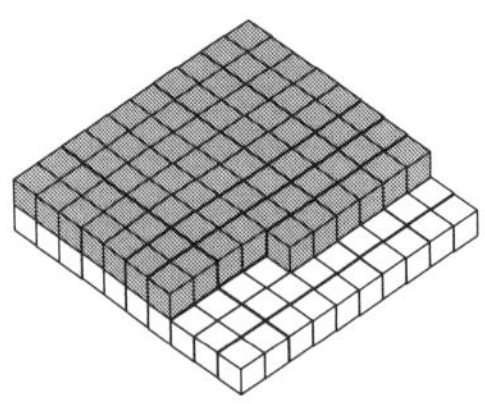

______

26:2   ☐ out of 16

1. 23 + 3 ______
2. 16 − 8 ______
3. 9 × 4 ______
4. 10 × 6 ______
5. 49 − 7 ______
6. 8 lots of 5. ______
7. 4 rows of 4. ______
8. 40 shared by 5. ______
9. 40 ÷ 10 ______
10. 3 × 8 ______
11. The next hundredth after 17 hundredths. ______
12. How many minutes after two o'clock? ______

13. 36 months = ______ years.
14. Is 46 354 or 49 012 larger? ______
15.

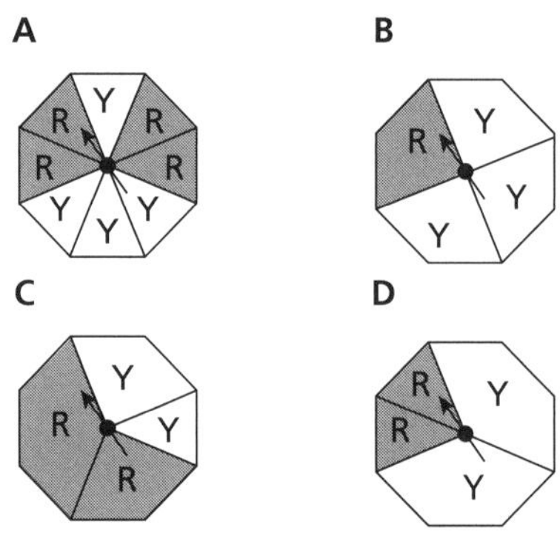

a Which spinner is more likely to land on R than Y? ______

b Which spinner is as likely to land on R as Y? ______

16. $1\frac{3}{10}$ as a decimal. ______

Roman Numerals

1	I	one finger	
5	V	one hand	
10	X	two V's	
50	L	half of a C	
100	C	centum = 100	

Write our numeral for:

a V ______ **b** XV ______ **c** LX ______

d CLI ______ **e** CLXV ______ **f** CLXVI ______

Write the Roman numeral for:

g 25 ______ **h** 110 ______ **i** 221 ______

j 207 ______ **k** 67 ______ **l** 333 ______

 ISBN 978 1 4886 2186 4

26:3 ☐ out of 8

1

H	T	U
3	8	5
– 2	9	7

2

H	T	U
4	0	3
– 1	7	4

3 Hours from 11:00 am to 2:30 pm. ______

4

a 2 of A plus 3 of B. ______

b 9 of E plus 2 of B. ______

c 4 of D plus 6 of A. ______

d 5 of E plus 4 of C. ______

5 Write 89 025 in words. ______

______

______

6 80 000 + 2000 + 300 + 10 + 5 ______

7 Colour 3 tenths of this hundreds block and write the label.

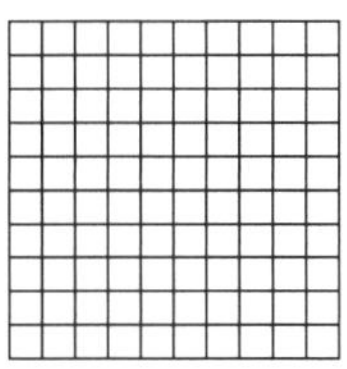

___ . ___

8 $\frac{9}{10}$ as a decimal. ______

26:4 Extension ☐ out of 6

1 If 25 − □ = 5, and △ + 17 = 21, the answer to □ ÷ △ is ______.

2 **a** 34 minutes after 2:06.

______

b 10 minutes before 2:06.

______

3 **a** The Roman numeral for 5. ______

b The Roman numeral for 10. ______

4 If 197 + 803 = 1 000, then:

a 1 000 − 803 = ______

b 1 000 − 197 = ______

5 We make small, medium and large masks. Each can be red, white, blue or yellow. How many different types of mask do we sell? ______

6 If the day after tomorrow will be Friday, what day was it 10 days ago? ______

Challenge

What do you know about the number 49?

______

______

______

______

______

______

- Throw one dice.
- From the start, move forward the number of spaces shown on the dice.

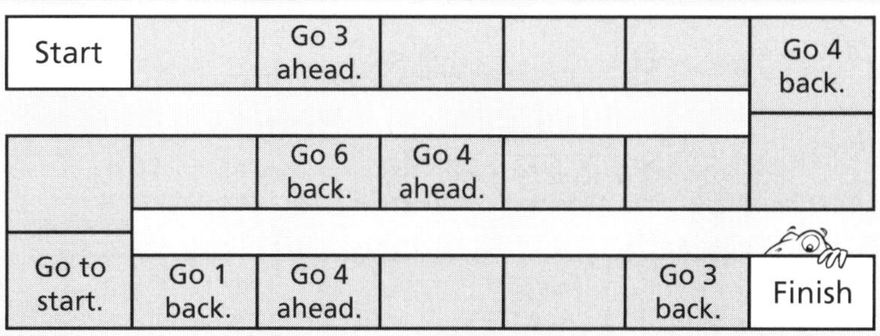

What is the least number of throws needed to reach the finish? ______

27:1

☐ out of 18

1. 8 × 0 ______
2. 19 + 2 ______
3. 17 − 3 ______
4. 7 × 5 ______
5. $\begin{array}{r} 63 \\ +\ 36 \\ \hline \end{array}$
6. 18 − 10 ______
7. 16 + 4 ______
8. Divide 14 by 7. ______
9. 78 kg − 10 kg ______
10. $\begin{array}{r} 94 \\ -\ 71 \\ \hline \end{array}$

11. 10 000 + 4000 + 700 + 70 + 3 __________
12. What is the time?
    a digital:

    ________ : ________

    b analogue:

    ________ past ________

Morning

13. 2 years = ________ months
14. Complete:

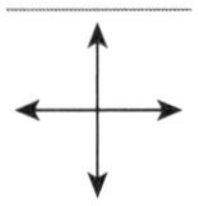

south

15. Share 9 lollies among 3 girls.

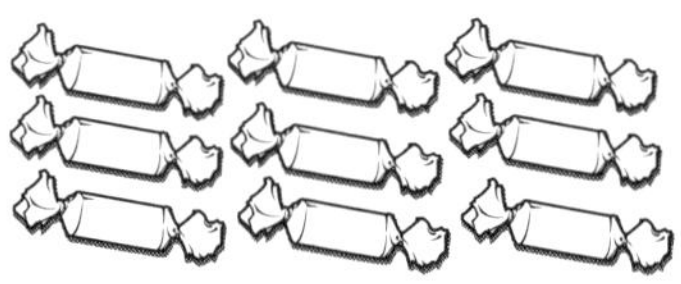

One share = ________ 9 ÷ 3 = ______

16. The ordinal number before 28th. ________
17. Write 785c in decimal form. ________
18. Weeks in 14 days. ________

27:2

☐ out of 17

1. 16 + 4 ______
2. 18 − 3 ______
3. 7 + 13 ______
4. 9 + 12 ______
5. $\begin{array}{r} 62 \\ +\ 14 \\ \hline \end{array}$
6. 3 groups of 5. ______
7. 6 × 10 ______
8. 32 ÷ 8 ______
9. 45 ÷ 9 ______
10. $\begin{array}{r} 6 \\ \times\ 6 \\ \hline \end{array}$
11. Show each time on the clock.
    a 2:45

    b 10:25

12. Which day is three days after Wednesday? ________
13. The number of boxes in this stack.

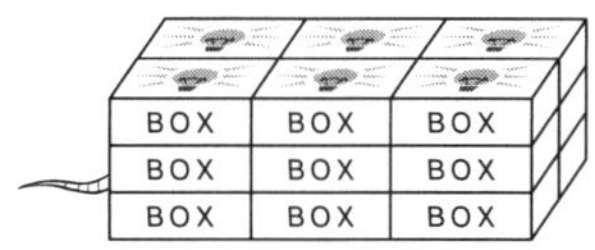

____

14. ÷ This is the d________ sign.
15. Is 29 879 or 30 214 larger? ________
16. Write the numeral for thirty thousand six hundred and twenty-one. ________
17. The decimal covered is:

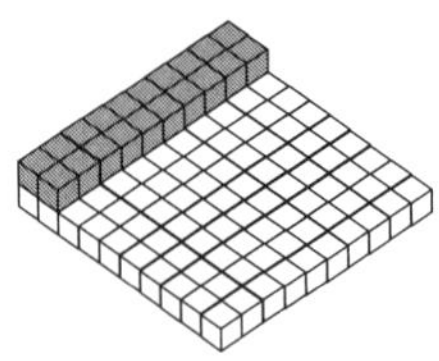

    a ______ tenths
    b ______ hundredths

3 cm	12 m
$1\frac{1}{2}$ m	100 m
2 m	50 m
30 m	5 m
3 m	8 mm
30 cm	10 mm
1 mm	10 cm

Choose a measurement from the table as an estimate for the height of a:

a door ______ **b** giraffe ______
c cat ______ **d** mouse ______
e mug ______ **f** power pole ______
g bus ______ **h** side fence ______

 ISBN 978 1 4886 2186 4

27:3 — out of 11

❶
```
  H T U
  1 9 9 +1
  2 0 0   (crossed out)
−   5 7
```

❷
```
  H T U
  6 9 9 +1
  7 0 0   (crossed out)
−   2 4
```

❸ The day before Sunday. ________

❹ What is the analogue time?

________ past ________

❺ 700 days = ________ weeks.

❻ How many twos in twenty? ________

❼ What direction is:

a Pai from A?

____

b Mun from A?

____

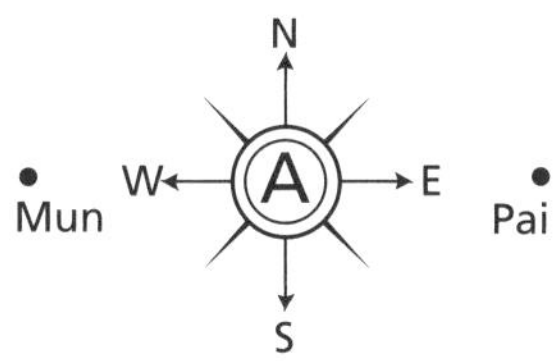

❽ Write 41 608 in words. ________

____

____

❾ Write $1\frac{5}{10}$ as a decimal. ________

❿

a 4 rows of 5 ________

b 4 rows of 7 ________

⓫ Use the picture above to find how many groups of 4 are in 28. ________

27:4 — Extension — out of 6

❶ If 17 + □ = 22 and 10 ÷ △ = 5, find:

a the answer to □ − △. ________

b the answer to □ + △. ________

❷ a 25 minutes after 8:05.

____

b 5 minutes before 8:05.

____

❸ I rode 3 km north, 5 km south and then 8 km north. How far was I then from my starting point? ________

❹ How many pairs in 18 shoes? ________

❺ a The Roman numeral for 9. ________

b The Roman numeral for 12. ________

❻ 20 lots of 10. ________

Challenge

Make up a number story for 20 ÷ 5, then find the answer.

____

____

____

____

____

____

____

N E W S

The needle of a compass always points north.

This word is made from North, East, West, South

Which parts of Australia are in the:

a west? ________

b north? ________

c east? ________

d south? ________

28:1 — out of 15

1. 15 + 2 ____
2. 9 × 5 ____
3. 19 − 3 ____
4. 10 × 4 ____
5. 77 − 43
6. 18 − 6 ____
7. 11 + 7 ____
8. Subtract 4 from 9. ____
9. Increase 7 by 3. ____
10. 88 + 35

11. What is the time?
   a digital: ____ : ____
   b analogue: ____ past ____

12. Share 16 crayons between 2 girls.
   One share = ____

13. Find the area of this shape.
   ____ cm²

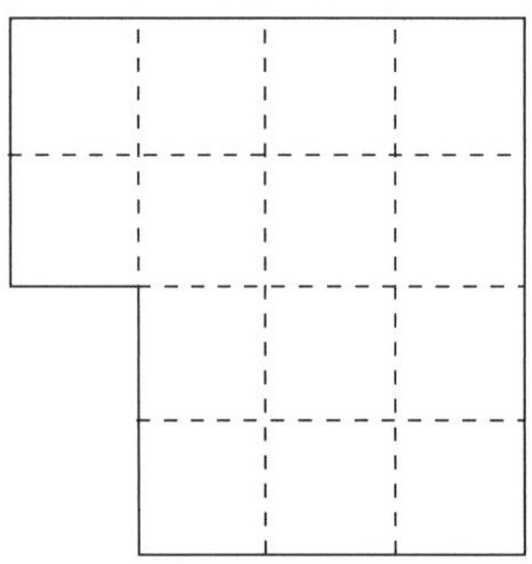

14. **Share among** means
   d____.

15. Complete:

north

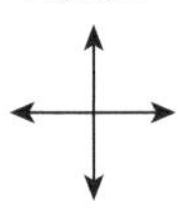

28:2 — out of 18

1. 18 + 2 ____
2. 3 + 12 ____
3. 8 × 7 ____
4. 5 × 6 ____
5. 80 − 6
6. 7 × 8 ____
7. 6 groups of 2. ____
8. 28 ÷ 7 ____
9. 18 shared by 9. ____
10. 9 × 5

11. What number multiplied by itself gives 49? ____
12. Minutes in 3 hours. ____
13. Share 30 tops among 5 children.

   One share = ____ 30 ÷ 5 = ____
14. 18 weeks = ____ fortnights.
15. The time 20 minutes before 9:10. ____
16. a 3 rows of 6. ____
   b 3 rows of 8. ____

17. What fraction of the bees above are:
   a shaded? ____
   b not shaded? ____
18. Use the bee picture above to find how many groups of 3 are in 24. ____

×	3	7	6	9	8	4
4						
6						
7						
8						
9						

Multiplying two odd numbers gives an odd answer.

Odd numbers end with 1, 3, 5, 7, 9.	Even numbers end with 2, 4, 6, 8.

21, 27, 3, 49, 63, 81

28:3 ☐ out of 9

1

	H	T	U	
	8	9	9	+ 1
	~~9~~	~~0~~	~~0~~	
−		4	6	
				+ 1
=				

2

	H	T	U	
	4	9	9	+ 1
	~~5~~	~~0~~	~~0~~	
−		6	9	
				+ 1
=				

3 Write five o'clock as digital time. ________

4

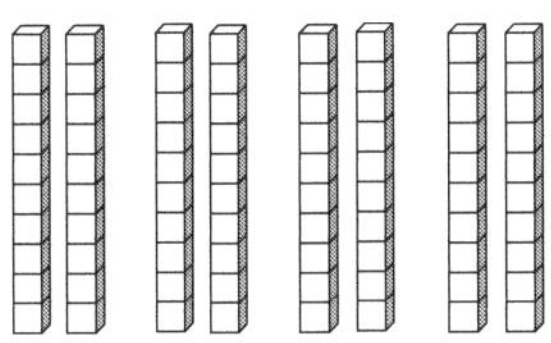

a How many fives in eighty? ________

b How many twos in eighty? ________

5 Which is larger:

a 3 × 6 or 7 × 2? ________

b 7 × 3 or 2 × 10? ________

6 Lia bought 4 mugs for $20. How much did one cost?

____

7 Decrease $20 by $7 and then double the result. ________

8 Degrees in a right angle. ________

9 The total value of the coins below. ________

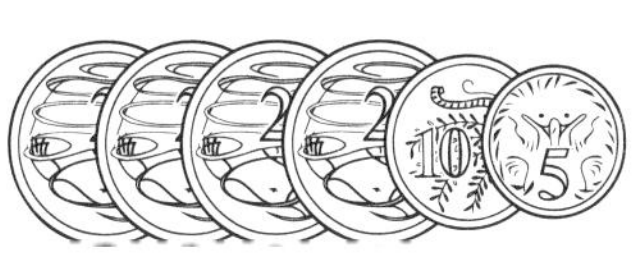

Extension

28:4 ☐ out of 3

1 Which number could go into all three boxes to make this sentence true? ☐ ÷ ☐ = ☐ ________

2 a The hour hand is pointing at 9. The minute hand and hour hand make a right angle.

What time is it? ________

b Is it possible for the hour hand to point at 6 and be at right angles to the minute hand? ________

3 I painted this 3 × 3 cube that is made of blocks. On how many blocks did I paint:

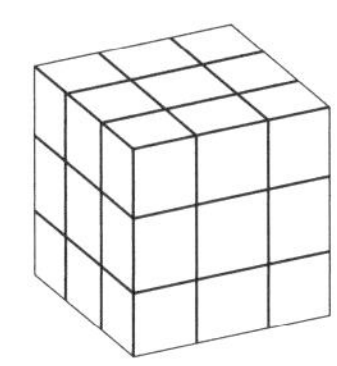

a 2 faces? ________

b no faces? ________

Challenge

Complete these columns of facts as quickly as you can. Once complete, check your answers and record your time.

2 × 7	______	8 × 2	______
6 × 5	______	3 × 7	______
5 × 8	______	10 × 7	______
9 × 7	______	6 × 7	______
4 × 7	______	3 × 8	______
6 × 6	______	8 × 7	______
6 × 8	______	7 × 8	______
7 × 7	______	5 × 7	______

Time = ______ seconds

Turn to ID Card B on page 7.
Give the answers for these numbers.

(20) ________ sixths shaded

(21) ______ hundredths shaded

(22) ________ tenths shaded

(23) 0· ______ shaded

(24) ________ hundredths shaded

(25) ________________

(26) ________________

(27) ________________

29:1 ☐ out of 16

1. 16 − 2 ____
2. 12 + 8 ____
3. 4 × 7 ____
4. 11 − 9 ____
5. $\begin{array}{r} 62 \\ +\ 35 \\ \hline \end{array}$
6. 10 + 6 ____
7. 8 × 9 ____
8. Triple 5. ____
9. 16 minus 7. ____
10. $\begin{array}{r} 65 \\ -\ 13 \\ \hline \end{array}$

11. Complete the label.

    ________ past ________

12. What is the value of the 4 in 34 569? ____

13. How many blocks have been used to make this model?

    ____

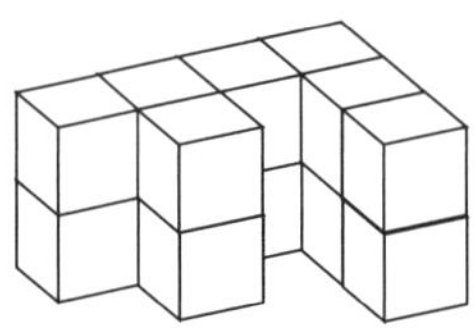

14. Aziz had 17 marbles. He lost 2 on Monday, 3 on Tuesday, 3 on Wednesday and 4 on Thursday. How many did he have left? ____

15. 2 × 3 = ____

    6 ÷ 2 = ____

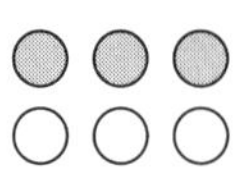

16. If 8 cakes were shared equally among four people, how many would each person get? ____

29:2 ☐ out of 17

1. 19 + 11 ____
2. 3 + 17 ____
3. 5 × 5 ____
4. 7 × 4 ____
5. $\begin{array}{r} 71 \\ -\ \ 4 \\ \hline \end{array}$
6. 10 × 9 ____
7. 9 × 4 ____
8. 6 shared by 3. ____
9. 60 ÷ 10 ____
10. $\begin{array}{r} 7 \\ \times\ \ 5 \\ \hline \end{array}$

11. 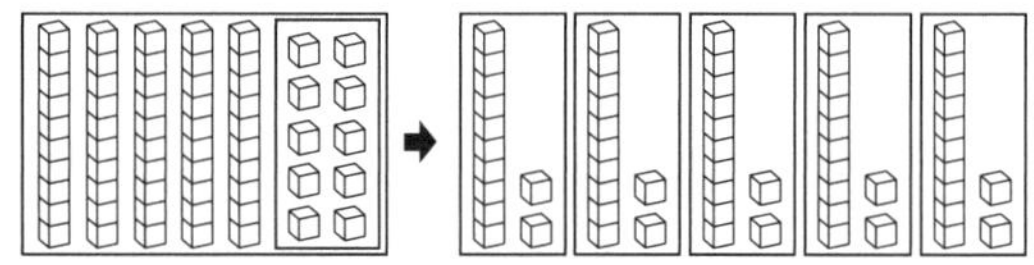

    How many 12s are in 60? ____

12. 70 000 + 2 000 + 400 + 90 + 2 ____

13. Write 14 874 in expanded form.

    ____

    ____

    ____

14. 32 ÷ 4 = ____ or ____ × 4 = 32

15. How many days in spring? ____

16. The total value of these notes. ____

17. 3 × 4 = ____

    12 ÷ 3 = ____

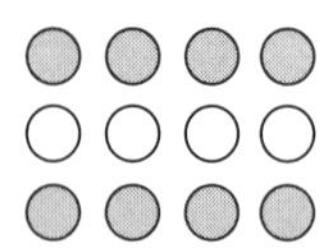

Turn to ID Card A on page 6.

Give the answers for these numbers.

(1) ________ (2) ________

(3) ________ (4) ________

(5) ________ (6) ________

(7) ____ ____ (8) ____ ____

 • *AUSTRALIAN SIGNPOST MATHS 4 MENTALS* • ISBN 978 1 4886 2186 4

29:3

[   ] out of 12

❶

	H	T	U	
	8	9	9	+ 1
	~~9~~	~~0~~	~~0~~	
−		4	6	
	___	___	___	+ 1
=	___			

❷

	H	T	U	
	4	9	9	+ 1
	~~5~~	~~0~~	~~0~~	
−		6	9	
	___	___	___	+ 1
=	___			

❸ $1\overline{)9}$ ❹ $5\overline{)15}$ ❺ $4\overline{)8}$

❻ 20 ÷ 5 = ________ or ________ × 5 = 20

❼ How many cubic centimetres are in this stack? ________

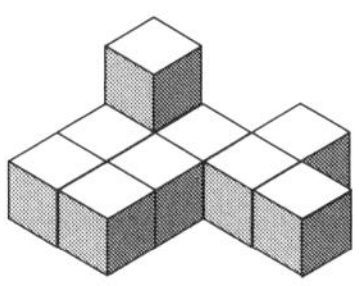

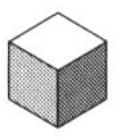 = 1 cm³

❽ Years in 2 decades. ________

❾ How many 5c lollies for 50c? ________

❿ True (T) or false (F)? 40 024 < 39 879 ________

⓫ **a** The digital time is ______ : ______.

b The analogue time is ______ past ______.

⓬

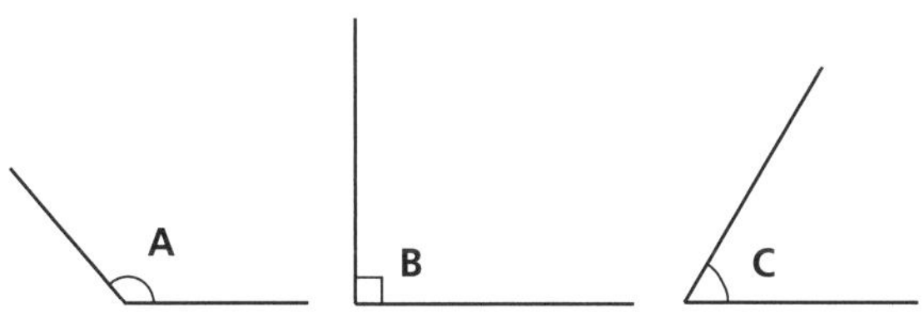

a Write the angles in order of size with the smallest first. ________

b Which angle is a right angle? ________

29:4

Extension

[   ] out of 5

❶ Which of the numbers 15, 18, 19 and 27, go in the spaces in each number sentence?

a ________ + ________ = 34

b ________ − ________ = 9

❷ Naomi walked 15 km east and then 23 km west. How far was she then from her starting point? ________

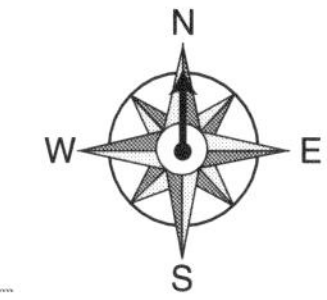

❸ If 13 + 13 + 13 + 13 + 13 + 13 = 78, then how many 13s in 78? ________

❹ I need $12 to buy one tie. How many ties can I buy with $79?

____

❺ Which is larger, an angle of a square or a regular hexagon? ________

Challenge

Represent the number 21 320 in as many ways as you can.

One hundred coins are placed in a row.

The flea as it jumps, lands on every second coin.
How many jumps are needed for the flea to get from the first coin to the:

a 5th coin? ______ **b** 11th coin? ______

c 15th coin? ______ **d** 19th coin? ______

30:1

out of 17

1. 7 + 6 ______
2. 2 × 2 ______
3. 11 − 4 ______
4. 6 ÷ 2 ______
5. 73 + 25 = ______
6. 9 kg − 4 kg ______
7. 25c + 10c ______
8. Half of 30. ______
9. 3 × 7 ______
10. 66 − 42 = ______

11. 20 000 + 6 000 + 100 + 90 + 7 ______
12. 2 × 4 = ______
    8 ÷ 2 = ______

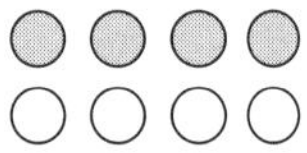

13. Write zero point two as a decimal. ______
14. How many 20c coins make $1? ______
15. 
    This tally stands for ______.
16. A minibus carries 8 people. How many people can fit on 4 minibuses?

______

17. Complete the labels.

a 

______ past ______

b 

______ past ______

30:2

out of 16

1. 15 + 5 ______
2. 7 + 23 ______
3. 9 × 5 ______
4. 7 × 6 ______
5. 34 + 14 = ______
6. 8 × 5 ______
7. 9 groups of 6. ______
8. 20 ÷ 10 ______
9. 54 ÷ 9 ______
10. 7 × 7 = ______
11. What is the value of the 8 in 71 298? ______
12. True (T) or false (F)? 23 956 > 23 781 ______
13. If $\eta \times 3 = 24$, then $\eta =$ ______.
14. Some cubes are stacked in a box. How many cubes are in this box?

______

15. 3 × 6 = ______
    18 ÷ 3 = ______

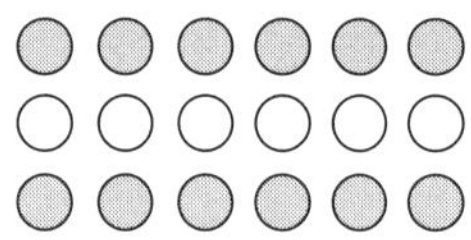

16. How many minutes before 5 o'clock?

a 
______

b 
______

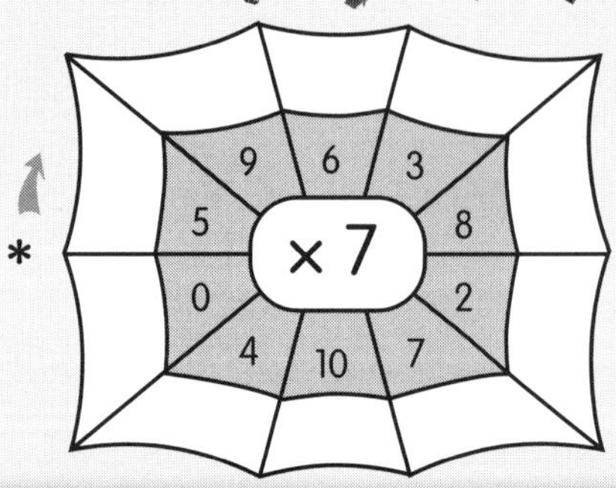

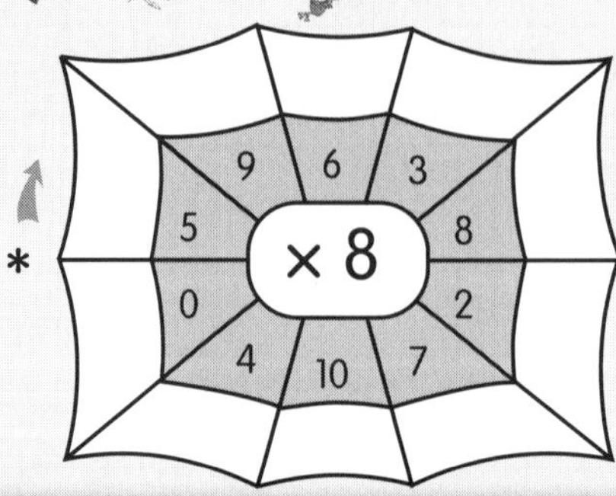

ISBN 978 1 4886 2186 4

30:3 ☐ out of 10

1

H	T	U
5	4	3
	2	3
+	1	2

2

H	T	U
6	8	1
–	3	7

3 $5\overline{)10}$ **4** $6\overline{)24}$ **5** $8\overline{)48}$

6 15 ÷ 3 = ______ or ______ × 3 = 15

7 What is in position:

a 2C? ______

b 3B? ______

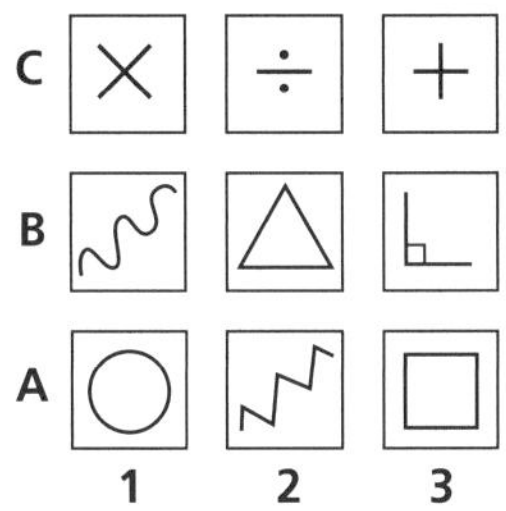

From the grid above, give the position of the:

c triangle. ______

d wavy line. ______

8 Write the numeral for the number shown. ______

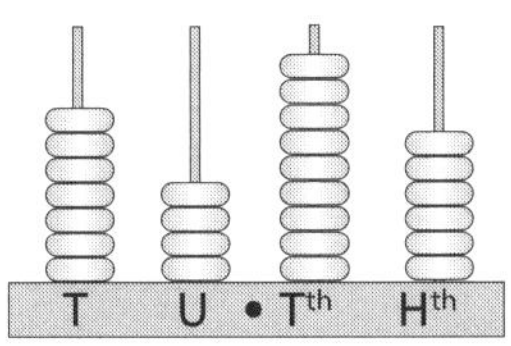

9 Share 55 lollies among 5 children.

One share = ______

10 Write the numeral for (7 × 10 000) + (5 × 1 000) + (3 × 100) + (5 × 10) + 5

______

30:4 Extension ☐ out of 6

1 a Find the total area of the faces. ______

b Find the total length of the edges. ______

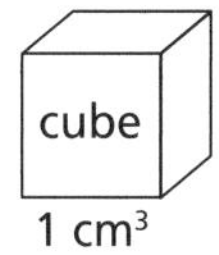

2 Does 3 hundredths equal 0·03? ______

3 The Roman numeral for:

a 4 ______ b 7 ______

4 If 6 February was a Friday, what day was 28 January? ______

5 If we choose one number from each column:

a which numbers give a total of 16? ______

b how many totals occur twice? ______

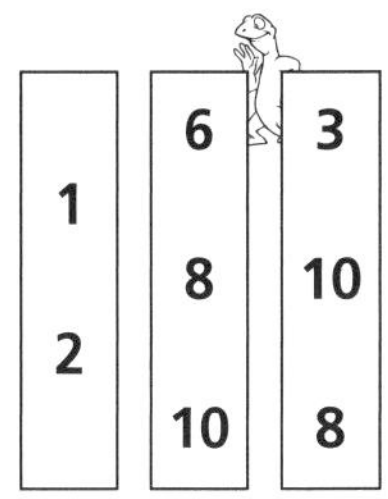

6 If 9 × 23 = 207, what does 8 × 23 equal? ______

Challenge

Follow these tracks, writing an answer in each circle.

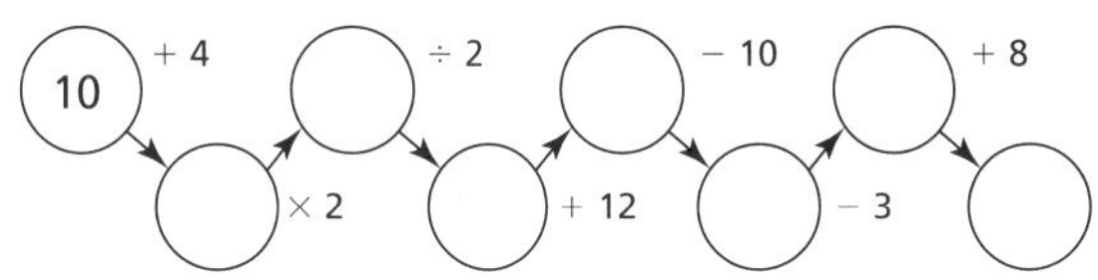

Write your own instructions, then complete.

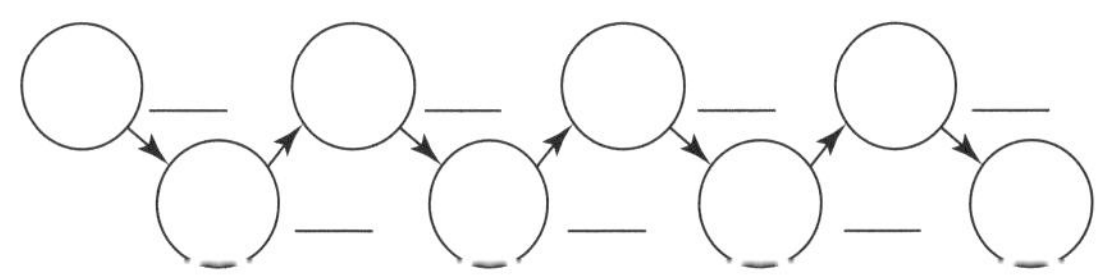

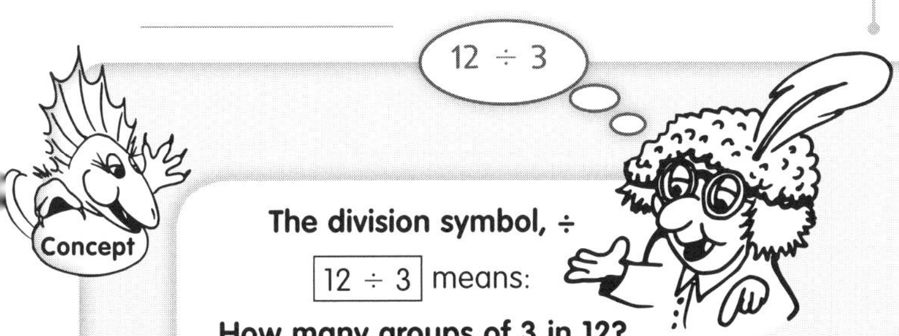

Concept

The division symbol, ÷

12 ÷ 3 means:

How many groups of 3 in 12?
OR **What is one share, if 12 is shared among 3?**

Therefore: **12 ÷ 3 = 4**

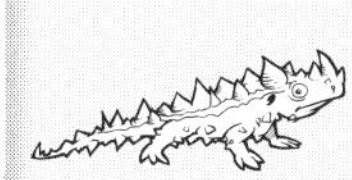

a 12 ÷ 4 ______	**b** 12 ÷ 2 ______
c 12 ÷ 6 ______	**d** 12 ÷ 3 ______
e 20 ÷ 2 ______	**f** 20 ÷ 10 ______
g 15 ÷ 3 ______	**h** 15 ÷ 5 ______
i 28 ÷ 4 ______	**j** 70 ÷ 10 ______

31:1

☐ out of 13

1. 16 − 6 ______
2. 20 ÷ 2 ______
3. 4 × 3 ______
4. 13 + 4 ______
5. $\begin{array}{r} 89 \\ +\ 62 \\ \hline \end{array}$
6. $7 + $10 ______
7. 5 × 7 ______
8. Divide 6 by 3. ______
9. 500 g − 300 g ______
10. $\begin{array}{r} 34 \\ +\ 34 \\ \hline \end{array}$

11. Seconds in one minute. ______
12.

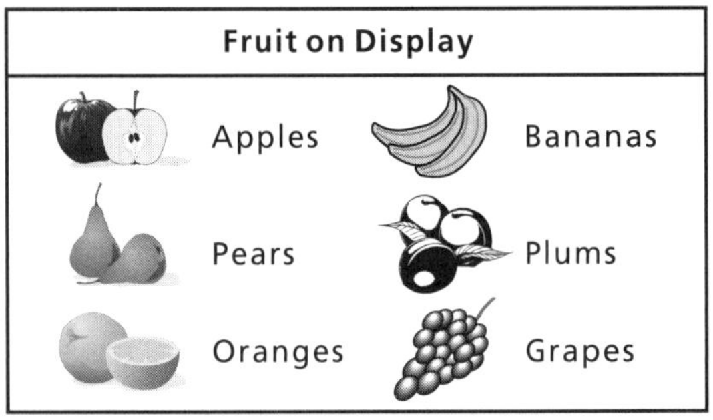

a Which fruit is on the bottom right? ______

b Which fruit is opposite the pears? ______

c Which fruit is above the plums? ______

d How many of the names of these fruits start with "p"? ______

e What fraction of the names starts with "p"? ______ out of ______

13. Six people shared 18 pencils. How many did each person get? ______

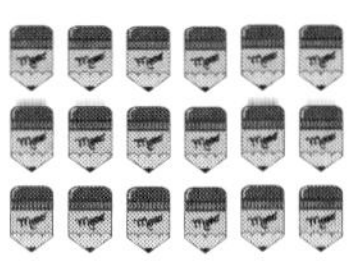

31:2

☐ out of 17

1. 13 + 7 ______
2. 20 − 6 ______
3. 10 × 4 ______
4. 2 × 9 ______
5. $\begin{array}{r} 60 \\ -\ 8 \\ \hline \end{array}$
6. 10 rows of 10. ______
7. 8 × 9 ______
8. 15 ÷ 3 ______
9. 81 ÷ 9 ______
10. $\begin{array}{r} 7 \\ \times\ 6 \\ \hline \end{array}$

11. How many triangles like this are needed to cover the second shape? ______

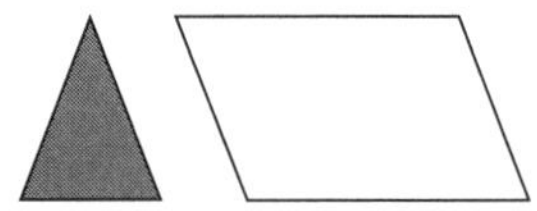

12. Write the numeral shown on the abacus.

______

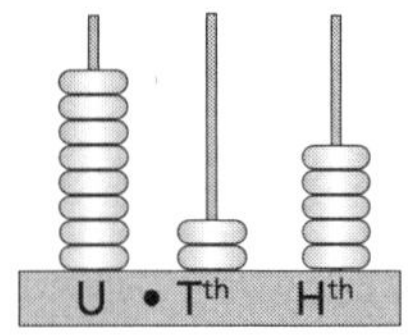

13. 卌 卌 卌 卌 II

This tally stands for ______.

14.

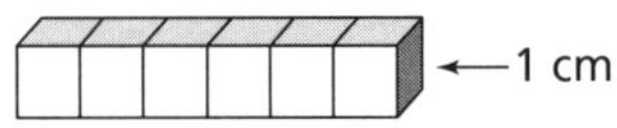

The total volume of this shape. ______

15. 3 × 5 = ______

15 ÷ 3 = ______

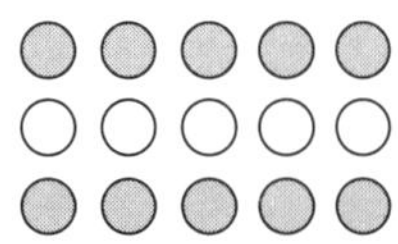

16. Draw the analogue time, 5 minutes past 9.

17. Make the largest number possible using 1, 7, 3 and 9. ______

☐ groups of 6 = 24

☐ × 6 = 24

The answer is 4.

Multiplication Linked with Division

a How many groups of 5 in 30?

☐ groups of 5 = 30

☐ × 5 = 30

The answer is ______.

b Share 28 among 4 boys.

4 shares of ☐ = 28

4 × ☐ = 28

The answer is ______.

c How many rows of 6 in 42?

☐ rows of 6 = 42

☐ × 6 = 42

The answer is ______.

d Share 27 among 3 girls.

3 shares of ☐ = 27

3 × ☐ = 27

The answer is ______.

31:3 ☐ out of 10

1

H	T	U
	6	7
+	3	1

2

H	T	U
	4	3
+	7	2

3 $2\overline{)16}$ **4** $2\overline{)4}$ **5** $4\overline{)16}$

6 Write the numeral shown. ________

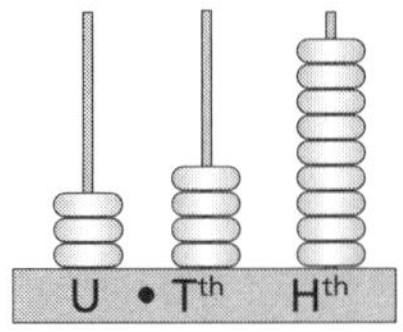

7 List the value of the notes and coins needed to make $53.10. ________

____

8

$1.20 $1.50 $2.40

The total cost of this fruit? ________

9 Give the coordinates of:

a W ________

b X ________

c Y ________

d Z ________

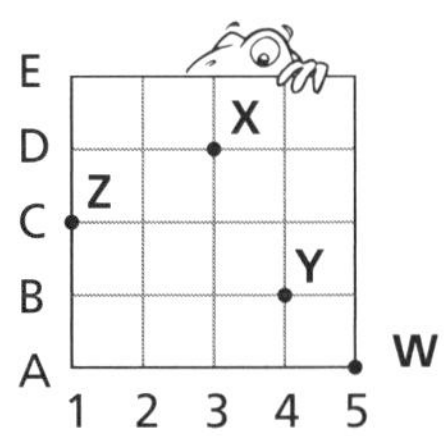

10 24 ÷ 3 = ________ or ________ × 3 = 24

31:4 Extension ☐ out of 4

1 If three cars will fill a semi-trailer, how many semis can be filled using 21 cars? ________

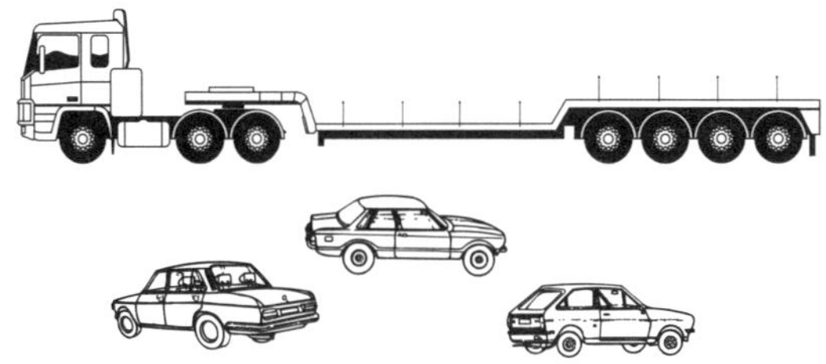

2 4, 8, 12, 16, 20, ____

If this number pattern continued, what would be the:

a 8th number? ________

b 10th number? ________

3 Eight friends gave either $4 or $5 each. If $38 was given, how many gave $5? ________

4 How many different ways are there of choosing two of these squares side by side for a hand-ball court?

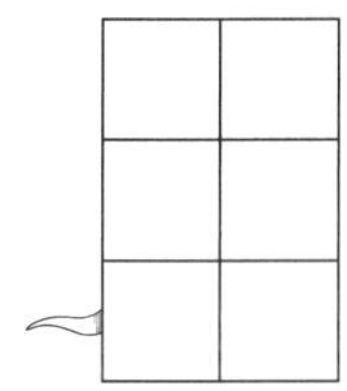

____

Challenge

What do you know about the decimal 261·73?

____

____

____

____

 • *AUSTRALIAN SIGNPOST MATHS 4 MENTALS* • ISBN 978 1 4886 2186 4

32:1 ☐ out of 16

❶ 6 × 4 ______

❷ 12 + 6 ______

❸ 9 ÷ 3 ______

❹ 15 − 2 ______

❺
```
   95
 − 43
```

❻ Subtract 3 from 9. ______

❼ 8 more than 7. ______

❽ 9 × 3 ______

❾ Total 3, 4 and 5. ______

❿
```
   73
 + 25
```

⓫ Days in 2 weeks. ______

⓬ Five more than fifteen. ______

⓭ **a** Months in half a year. ______

b Months in $2\frac{1}{2}$ years. ______

⓮ 300 000 + 30 + 9 ______

⓯

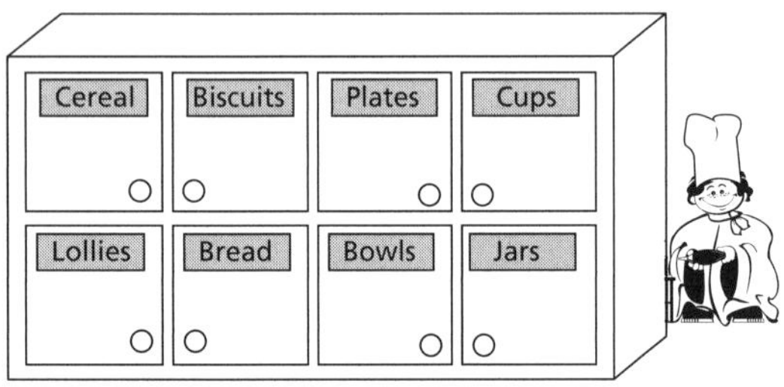

a What is kept second from the left, on the top row? ______

b Where is the bread kept? ______

______

⓰ Write the volume on this model in cm³. ______

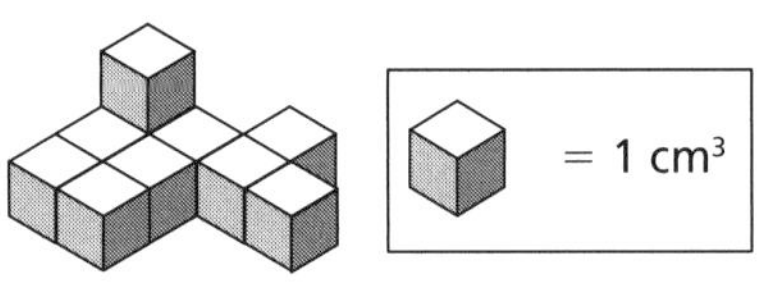

32:2 ☐ out of 16

❶ 6 + 14 ______

❷ 20 − 7 ______

❸ 10 × 7 ______

❹ 3 × 4 ______

❺
```
   33
 + 22
```

❻ 6 rows of 8. ______

❼ 7 × 5 ______

❽ 15 ÷ 5 ______

❾ 72 ÷ 9 ______

❿
```
    6
 ×  6
```

⓫ Days in August. ______

⓬

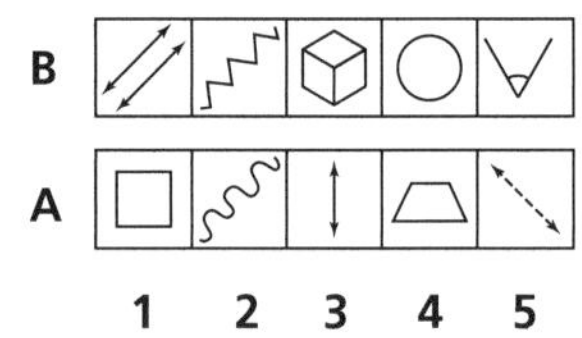

What shape has coordinates:

a 3B? ______ **b** 1A? ______

Write the coordinates for the:

c trapezium ______

d parallel lines ______

⓭ Estimate how many of your Mentals Book would be needed to cover one square metre. ______

⓮ List the value of the notes and coins needed to make $231.25. ______

______

⓯ 5 tenths as a decimal. ______

⓰ Share 12 lollies among 3 boys.

One share = ______

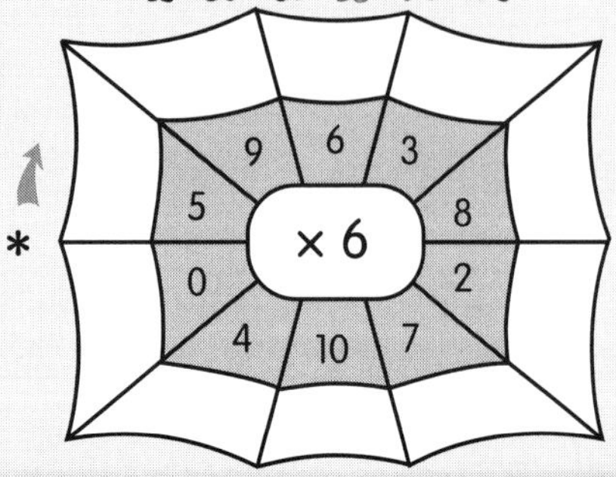

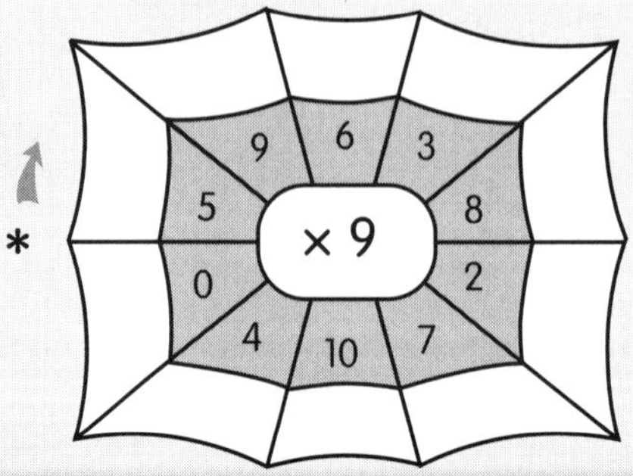

32:3   ☐ out of 12

1
```
   671
 − 156
```

2
```
   637
   141
 + 242
```

3
```
   321
   434
 + 157
```

4 6)36   **5** 2)14   **6** 3)15

7 Circle the shape that has been cut out.

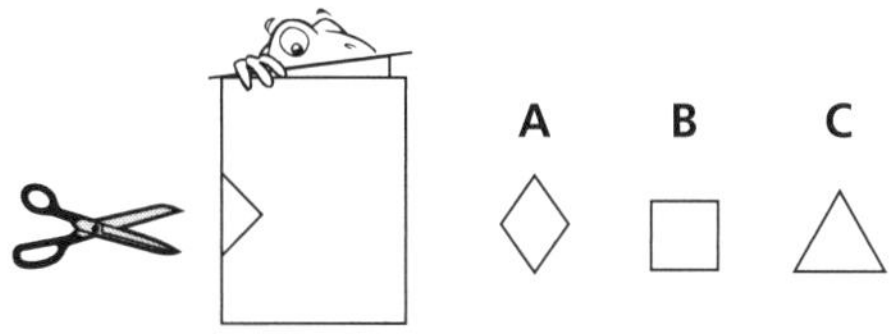

8 Estimate your height. ______

9 900 000 + 30 000 + 600 + 9 ______

10 50 cards are shared equally. If each player has 5 cards, how many players are there? ______

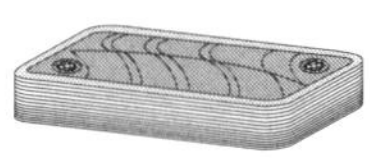

11 How long does it take to travel from:

a Blacktown to Pendle Hill? ______

b Seven Hills to Parramatta? ______

c Toongabbie to Westmead? ______

Train Timetable	
Blacktown	8:51
Seven Hills	8:54
Toongabbie	8:57
Pendle Hill	8:59
Wentworthville	9:01
Westmead	9:03
Parramatta	9:06

12 What is the change from $50 if I spend $5.30? ______

Extension

32:4   ☐ out of 6

1 Share 56 dolls among 4 shops. Each shop is given ______.

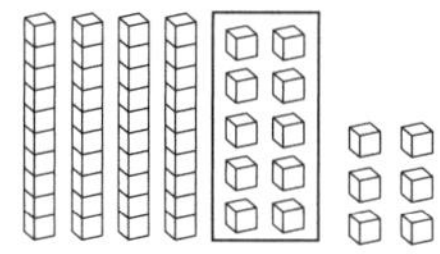

2 Of the 39 houses in a street, how many have even numbers? ______

3 If one pizza is needed to feed 5 people, how many are needed to feed 45 people? ______

4 If 17 × 18 = 306, what does 18 × 18 equal? ______

5 If 2 × □ = 18, 3 × △ = 24 and 6 × ◇ = 36, find □ + △ − ◇. ______

6 197 + 46 ______

Challenge

What do you know about the number 34 802?

______

______

______

______

______

______

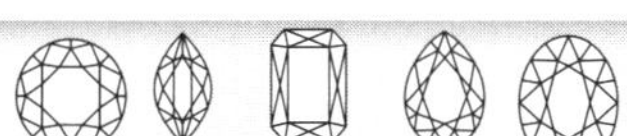

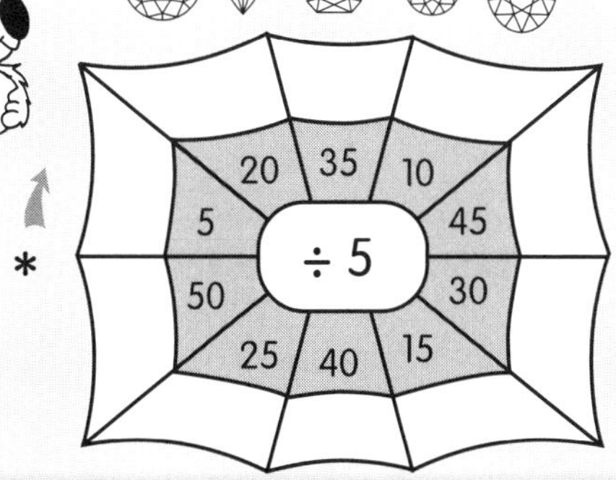

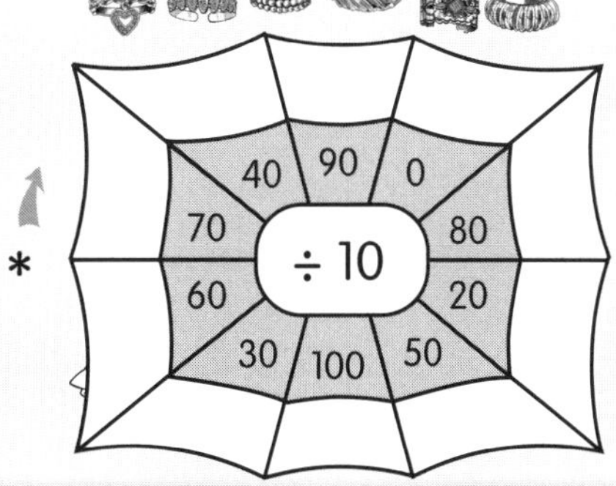

33:1 — ☐ out of 18

1. $8 \div 4$ ______
2. $14 - 3$ ______
3. $13 + 2$ ______
4. 6×5 ______
5. $\begin{array}{r} 86 \\ -\ 30 \\ \hline \end{array}$
6. 8×7 ______
7. Sum of 5, 6 and 7. ______
8. 16 minus 8. ______
9. Triple 5. ______
10. $\begin{array}{r} 63 \\ +\ 36 \\ \hline \end{array}$
11. Write the numeral four hundred and thirty-seven thousand eight hundred and nine. ______
12. What type of angle is in a square? ______
13. Who is holding the horizontal line? ______

14. List all the factors of 24.
    1, ____, ____, ____, ____, ____, ____, ____
15. The product of 6 and 2.
    ______

16. What units do we use to measure milk? ______
17. What four coins could you use to make up 75 cents? ______
18. One share in ten. How many in seven shares? ______

33:2 — ☐ out of 19

1. $15 + 5$ ______
2. $20 - 1$ ______
3. 5×4 ______
4. 2×8 ______
5. $\begin{array}{r} 55 \\ -\ 6 \\ \hline \end{array}$
6. 7 groups of 6. ______
7. 8×6 ______
8. 4×10 ______
9. $63 \div 9$ ______
10. $\begin{array}{r} 8 \\ \times\ 5 \\ \hline \end{array}$
11. How many days in July? ______
12. **a** The day after Sunday. ______
    b Ten days before Friday. ______
13. 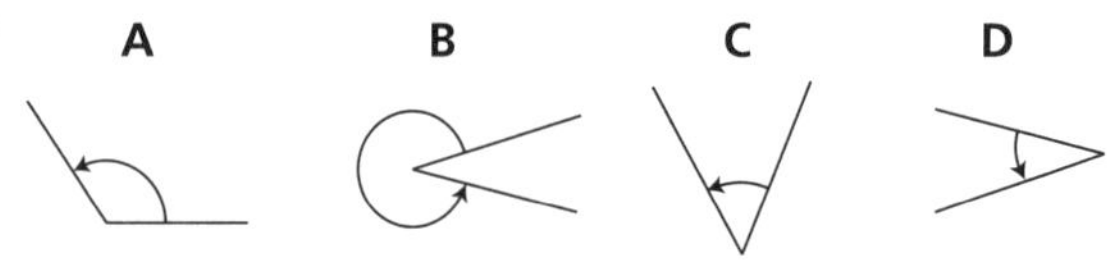

    Put these angles in order with the smallest first. ______
14. What type of angle (above) is:
    a A? ______ **b** D? ______
15. **a** The factors of 8. ______
    b The first six multiples of 5. ______
16. Minutes in half an hour. ______
17. How many 10 L bins will fill the 100 L bin? ______

18. What is the change from $100 if I spend $81.75? ______
19. We share 30 cards equally and each of us has 6 cards. How many of us were there? ______

Division Linked with Multiplication

If 7 × 9 = 63, then 63 ÷ 7 = 9
63 ÷ 9 = 7.

a 7 × 6 = ☐ | 42 ÷ 7 = ____ | 42 ÷ 6 = ____

b 4 × 7 = ☐ | 28 ÷ 4 = ____ | 28 ÷ 7 = ____

c 6 × 8 = ☐ | 48 ÷ 6 = ____ | 48 ÷ 8 = ____

d 9 × 6 = ☐ | 54 ÷ 9 = ____ | 54 ÷ 6 = ____

e 8 × 9 = ☐ | 72 ÷ 8 = ____ | 72 ÷ 9 = ____

f 8 × 7 = ☐ | 56 ÷ 8 = ____ | 56 ÷ 7 = ____

 ISBN 978 1 4886 2186 4

33:3 ☐ out of 13

1

$$\begin{array}{r} 629 \\ 231 \\ +\ 117 \\ \hline \end{array}$$

2

$$\begin{array}{r} 800 \\ -\ 298 \\ \hline \end{array}$$

3

$$\begin{array}{r} 564 \\ -\ 159 \\ \hline \end{array}$$

4 Write 689c in decimal form. ______

5 Is 637 closer to 635 or 640? ______

6 Write the division sign. ______

7 In which season is April? ______

8 Share 20 cards among 5 players.

One share = ______

9 1, 12, 2, 6, 3 and 4 are the f______ of 12.

10 200 000 + 7 000 + 100 + 6 ______

11 A mouse was balanced by 6 coins. A book was balanced by 24 coins. How many mice would balance the book?

______

12 List the value of the notes and coins needed to make $84.65. ______

______

13 Three girls shared 15 cards. How many did each girl get? ______

33:4 Extension ☐ out of 4

1 3 students shared 600 mL of drink equally. How much did each student drink?

______

2 Circle the best estimate of how many books like this one you need, to have a mass of 1 kg.

2 4 10 50

3 If we multiply together a number from each column, in how many ways can we get a product of 24?

2	1	2
8	2	3
4	3	4
	4	6
	6	

______

4 289 + 43 ______

Challenge

Write 6-digit numbers using the expanded form.

e.g. 400 000 + 20 000 + 50 + 2

______

______

______

______

______

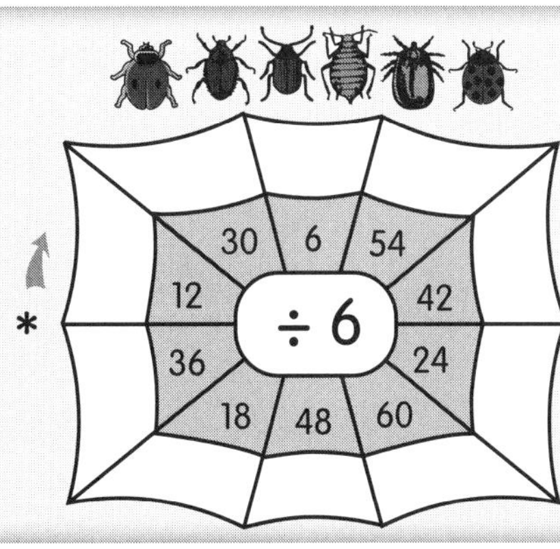

How many groups of 3?
How many rows of 6?

34:1 out of 17

1. 10 + 9 ______
2. 7 × 2 ______
3. 19 − 8 ______
4. 15 ÷ 5 ______
5. $\begin{array}{r} 51 \\ +\ 28 \\ \hline \end{array}$
6. Add 4, 5 and 6. ______
7. 9 × 6 ______
8. 3 less than 7. ______
9. Double 8. ______
10. $\begin{array}{r} 49 \\ -\ 12 \\ \hline \end{array}$
11. What part is shaded?

______ out of ______

12. Is this time *before* midday or *after* midday?

______

13. Find the smallest number that is a multiple of both 3 and 5. ______
14. The abbreviation for **litre**. ______
15. DVDs TV Camera

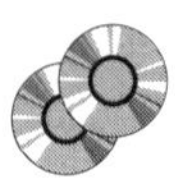

$39.90 $895 $95

Place these objects in order of value.

______

16. 14 stars are shared between 2 boys.

One share = ______

17. Days in May. ______

34:2 out of 17

1. 19 + 4 ______
2. 20 − 8 ______
3. 10 × 8 ______
4. 3 × 6 ______
5. $\begin{array}{r} 24 \\ +\ 13 \\ \hline \end{array}$
6. 6 rows of 6. ______
7. 5 × 10 ______
8. 36 ÷ 4 ______
9. 56 ÷ 8 ______
10. $\begin{array}{r} 9 \\ \times\ 3 \\ \hline \end{array}$
11. Fifteen less than 200. ______
12.

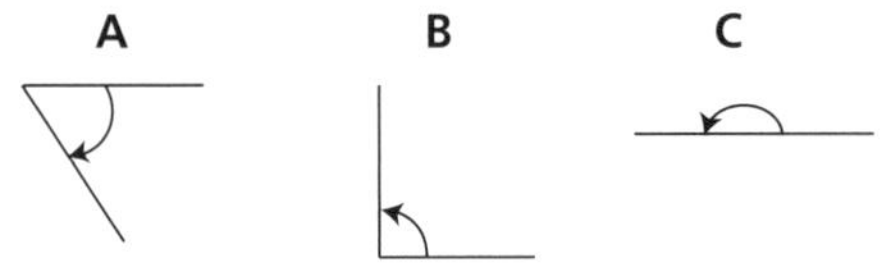

Which angle is:

a a straight angle? ______

b an acute angle? ______

13. The product of 4 and 8. ______
14. Halve 32. ______
15. Would your cupped hands hold about 7 mL, 7 L, 70 mL or 700 mL of water?

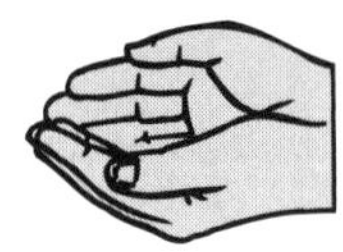

______

16. What is the change from $100 if I spend $47.80? ______
17. Four children shared forty shells. How many shells were in one share? ______

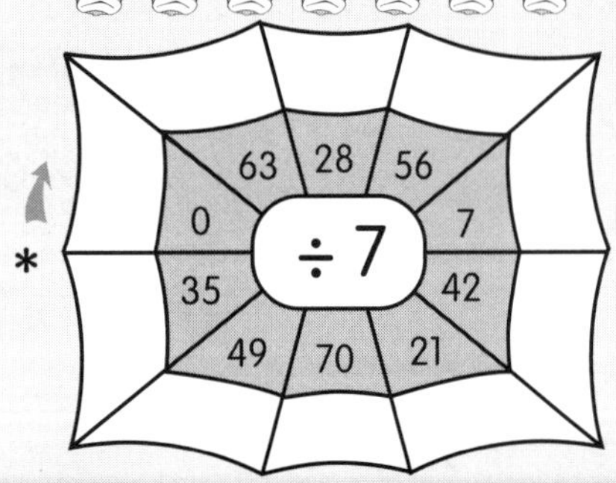

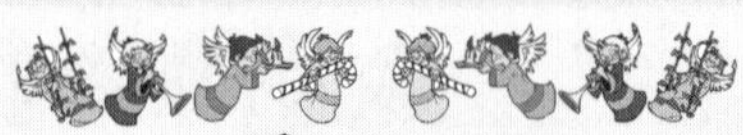

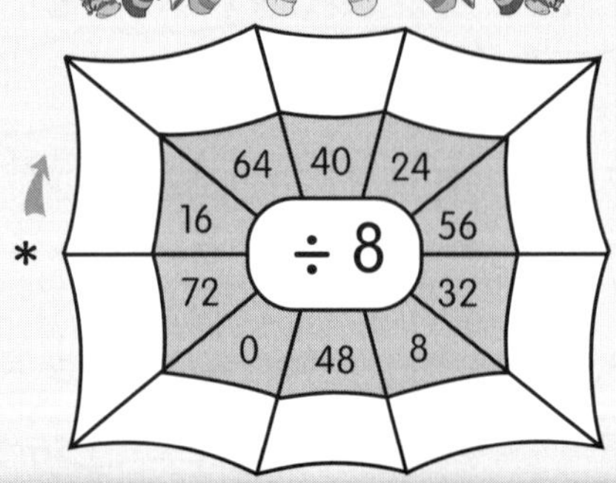

24 ÷ 3 = ☐

Ask: What × 8 = 24?

 ISBN 978 1 4886 2186 4

34:3 out of 10

1 617 + 280 + 131

$$\begin{array}{r} 617 \\ 280 \\ +\ 131 \\ \hline \end{array}$$

2

$$\begin{array}{r} 900 \\ -\ 299 \\ \hline \end{array}$$

3

$$\begin{array}{r} 678 \\ -\ 189 \\ \hline \end{array}$$

4 Write out and answer the number sentence for this problem.

45 people booked a trip on a bus. If the bus left with only 27 people on it, how many missed the bus? ________

____

5 This time is:

________ past ________.

6 Abbreviation for **ante meridiem**. ________

7 Which pipes are:

a horizontal? ________

b vertical? ________

c sloping? ________

d not horizontal? ________

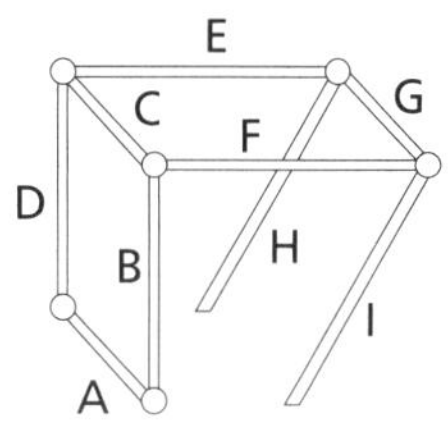

8 Write the factors of:

a 39 ________

b 77 ________

9 Is the height of a door about 2 metres? ________

10 Share 42 flowers among 6 girls.

One share = ________

34:4 out of 6

Extension

1 Rhonda has $36 and Alan has $15. How much must Rhonda give Alan if they are to have the same amount? ________

2 What is the value of 20 gold bars worth $1000 each? ________

3 If # means "times 2" and ^ means "divide by 3", then 12##^ = ________

4 **a** What two numbers add to give 13 and multiply to give 30? ________

b What two numbers add to give 14 and multiply to give 24? ________

5 **a** 247 + 32 ________

b 1218 + 34 ________

6 The Roman numeral for:

a 8 ________ **b** 9 ________

Challenge

Write a division number sentence and a matching number story.

____

____

____

____

____

____

____

Turn to ID Card A on page 6.

Give the answers for numbers 18 to 27.

(18) ________ (19) number ________

(20) ________ expander (21) ________ numbers

(22) ________ numbers (23) ________ numbers

(24) ________ numbers (25) ________

(26) ________ (27) ________

 ☐ out of 18

1. 15 − 4 ____
2. 24 ÷ 6 ____
3. 5 × 3 ____
4. 11 + 8 ____
5. $\begin{array}{r} 98 \\ -\ 63 \\ \hline \end{array}$
6. 3 × 6 ____
7. Increase 6 by 4. ____
8. Divide 30 by 3. ____
9. Multiply 2 by 9. ____
10. $\begin{array}{r} 38 \\ +\ 17 \\ \hline \end{array}$

11. Mum had 20 candles. She used 13 on my cake. How many candles were not used? ____

12. Round 971 086 to the nearest thousand. ____
13. Out of a litre of milk I drank 300 mL. How much is left? ____

14. 800 000 + 4000 + 600 + 50 + 4 ____
15. What is the value of the 7 in 732 865? ____
16. Millimetres in 9 cm 5 mm. ____
17. Abbreviation for **post meridiem**. ____
18. Find the smallest number that is a multiple of both 2 and 4. ____

 ☐ out of 18

1. 20 + 0 ____
2. 18 − 6 ____
3. 10 × 9 ____
4. 3 × 7 ____
5. $\begin{array}{r} 77 \\ -\ 6 \\ \hline \end{array}$
6. Multiply 5 by 7. ____
7. 9 × 6 ____
8. 7 × 7 ____
9. 21 ÷ 3 ____
10. $\begin{array}{r} 9 \\ \times\ 7 \\ \hline \end{array}$
11. Is it equally likely that the spinner will land on 1, 2 or 3? ____

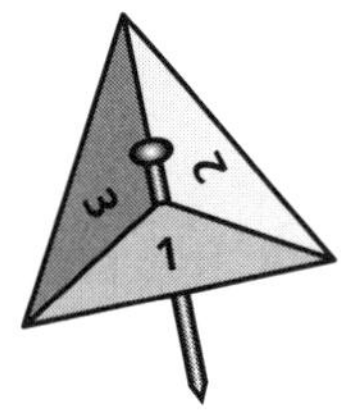

12. Write 4 cm 1 mm in millimetres. ____
13. The length of this pencil.

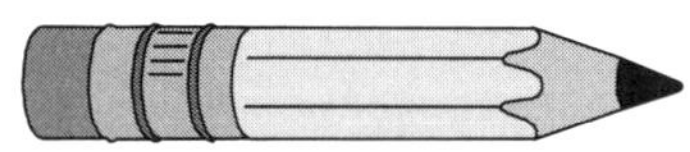

Estimate = ____ mm

Measure = ____ mm

14. **pm** means ____.
15. Name the angle type used in each shape.

a b c

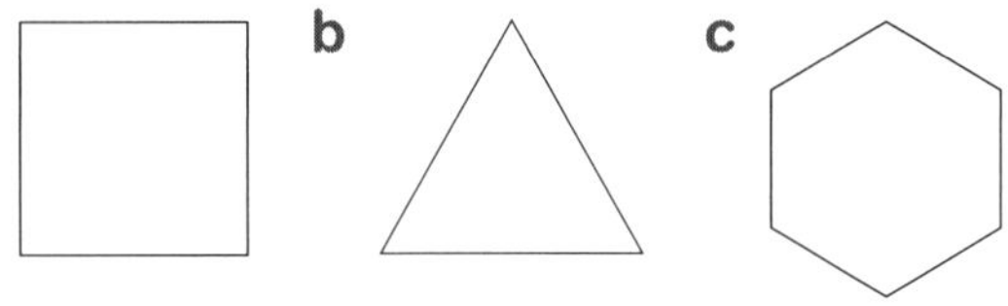

____ ____ ____

16. Is a flag pole more likely to be horizontal or vertical? ____
17. The product of 7 and 8. ____
18. The total value of four 10c coins and four 5c coins. ____

÷/× tables

☆☆☆☆☆☆☆☆☆

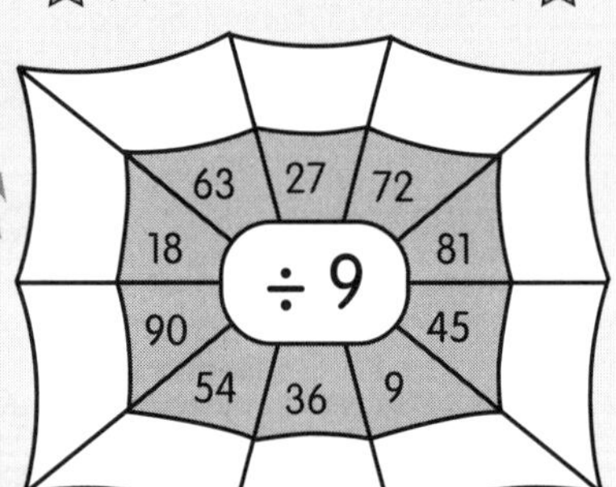

	4	1	9	0	7	5	2	11	6	3	8	10
× 4												

	8	4	7	1	11	0	5	10	2	3	6	9
× 7												

	3	0	4	8	5	10	7	1	6	11	2	9
× 9												

 • *AUSTRALIAN SIGNPOST MATHS 4 MENTALS* • ISBN 978 1 4886 2186 4

35:3 ☐ out of 10

1. $3\overline{)24}$
2. $6\overline{)30}$
3. $8\overline{)32}$
4. $3\overline{)12}$
5. $4\overline{)32}$
6. $6\overline{)48}$
7. **Dolls Sold**

   a On which day was the greatest number of dolls sold? ______

   b How many dolls were sold on Wednesday? ______

   c What was the total number of dolls sold? ______

8. a How many minutes past 3? ______

   b How many minutes before 4? ______

9. Find the smallest number that is a multiple of both 2 and 4. ______
10. Using 5c, 10c or 20c coins, in how many different ways can 30 cents be paid? ______

35:4 Extension ☐ out of 5

1. 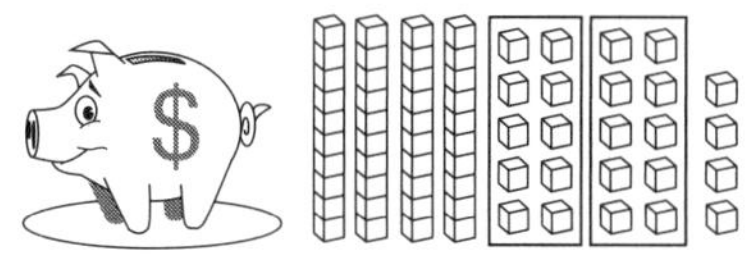

   Share $64 among 4 money boxes.

   One share = ______

2. Teagan has 33 birds. This is 3 times as many as Bill. How many does Bill have? ______

3. Multiples of 7 are 7, 14, 21, … . Which of 94, 96 and 98 is the sum of two multiples of 7? ______
4. If you look at this watch once every minute from 8:40 pm until 9:00 pm, how many fives would you see? ______

5. a $80 - \square = 24$

   b $\square - 32 = 17$

Challenge

Write related multiplication facts.
e.g. $2 \times \underline{4} = 8$ so $2 \times \underline{8} = 16$

______
______
______
______
______

Factors of a Number

Write all the factors of:

a 15 ____, ____, ____, ____

b 21 ____, ____, ____, ____

c 16 ____, ____, ____, ____, ____

d 12 ____, ____, ____, ____, ____, ____

If two numbers multiply to give 24, then they are factors of 24.

Now 24 = **1** × **24**, 24 = **2** × **12**,
24 = **3** × **8**, 24 = **4** × **6**

The factors of 24 are 1, 24, 2, 12, 3, 8, 4 and 6.

36:1 ☐ out of 15

1. 17 − 4 ______
2. 3 × 6 ______
3. 13 + 4 ______
4. 36 ÷ 4 ______
5. $\begin{array}{r} 46 \\ +\ 25 \\ \hline \end{array}$
6. Triple 5. ______
7. $21 ÷ 7 ______
8. 4 × 6 ______
9. Half of 18. ______
10. $\begin{array}{r} 96 \\ -\ 63 \\ \hline \end{array}$

11. Double each time.

    1, 2, ______, ______, ______

12. Hours in 1 day. ______
13. 2 × 2 = 4 so 2 × 4 = ______
14. 

    a How many books were read by Tom and Deb altogether? ______

    b How many books read, does one picture stand for? ______

    c How many books were read altogether? ______

15. If the time is 2:20, it is also

    ______ minutes past ______.

36:2 ☐ out of 17

1. 22 + 8 ______
2. 20 − 5 ______
3. 6 × 4 ______
4. 9 × 7 ______
5. $\begin{array}{r} 34 \\ +\ 23 \\ \hline \end{array}$
6. Multiply 6 by 4. ______
7. 10 × 7 ______
8. 8 × 8 ______
9. 32 ÷ 4 ______
10. $\begin{array}{r} 10 \\ \times\ \ 7 \\ \hline \end{array}$
11. In this maze, Naomi started at A. Where did she end up if she turned left at the first corner, then right at the next, then left at the next?

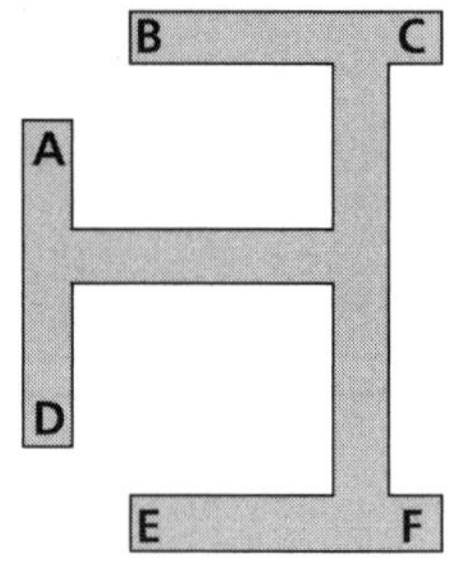

    ______

12. 2 × 6 = 12 so 4 × 6 = ______
13. Multiply by 2 each time.

    2, ______, ______, ______

14. Round 657 893 to the nearest thousand. ______
15. The time on this clock face is: ______ past ______

    or ______.

16. Is your teacher taller than 1 m? ______
17. Find the smallest number that is a multiple of both 5 and 10. ______

Turn to ID Card A on page 6.
Give the answers to these numbers.

(9) ______ ______ (10) ______ ______ of ______

(11) ______ ______ of ______ (12) ______ ______

(13) ______ ______ (14) 5 ______ 7

(15) is ______ ______ (16) is ______ ______

 • *AUSTRALIAN SIGNPOST MATHS 4 MENTALS* • ISBN 978 1 4886 2186 4

36:3 out of 13

❶ 620 + 395 =

❷ 348 + 254 =

❸ 624 + 159 =

❹ Centimetres in 1 m 19 cm. ______

❺ The height of a door is closest to:
A 4 m? **B** 2 m? **C** 6 m? **D** 1 m? ______

❻ 6 × 3 = 18 so 12 × 3 = ______

❼ I have 49 marbles. How many more do I need to make 160? ______

❽ Write 506 400 in words. ______

______

______

❾ Is it equally likely that the number rolled on a 6-sided die will be 1, 2, 3, 4, 5 or 6? ______

❿ Estimate then measure this length in mm.

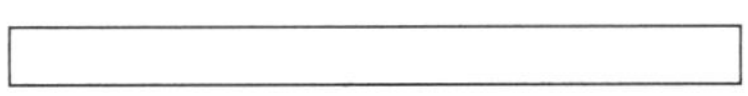

Estimate: ______ Measure: ______

⓫ Write 7 cm 5 mm in mm. ______

⓬ **a** The time seven hours after noon. ______

b The time three hours before noon. ______

⓭ An angle larger than a right angle but less than a straight angle is called an ______ angle.

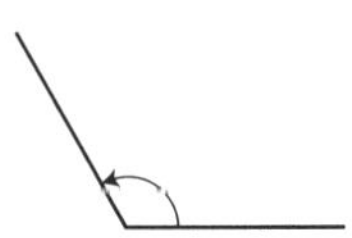

36:4 out of 8

Extension

❶ Find the smallest number that is a multiple of both 6 and 8. ______

❷ 40 lots of 10. ______

❸ What is the value of 70 gold bars worth $1 000 each? ______

❹ 1, 2, 4, 8, ______, ______, ______, ______

❺ **a** The Roman numeral for 7. ______

b The Roman numeral for 4. ______

❻ There are 12 chocolates on each of the two layers in a box. How many chocolates are in 3 boxes? ______

❼ Our zoo has 63 eels. Their zoo has 26 less. How many eels in both zoos? ______

❽ If # means "add 3" and ~ means "subtract 2", then 8###~~~ = ______

Challenge

Create and answer your own questions using the code in question 8 above.

______

______

______

______

______

______

______

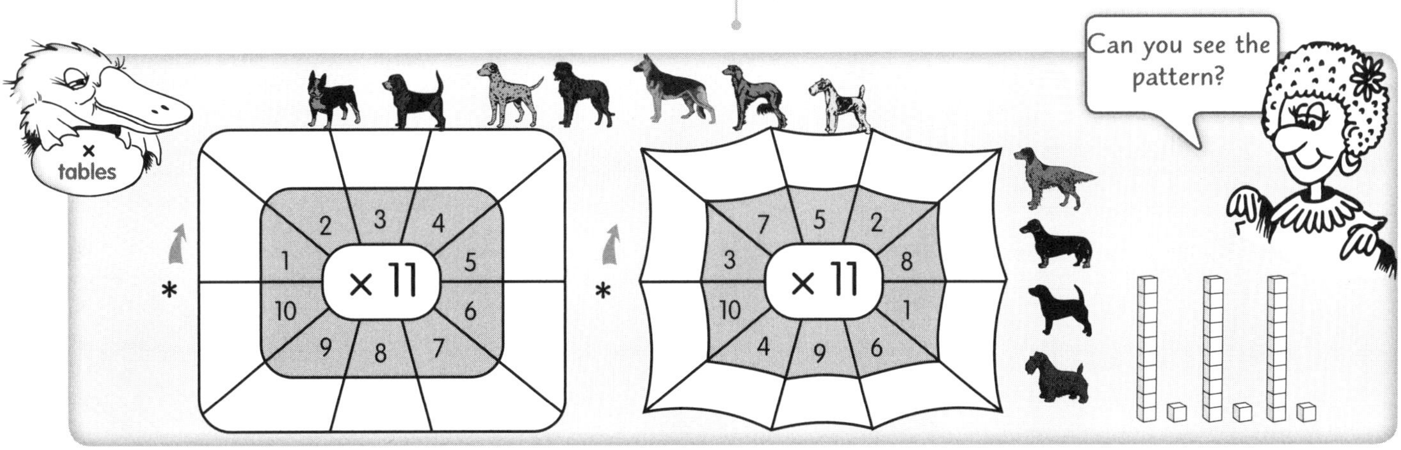

37:1 ☐ out of 18

1. 15 − 6 ______
2. 12 + 7 ______
3. 42 ÷ 6 ______
4. 6 × 9 ______
5. $\begin{array}{r} 87 \\ -\ 55 \\ \hline \end{array}$
6. \$81 ÷ 9 ______
7. 15 ÷ 3 ______
8. 5 × 5 ______
9. 100 − 30 ______
10. $\begin{array}{r} 32 \\ +\ 45 \\ \hline \end{array}$

11. Another name for "0" is z__________.
12. Is 7:30 am, morning, afternoon or evening? ______
13. 5, 10, 15, ____, ____, ____, ____
14. Complete the pattern by shading.

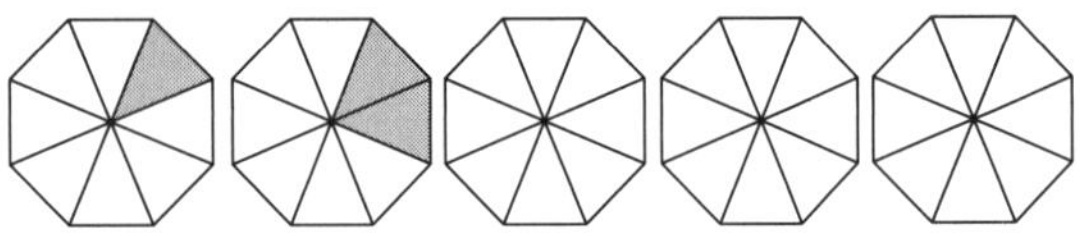

$\frac{1}{8}$ $\frac{2}{8}$ $\frac{3}{8}$ $\frac{4}{8}$ $\frac{5}{8}$

15. Write the mixed numeral for:
    a two and three tenths ______
    b six and three quarters ______
16. Colour $2\frac{1}{2}$ tigers.

17. What is the value of the 2 in 405 200? ______
18. Is 8:30 pm, morning, afternoon or evening? ______

37:2 ☐ out of 18

1. 15 + 4 ______
2. 20 − 9 ______
3. 7 × 4 ______
4. 8 × 9 ______
5. $\begin{array}{r} 70 \\ -\ 9 \\ \hline \end{array}$
6. 8 groups of 4. ______
7. 9 × 9 ______
8. 27 ÷ 3 ______
9. 64 ÷ 8 ______
10. $\begin{array}{r} 9 \\ \times\ 3 \\ \hline \end{array}$
11. Days in four weeks. ______
12. To make \$2, what must we add to 75 cents? ______
13. The factors of 16. ______
14. If you add two even numbers, your answer is ______.
15. Count back by 2s from 27
    27, ____, ____, ____, ____
16. $\frac{1}{5}, \frac{2}{5}, \frac{3}{5}, \frac{\square}{\square}, \frac{\square}{\square}, \frac{\square}{\square}$
17. Write the improper fraction for the shaded part.
    a

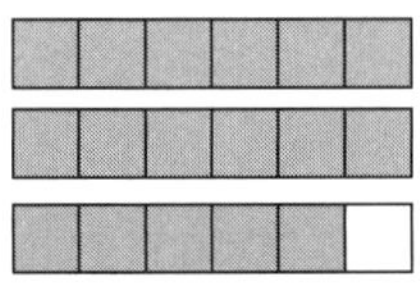

    b

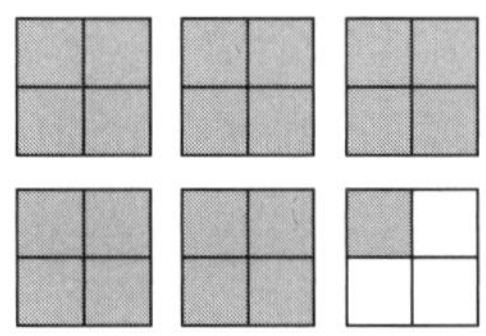

______ ______

18. The length of this bar is:
    a ____ mm
    b ____ cm

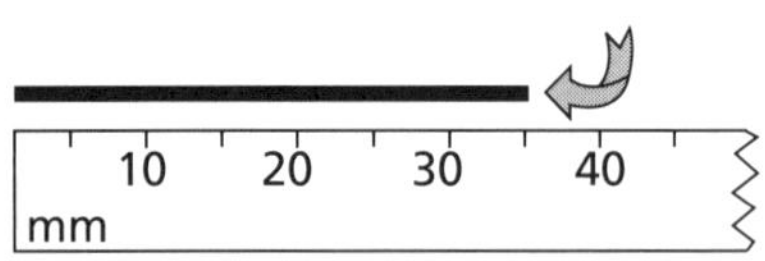

Turn to ID Card B on page 7.
Give the answers for these numbers.

(11) ______ angle (12) ______ angle
(13) ______ angle (14) ______ angle
(15) ______ of an angle (16) ______ of an angle
(17) ______ of ______ (18) ______

The angle at a square corner is called a right angle.

© PEARSON AUSTRALIA 2018 • *AUSTRALIAN SIGNPOST MATHS 4 MENTALS* • ISBN 978 1 4886 2186 4

37:3 ☐ out of 12

1
```
  731
  603
+  24
-----
```

2
```
  233
  147
+   2
-----
```

3
```
  222
  317
+ 404
-----
```

4 What is the number before:

a 230? ______ **b** 1011? ______

5 **a** Months in 1 year. ______

b Months in a decade. ______

c Years in 4 decades. ______

6 If you add an even and an odd number, your answer is ______.

7 Fill in the missing numbers.

3, 6, 9, ____, ____, 18, 21, ____

8 Write each improper fraction as a mixed number.

a $\frac{7}{4}$ ______ **b** $\frac{5}{3}$ ______

9 Write as an improper fraction.

a $1\frac{1}{4}$ ______ **b** $2\frac{3}{10}$ ______

10 Write 403 720 in words.

______

______

______

11 Write as cm.

a 45 mm ______ **b** 87 mm ______

12 We write **ante meridiem** as ______.

37:4 ☐ out of 7

Extension

1 Of which counting numbers is 12 a multiple? ______

2 If this pattern continues, how many hexagons would be in row:

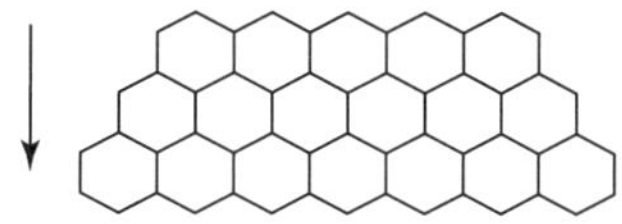

a 10? ______ **b** 100? ______

3 I make 4 sandwiches from 2 slices of bread. How many can I make from 46 slices? ______

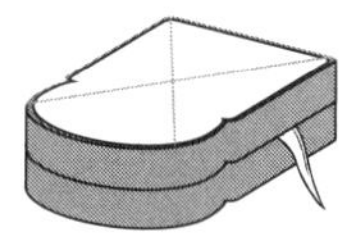

4 If you multiply two odd numbers, your answer is: ______

5 100 − 35 − 35 ______

6 50 − 15 − 15 − 15 ______

7 **a** 206, 308, 410, ____, ____

b Write a rule for this pattern. ______

______

Challenge

Ask at least four people to tell you their favourite fruit. List their answers.

______

______

______

______

______

______

Fill out this table about yourself, a relative or a friend.
Compare your answers to those on page 11 in Unit 1.

Name: ______ **Date:** ______

Age: ______	Mass: ______ kg	Shoe size: ______
Height: ______ cm	Waist: ______ cm	Neck size: ______ cm

Tables of Number and Measurement

Length

1 centimetre = 10 millimetres
1 metre = 100 centimetres
1 kilometre = 1 000 metres

The **freezing point** of water is **0°C**.
The **boiling point** of water is **100°C**.

°C means degrees Celsius.

A temperature of **5°C** is a **cold** day.
A temperature of **35°C** is a **hot** day.

Area

1 hectare = 10 000 m²
1 square metre = 10 000 cm²

Mass

1 kilogram = 1 000 grams
1 tonne = 1 000 kilograms

Roman Numerals

1	= I	**6**	= VI	**20**	= XX	**90**	= XC
2	= II	**7**	= VII	**30**	= XXX	**100**	= C
3	= III	**8**	= VIII	**40**	= XL	**200**	= CC
4	= IV	**9**	= IX	**50**	= L	**500**	= D
5	= V	**10**	= X	**60**	= LX	**1 000**	= M

Capacity and Volume

1 000 millilitres = 1 litre
1 000 litres = 1 kilolitre
1 millilitre = 1 cm³
1 litre = 1 000 cm³

5 mL

Months of the Year

Thirty days have September, April, June and November. All the rest have thirty-one, except February alone, which has twenty-eight days clear and twenty-nine days each leap year.

You can use the knuckles of your hands to find the number of days in each month.

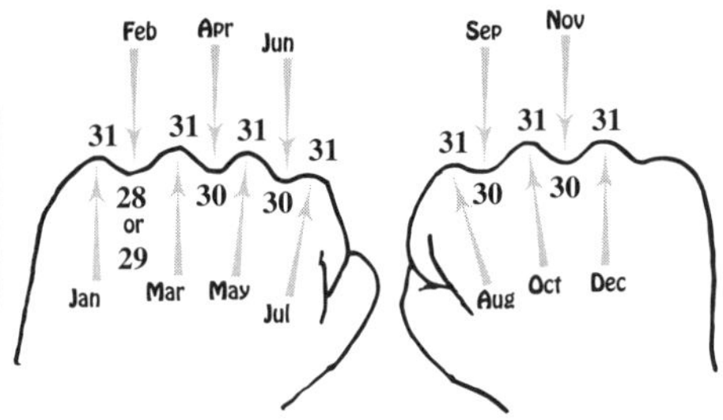

Time

1 minute = 60 seconds
1 hour = 60 minutes
1 day = 24 hours
1 week = 7 days
1 fortnight = 2 weeks
1 year = 52 weeks
1 year = 365 days
1 leap year = 366 days
1 decade = 10 years
1 century = 100 years

am stands for **ante meridiem**.
am means **before midday**.

pm stands for **post meridiem**.
pm means **after midday**.

Seasons

Summer: December, January, February
Autumn: March, April, May
Winter: June, July, August
Spring: September, October, November

Multiplication Tables

1 × 2 = 2	1 × 3 = 3	1 × 4 = 4	1 × 5 = 5	1 × 6 = 6	1 × 7 = 7	1 × 8 = 8	1 × 9 = 9	1 × 10 = 10
2 × 2 = 4	2 × 3 = 6	2 × 4 = 8	2 × 5 = 10	2 × 6 = 12	2 × 7 = 14	2 × 8 = 16	2 × 9 = 18	2 × 10 = 20
3 × 2 = 6	3 × 3 = 9	3 × 4 = 12	3 × 5 = 15	3 × 6 = 18	3 × 7 = 21	3 × 8 = 24	3 × 9 = 27	3 × 10 = 30
4 × 2 = 8	4 × 3 = 12	4 × 4 = 16	4 × 5 = 20	4 × 6 = 24	4 × 7 = 28	4 × 8 = 32	4 × 9 = 36	4 × 10 = 40
5 × 2 = 10	5 × 3 = 15	5 × 4 = 20	5 × 5 = 25	5 × 6 = 30	5 × 7 = 35	5 × 8 = 40	5 × 9 = 45	5 × 10 = 50
6 × 2 = 12	6 × 3 = 18	6 × 4 = 24	6 × 5 = 30	6 × 6 = 36	6 × 7 = 42	6 × 8 = 48	6 × 9 = 54	6 × 10 = 60
7 × 2 = 14	7 × 3 = 21	7 × 4 = 28	7 × 5 = 35	7 × 6 = 42	7 × 7 = 49	7 × 8 = 56	7 × 9 = 63	7 × 10 = 70
8 × 2 = 16	8 × 3 = 24	8 × 4 = 32	8 × 5 = 40	8 × 6 = 48	8 × 7 = 56	8 × 8 = 64	8 × 9 = 72	8 × 10 = 80
9 × 2 = 18	9 × 3 = 27	9 × 4 = 36	9 × 5 = 45	9 × 6 = 54	9 × 7 = 63	9 × 8 = 72	9 × 9 = 81	9 × 10 = 90
10 × 2 = 20	10 × 3 = 30	10 × 4 = 40	10 × 5 = 50	10 × 6 = 60	10 × 7 = 70	10 × 8 = 80	10 × 9 = 90	10 × 10 = 100